Rhetoric and Communication Perspectives on Domestic Violence and Sexual Assault

This book brings rhetorical, legal, and professional communication perspectives to the discourse surrounding policymaking efforts within the United States around two types of violent crimes against women: domestic violence and sexual assault. The authors propose that such analysis adds to our understanding of rhetorical concepts such as *kairos*, risk perception, moral panic, genre analysis, and identity theory. Overall, the goal is to demonstrate how rhetorical, legal, and professional communication perspectives work together to illuminate public discourse and conflict in such complicated and ongoing dilemmas as how to aid victims of domestic violence and sexual assault, and how to manage the offenders of such crimes—social and cultural problems that continue to perplex the legal system and the social environment.

Amy D. Propen is Assistant Professor in the Writing Program at the University of California, Santa Barbara, USA.

Mary Lay Schuster is Professor in the Department of Writing Studies and Faculty Fellow in the Law School at the University of Minnesota, USA. She and Amy D. Propen are also co-authors of *Victim Advocacy in the Courtroom: Persuasive Practices in Domestic Violence and Child Protection Cases*.

Routledge Studies in Technical Communication, Rhetoric, and Culture
Series Editors: Miles A. Kimball and Charles H. Sides

This series promotes innovative, interdisciplinary research in the theory and practice of technical communication, broadly conceived as including business, scientific, and health communication. Technical communication has an extensive impact on our world and our lives, yet the venues for long-format research in the field are few. This series serves as an outlet for scholars engaged with the theoretical, practical, rhetorical, and cultural implications of this burgeoning field. The editor welcomes proposals for book-length studies and edited collections involving qualitative and quantitative research and theoretical inquiry into technical communication and associated fields and topics, including user-centered design; information design; intercultural communication; risk communication; new media; social media; visual communication and rhetoric; disability/accessibility issues; communication ethics; health communication; applied rhetoric; and the history and current practice of technical, business, and scientific communication.

1 **Computer Games and Technical Communication**
Critical Methods and Applications at the Intersection
Edited by Jennifer deWinter and Ryan M. Moeller

2 **Visible Numbers**
Essays on the History of Statistical Graphics
Edited by Miles A. Kimball and Charles Kostelnick

3 **Communicating Mobility and Technology**
A Material Rhetoric for Persuasive Transportation
Ehren Helmut Pflugfelder

4 **Topic-Driven Environmental Rhetoric**
Edited by Derek G. Ross

5 **Rhetoric and Communication Perspectives on Domestic Violence and Sexual Assault**
Policy and Protocol Through Discourse
Amy D. Propen and Mary Lay Schuster

Rhetoric and Communication Perspectives on Domestic Violence and Sexual Assault

Policy and Protocol Through Discourse

Amy D. Propen
and Mary Lay Schuster

Routledge
Taylor & Francis Group
LONDON AND NEW YORK

First published 2017
by Routledge

2 Park Square, Milton Park, Abingdon, Oxfordshire OX14 4RN
52 Vanderbilt Avenue, New York, NY 10017

Routledge is an imprint of the Taylor & Francis Group, an informa business

First issued in paperback 2019

Library of Congress Cataloging-in-Publication Data
CIP data has been applied for.

ISBN: 978-1-138-71498-4 (hbk)
ISBN: 978-0-367-88704-9 (pbk)

Typeset in Sabon
by codeMantra

Contents

Acknowledgments

Many people helped and encouraged us with this project and the resulting book. We are most grateful to our interviewees who shared their stories and impressions with us in the first place; this project would not have been possible without them, and we have tried our best to allow the uniqueness of each of their ideas to resonate throughout this book. In addition, two people introduced us to the challenges faced by the Minnesota Sex Offender Program and the excitement about the Lethality Assessment Protocol: Eric Janus, former president of what is now St. Paul's Mitchell Hamline School of Law and an expert on all things relating to civil commitment, and Sergeant Randy McAllister, of the College Grove Police Department, who was instrumental in bringing LAP to Minnesota and was always available to talk with us. We also thank Charles Sides of Fitchburg State University who, in his role with Baywood Publishing, saw merit in our work and shared those impressions when we needed them the most. At Routledge/Taylor & Francis Group, Felisa Salvago-Keyes and Christina Kowalski shepherded our work through with professionalism and warmth. The Maryland Network Against Domestic Violence allowed us to display the lethality screen in Figure 2.1. Finally, portions of our Chapter 1 appear in our article, "Expanding Our Understanding of *Kairos*: Tracing Moral Panic and Risk Perception in the Debate over the Minnesota Sex Offender Program," which was published in a 2015 issue of the *Journal of Technical Writing and Communication* (volume 45, pp. 3–30).

Mary received a semester leave in Spring 2015 from the University of Minnesota to complete this project. She thanks Laura Gurak, Chair of the Department of Writing Studies, and her colleagues there and at the Law School at the University of Minnesota for their encouragement. Mary's husband, Slade Schuster, spent many hours proofreading the book manuscript and encouraging Mary for the five years she was involved in traveling to interviews, drafting chapters, and finding a home for this book. Mary's late mother and father, Doris and Charles Lay, and were always her greatest cheerleaders throughout her professional career.

Amy would like to thank her friends and colleagues in the Writing Program at the University of California, Santa Barbara and in the Department of English and Humanities at York College of Pennsylvania for their support, collegiality, and conversation. She, too, thanks Mary's husband Slade for his proofreading prowess. Amy would also especially like to thank her parents, Beverly and Michael, for their ongoing support and for always encouraging her to write.

Policy and Protocol Through Discourse

An Introduction

On September 22, 2006, Steven Van Keuren broke into his former girlfriend Teri Lee's home in West Lake Township, MN, and killed her and her current boyfriend. Teri Lee, boyfriend Timothy Hawkinson, Sr., and Lee's four children were asleep in the home, located along the Minnesota side of the St. Croix River in east central Washington County. The new security system Lee had installed failed to alert the family that Van Keuren, armed with his father's .22-caliber gun, had entered the house. Van Keuren shot Lee six times and Hawkinson three times. The older daughter, twelve-year-old Taylor, who had had trouble sleeping that night, was in the bed with Lee and Hawkinson. When the shots began, Taylor ran to grab her younger sister and fled the house to alert the neighbors to call the police while Taylor's two brothers hid in a closet and were later found unharmed. Van Keuren, who refused to surrender his weapon, was wounded by the police, recovered, and on July 27, 2007, was convicted of two counts of first-degree premeditated murder and sentenced to two consecutive terms of life imprisonment in state prison without the possibility of release.

Also serving a life sentence at this time was sex offender Ming Sen Shiue. In 1980, Shiue kidnapped his former high school math teacher, Mary Stauffer, and her 8-year-old daughter, Beth, from outside a beauty salon in Roseville, a suburb of St. Paul, MN. Shortly afterwards, in nearby Anoka County, Shiue killed 6-year-old Jason Wilkman when the boy spotted the Stauffers in the trunk of Shiue's car. Once Shiue returned to his Roseville home, he locked the Stauffers in a closet and repeatedly raped his former teacher during seven weeks of confinement, videotaping some of the attacks. During the criminal trial for the murder of young Wilkman, Shiue attacked Mary Stauffer with a knife while she was on the witness stand; her wounds required 62 stitches. Shiue is eligible for parole from federal prison every two years, but his requests have always been denied. In 2010, the Minnesota Tenth District Court also ruled that if Shiue were ever paroled, he would be immediately civilly committed to the Minnesota Sex Offender Program (MSOP) where he would be treated in the high-security facility until he could safely be reintroduced into the community.

Using theoretical perspectives from rhetoric, law, and professional communication, we analyze attempts to manage such sex offenders as Ming Sen Shiue and to prevent such domestic homicides as committed by Steven Van Keuren. Although professional communication is usually defined as written, oral, visual, and digital communication within the workplace setting or the corporate world, we extend this definition to include how such settings affect and are affected by cultural and social contexts and constraints. For example, we emphasize the legal arena as a professional system, much as Andrew Abbott (1988) has described how such systems establish jurisdictional boundaries in their social contexts:

> In claiming jurisdiction, a profession asks society to recognize its cognitive structure through exclusive rights; jurisdiction has not only a culture, but also a social structure. These claimed rights may include absolute monopoly of practice and of public payments, rights of self-discipline and of unconstrained employment, control of professional training, of recruitment, and of licensing, to mention only a few.
>
> (59)

According to Abbott, the ability of a profession to establish and sustain its jurisdiction has, in part, depended on prestigious academic knowledge and on exclusive claim to aspects of science and technology. That claim grants the profession the authority to monitor its own practice, to select those practitioners it wants to recognize and recruit, and to direct what voices it wants to include and to whom it would grant agency and decision-making.

We propose that such rhetorical, legal, and professional communication analysis adds to our understanding of such rhetorical concepts as exigence and *kairos* as well as risk perception and assessment, and we apply and extend genre and identity theories within that analysis to reveal the discursive complexities surrounding two types of violent crimes against women: domestic violence and sexual assault. Specifically, we add what we call kairotic cycles to current understandings of *kairos* by pointing out how moral panic prevents stakeholders from creating more productive arguments. Moreover, we illuminate how misconceptions of risk evolve and then can derail effective systemic change. We extend genre theory by illuminating how a genre, based on specific persuasive elements, can not only disrupt but also challenge behaviors and potentially change core ideologies within a system and among individuals. Finally, we contribute to identity theory by pointing out how those in power actually diminish their power to conduct productive discourse and reach resolution by stereotyping or "Othering" groups and individuals. Within our analysis, some readers might appreciate the solutions that emerge, such as a public health approach to domestic violence and a public education effort to correct misperceptions of the recidivism rate among sex offenders. Overall, however, our goal is to demonstrate how rhetorical, legal, and professional communication perspectives work together to illuminate public discourse and conflict in such complicated and ongoing dilemmas as how to aid victims of domestic violence and sexual assault, and how to manage the offenders of such crimes—social and cultural problems that continue to perplex the legal system and the social environment.

Although we examine these problems and efforts broadly, for a number of reasons the description and analysis of these efforts are grounded frequently in the state of Minnesota. On the one hand, in 2015 Minnesota had the highest per capita number of sex offenders confined in, but the lowest number of offenders discharged from, civil commitment to a secure treatment facility, and the federal courts have more than once threatened takeover of what appears to be a failed system. According to U.S. Federal Judge Donovan Frank, the state system is "clearly broken" and "draconian" (Serres 2014, February 20, n.p.). In the summer of 2015, Judge Frank, deciding a civil suit against MSOP brought by 14 offenders civilly confined and not making progress toward discharge, concluded that the Minnesota statutes governing civil commitment and treatment of sex offenders were unconstitutional as written and as applied (*Karsjens et al. v. Jesson et al.* 2015, 2). Currently, Judge Frank's remedies to improve the system are stayed until the Eighth Circuit Court of Appeals can review the case, perhaps joined by a similar case coming out of Missouri. On the national level, *The New York Times* noted that at least 19 other states were following the case closely, "largely because questions of constitutionality, costs and effectiveness of holding sex offenders beyond their prison terms have long been debated" (Davey 2015, n.p.).

On the other hand, Minnesota is home to the Duluth Model, a coordinated community response to domestic violence, which was awarded the 2014 Future Policy Award for Ending Violence against Women and Girls, an international award that recognizes successful policies. Additionally, Washington and Anoka Counties, MN, where the Van Keuren and Shiue murder trials took place, are involved in a system-wide assessment of how such cases are handled and the implementation of a new genre to get domestic violence victims life-saving services immediately.

In a way, then, these Minnesota efforts represent the continuum between progress and misstep in addressing domestic violence and sexual assault, two highly related crimes. These challenges and resulting responses in the state and across the nation allow a close examination of systemic efforts to curtail the crimes. And, eventually, it becomes clear that excessive funding in one attempt can diminish necessary funding in another. Systemic efforts to curtail these crimes, however, no matter how successful or problematic, must also be set within the broad cultural construction of gender and violence as well as specific instances of public alarm and political response. And so, throughout this book we follow the advice of Indiana State Senator Karen Tallian (2013), who cautioned, "Good public policy requires that we look carefully at what we fear" (n.p.).

In particular, we bring rhetorical, legal, and professional communication perspectives to the discourse surrounding two policy-making efforts: (1) the civil commitment option available in 20 states as well as the federal courts, such as the one administered by MSOP, to protect the public by treating and confining dangerous sex offenders after they have served their prison sentences and before they are discharged into the community; and (2) a Lethality Assessment Protocol or LAP, created by the Maryland Network Against Domestic Violence and piloted in Washington and Anoka Counties as well as other counties across the nation, to identify domestic violence victims at high risk of being killed by their abusers and to convince these victims to take advantage of advocacy services immediately. These efforts illustrate the need for effective systemic responses in the broadest sense as well as revision of local legal and judicial policies and procedures, and a study of these efforts reveals the rhetorical, discourse, and legal constructs that either enhance or block such efforts.

Finally, we selected to examine these efforts because continued examination of domestic violence and sexual assault is essential to social welfare. This examination reflects the attempts of professional communication scholars to become activists, in a sense, or to reveal how, through productive discourse, the situations of research participants might be enhanced (see, for example, Propen and Schuster 2008). Although, certainly, men and children are victimized in domestic violence and sexual assault cases, as were Steven Hawkinson, the Lee children, Beth Stauffer, and Jason Wilkman, according to the American Psychological Association (2014) the statistics for adult female victims are quite high. Overall, one in three women has experienced sexual assault, stalking, and physical violence from an intimate partner, and more specifically, the 2015 Minnesota Coalition for Battered Women's "Femicide Report" documented 34 deaths linked to domestic violence statewide, the vast majority of whom were women (n.p.). As noted by Jennifer Vainik (2006–2007), "[W]omen are most likely to encounter violence in their own homes, perpetrated not by strangers, but by men whom the women know and love. These men are often women's long-term partners and the fathers of their children" (1114).

In addition, state and federal civil commitment laws mark offenders such as Ming Sen Shiue as dangerous sexual predators, the "worst of the worst" as often characterized by the media and the public. Across the US, legal and justice systems, including law enforcement, have introduced tools to prevent domestic homicide and to assess the likelihood of recidivism among sex offenders. These tools include orders for protection, no-contact orders, dedicated sexual assault or domestic violence units in police departments and probation offices, expedited hearings for domestic violence cases, enhanced sentences and higher bail for repeat and dangerous offenders, increased victim services, and updated forensic risk assessment tools. Some of these efforts appear to have succeeded more than others in managing the perpetrators who commit these crimes, in protecting the victims of such crimes, and in easing the public's fear. The challenges, however, are many, and the cases complicated, as seen again in the Van Keuren and Shiue cases. Therefore, a rhetorical and professional communication analysis of these challenges seems well worth the effort in extending our theoretical approaches and in revealing how such analysis might guide reform.

Challenges of Domestic Violence and Sexual Assault Cases

The September 22 murder of Teri Lee was not the first time that Van Keuren had assaulted her. That July, shortly after Lee had told Van Keuren that she no longer wanted to see him, he broke into the Lee home and attacked Lee with butcher knives that he wielded in both hands. When asked in a police interview why he brought the knives into Lee's house, Van Keuren answered: "Mostly to maybe straighten her out" (Kotb 2007, n.p.). Likewise, Shiue had been obsessed with Stauffer long before he kidnapped her and her daughter. Prior to the kidnapping, Shiue had burglarized the home of Stauffer's relatives to try to find her, attempted to break into her house, and wrote in his diary about his fantasies of hurting her.

Teri Lee escaped harm from the butcher knife attack, and Van Keuren was arrested at his home in Wisconsin, charged with assault and battery, released on $75,000 bail, and ordered to have no contact with Lee and her family. It took Van Keuren very little time to violate that no-contact order. When Van Keuren showed up at Taylor Lee's volleyball game, coach Judy White remembered Taylor saying: "That man is here. That man who tried to kill my mother. He's here. He's here. He's going to kill me" (Kotb 2007, n.p.). But because Minnesota police would not cross state lines to arrest Van Keuren at his Wisconsin home on a no-contact violation, he remained free.

In the Ming Sen Shiue case, the appellate judges cited psychological assessments and reports and noted in their ruling that Shiue "had engaged in disturbing behavior dating back to his adolescence, and that he was diagnosed with personality disorders, including sexual sadism" (Forliti 2011, n.p.). One psychologist who examined Shiue's file argued, for example, that Shiue "required intensive secured treatment and concluded that he is 'extremely dangerous'" (Chanen 2010, April 19, n.p.). Because Shiue had not undergone or pursued any psychological treatment services while in prison, he argued in his civil commitment appeal that the lack of availability of therapy in federal prison violated his right to due process.

The challenges of managing sexual assault and domestic violence cases and the discourse surrounding those efforts, as we discuss next, involve recognizing such forces as fear, power, and control, and such goals as individual and public safety. These forces and goals are creations, to a great extent, of discourse—public and professional. They are revealed, for example, in personal statements as well as expert testimony.

Individual and Public Safety

As Shuie's November 2010 parole hearing grew nearer, Mary Stauffer, her family, and the general public were understandably nervous at the prospect of Shiue's possible release: said Stauffer, "I don't know that any human institution can ensure total safety" (Martinez 2010, n.p.). Stauffer also expressed the fear that drives many civil commitment decisions: "It would be a huge concern to the public if he isn't ready ... It will just end up happening again" (Martinez 2010, n.p.). Concerns for individual and public safety continue to inform and shape discourse about civil commitment of sex offenders, and emotions in the public sphere can run high when considering the possible release of an offender into the community.

On the one hand, as Catherine West-Newman (2005) cautions, these emotions can often become a "powerful source of human actions and a strategic political resource," at times so powerful to override a reasonable response (314). On the other hand, citing confidence in the ability of the criminal justice system to do its job, one Anoka County assistant attorney who worked on Shiue's civil commitment hearing endorsed the accuracy of the many forensic risk assessments performed by criminal profilers and psychologists: "It's a good thing that the public is protected—that he won't get out unless there are a number of people who determine that he is no longer a risk to the public" (Forliti 2011, n.p.).

Finally, acknowledging not only the risk to public safety but also the controversy surrounding civil commitment, Eric Janus, faculty at Mitchell Hamline School of Law in St. Paul, MN, and an expert on civil commitment laws, asks the overriding question before the judicial system: "What if the judge mistakenly concludes he is not sufficiently dangerous and he goes out and hurts somebody?" (Chanen 2010, April 19, n.p.). However, Janus also notes of the Minnesota program, "If he is committed, it's tantamount to a life sentence," a violation of constitutionally protected rights (Chanen 2010, April 19, n.p.). After all, as the Minnesota Supreme Court earlier cautioned, "To live one's life free of physical restraint by the state is a fundamental right; curtailment of a person's liberty is entitled to substantive due process protection"

(*In re Blodgett* 1994, 914). Judge Frank later confirmed this perspective in his opinion in *Karsjens et al. v. Jesson et al.* (2015), the civil suit brought MSOP clients:

> But our constitutional preservation of liberty requires that we carefully scrutinize any such deprivation of an individual's freedom to ensure that the civil commitment process is narrowly tailored so that detention is absolutely limited to a period of time necessary to achieve these narrow governmental objectives.
>
> (2)

Just as Mary Stauffer and her family feared Shiue's potential release given his past crimes and his potential for recidivism, Teri Lee feared Van Keuren, based on the concerning behaviors she began to notice. When Lee met Van Keuren in 2002, she was raising her four children alone after her husband had died in a car crash. Van Keuren assumed the role of disciplinarian for the children and expected that he and Lee would marry. But Lee's sister, Vicki, noted that after Van Keuren entered Lee's life, the family heard from her less and less, and Lee confided in a friend that Van Keuren had become very controlling. "I can never do anything right," Lee lamented (Kotb 2007, n.p.). Even daughter Taylor noted that Van Keuren "put down a lot of new rules, I think, like we couldn't go barefoot in the house and stuff … I think he just liked being the boss of everything and that made him feel good" (Kotb 2007, n.p.). Teri Lee tried to separate from Van Keuren several times before she finally broke off the relationship, but Van Keuren continued to assert power over Lee and her children and controlled them through fear.

Although friends and family as well as the victim often know that a relationship has become controlling and even dangerous, the victim might stay with her abuser for a number of reasons. On the one hand, domestic violence victims may lack the confidence to leave, as Kim Scheppele (1992) notes: Victims

> repress what happened; they cannot speak; they hesitate, waver and procrastinate: they hope the abuse will go away; they cover up for their abusers; they try hard to be 'good girls' and they take the blame for the abuse upon themselves.
>
> (127)

On the other hand, the victim might be asserting agency by staying with the abuser—keeping the abuser close so as to predict and control abuse. As Elizabeth Schneider (1993) concludes, "The exclusive focus on a particular form of agency—exit—renders invisible all the other active efforts that the woman may have made to protect herself and her children" (390). Moreover, as Lee sensed when she spoke in Van Keuren's bail hearing, the time of separation is the point of extreme danger for the victim. Martha Mahoney (1991) defined this danger as "separation assault": "At the moment of separation or attempted separation—for many women, the first encounter with the authority of the law—the batterer's quest for control becomes most acutely violent and potentially lethal" (5–6).

In the case of Shiue, issues of power and control were also prominent and extreme. According to Pat Brown, a criminal profiler who worked on the case in depth, "Shiue was obsessed with his own sexual, psychopathic fantasies ... His very sadistic fantasy [was one] where he would have total power and control over one woman" (Martinez-Ramundo 2010, n.p.). Sexual violence has been often cited by feminist and cultural theorists as a means of subordinating women, and battery and rape are likewise understood as "acts of power and control" (Merry 2009, 43). The fact that Shiue abducted Stauffer's daughter was also linked to his desire for control. As Brown described,

> [A]bducting Stauffer's daughter was no accident. With the child in tow, Shiue expected Mary Stauffer to be more compliant. "You take the child so that you can have control over the female, because she will do a lot more if she's afraid for her child's life."
>
> (Martinez-Ramundo 2010, n.p.)

Moreover, Shiue raped Mary Stauffer on a daily basis, according to Brown, "not because of an interest in sex but rather because he wanted to humiliate her and exercise his power over her" (Martinez-Ramundo 2010, n.p.). It is not surprising, then, that as Shiue's parole hearing approached, Stauffer and her family counted on the legal and judicial system to keep them and the general public safe.

Moreover, in his trial for murder, Van Keuren testified that he did not intend to kill Lee but to commit suicide in front of her, perhaps the ultimate form of control over the relationship. He had left two suicide notes at his father's house, one of which declared simply: "I had it with her" (*State of Minnesota, Respondent v. Steven Van Keuren* 2008, n.p.). And so, Van Keuren claimed that when he entered Lee's bedroom he intended to shoot himself in the neck, and, on his third failed attempt, the bullet accidently struck Hawkinson. In the sentencing hearing, however, Lee's sister stressed to the judge that "Teri's death had aged each one of us" and that the Lee children "have lost out on a lifetime of firsts to experience with their mom that will now never be shared" (Kathman 2007, n.p.).

Again, these expressions of power and control extend beyond the needs of the individual victim to the demands for public safety in general. In cases such as Shiue's, the legal and judicial systems function to protect the victim and the public by invoking the authority and expertise of legal, criminal, and mental health professionals from across systems and areas of practice. For example, as Mary Kenning, a psychologist who has worked on more than 100 civil commitment cases has stated, the public should realize that in civil commitment cases, "they go over every page of the person's prison file with a fine-tooth comb" (Chanen 2010, April 19, n.p.). Professionals such as Kenning review a perpetrator's prison treatment, discipline and medical records, and visitor logs. They administer personality assessments and other tests that measure the risk of recidivism, and they ultimately consider whether the offender will successfully adjust to life outside of prison. Psychologist Amanda Powers-Sawyer, for example, who helped evaluate Shiue's risk of recidivism and who diagnosed Shiue with sexual sadism and anti-social personality disorder, argued that research indicates that these problems "don't go away with the passage of time" (Chanen 2010, April 19, n.p.).

Teri Lee did as much as she could before the final assault, personally and through the resources offered by the legal and judicial systems, to protect herself, her family, and her support system. As well as having a no-contact order, she asked boyfriend Hawkinson to stay over many nights, or she stayed at his house. She had installed the security system at the house and alerted neighbors to her situation. She gathered photos of Van Keuren to distribute to the children's teachers and had warned them about his potential for violence, and she kept in touch with law enforcement and reported each sighting of Van Keuren. The detective handling her case arranged for extra patrols to drive by her house, and the prosecutor's office had given Lee information about a women's shelter as well as the phone number of a domestic violence hotline. But, much like Lee, many women are uneasy about leaving their homes. Maria Galano et al. (2013), for example, completed a study of 113 women, half of whom resided in a shelter for over a year, and found that rather than violence exposure, such factors as ethnicity, income, housing stability, and mental health determine whether women move into shelters (518). Moreover, as Linda Vinton and Dina Wilke (2014) note, even professionals "may not realize that case management services are even available in domestic violence shelters" (726) and so not be able to explain fully, particularly at a time of high emotion for the victim, just how much help she might have.

With the goal of individual and public safety in mind, the legal system reflects upon and revises the procedures and practices engaged by law enforcement, the rules and statutes created by legislatures, and the responses offered by the judicial system to curtail domestic violence and sexual assault and to better manage the cases when the crimes do occur, illustrated by the Shiue and Van Keuren cases. As we see next and throughout this book, these procedures and practices are reflected in the discourse surrounding systemic efforts and change.

Systemic Efforts and Change

The Minnesota legislature, as do legislatures in 19 other states, provides the criteria for civil commitment of such sex offenders as Ming Sen Shiue by defining the features that distinguish these offenders from those who are able to leave prison to reenter their communities under supervised release or parole. Minnesota offenders confined to state civil commitment facilities are identified as (1) the sexually dangerous person (SDP), who "has engaged in a course of harmful sexual conduct," "has manifested a sexual, personality, or other mental disorder or dysfunction," and, as a result, "is likely to engage in acts of harmful sexual conduct"; and/or (2) the sexual psychopathic personality (SPP), who exhibits emotional instability or impulsiveness such that the person "ha[s] evidenced, by a habitual course of misconduct in sexual matters, an utter lack of power to control the person's sexual impulses and, as a result, is dangerous to other persons" (Minnesota Statutes 2014, section 253D.02, subds. 16 and 15).

The 50-page commitment petition against Shiue filed by the Anoka County Attorney's office illustrates how these systemic efforts are operationalized. The report offered explicit details of Shiue's crimes, including portions of a July 2008 evaluation of Shiue conducted by psychologist Paul Reitman from El Reno prison in Oklahoma. Reitman had reviewed psychological diagnoses made at the time of Shiue's criminal trials and subsequent screenings conducted by the U.S. Bureau of Prisons. Reitman then determined that Shiue "exhibits utter lack of power to control sexual impulses, refusal of treatment opportunities, lack of a relapse prevention plan, violence demonstrated towards his victims, obsession and compulsion, [and] belief that no problem exists" (Chanen 2010, April 19, n.p.). Given the clear directive of the petition and the tenor of its findings, Stauffer and the public could perhaps take some comfort that the legal system would function in the best interest of public safety.

Current systemic efforts, however, failed in the Van Keuren case, a failure that in turn served as a catalyst for systemic change. The case brought not only criticism of law enforcement and the legal system but also resolve to handle domestic violence cases differently in Washington County, MN. On the one hand, upon pronouncing Van Keuren's sentence, Judge Elizabeth Martin expressed to Van Keuren the wish that "you could have done something different to handle the breakup [with Lee] instead of ultimately becoming both suicidal and homicidal" (Kathman 2007, n.p.), placing responsibility for the tragedy solidly on Van Keuren's shoulders. On the other hand, Judge Martin told Van Keuren, and in essence the whole county, that there was one good thing to come out of the publicity surrounding the trial: "This whole situation has raised the collective consciousness in our community regarding no contact orders ... It's brought people together to examine ways we can improve in the future" (Kathman 2007, n.p.). In response, Washington

County Attorney Doug Johnson said that he would like to change the process of handling domestic violence cases, focusing on training first responders to take victims' statements at the scene of the incident and putting victims immediately in contact with advocacy resources. Washington County Sheriff Bill Hutton concurred that domestic violence procedures "should never stop being reviewed" and that throughout the county there should be "some continual process" in terms of handling such incidents (Kathman 2007, n.p.). Law enforcement would no longer stop at the Wisconsin border, for example, when picking up someone for violating a no-contact order in Minnesota.

The degree of success in curtailing domestic violence and sexual assault lies in how such tools and efforts lead to or stem from effective systemic change, change that is defined through professional communication. Success seems better ensured when the legal and judicial systems not only address ways to manage offenders and curtail sexual assault and domestic violence but also use these ways to help adjust perceptions of such cultural aspects as gender roles and rape myths, to avoid marginalization of victims and even perpetrators, and to engage in early intervention and education about the causes of violence. In this book, we draw on the civil commitment laws and the lethality assessment protocol to illustrate the need for and effects of broad systemic change. And again, rhetorical and professional communication analysis inform just how such changes are articulated.

Rhetorical and Communication Perspectives on Domestic Violence and Sexual Assault

We use a rhetorical lens, or rhetorical analysis, throughout this book to illuminate further how discursive acts and textual artifacts shape and reflect the shifting views on domestic violence and sexual assault. In a way, we examine the symbolic artifacts of discourse as well as show how well such artifacts work to persuade an audience. We also stress how such analysis can further rhetorical and professional communication theory and application of that theory to similar cases. Thus, our approach to this analysis understands a text as an artifact "whose meaning is created in a historical context of interactions with different readers" at different times, as characterized by feminist scholar Sandra Harding (qtd. in Hirsh and Olson 1995, 194). Finally, such analysis involves an exploration of the various genres and stylistic choices, audiences, and cultural contexts that so often shape and reflect views and policymaking.

Analysis of Persuasive Communication

As we explore in later chapters, both the questionnaire administered to domestic violence victims during the Lethality Assessment Protocol

(LAP) in Anoka and Washington Counties, MN, and the media articles about the civil commitment debate are documents and discursive artifacts that reflect, in textual form, the views of the public and policymakers on these changing issues. Thus, to explore the social and cultural factors influencing shifting ideas about these issues, we rely predominantly on rhetorical analysis as well as several interdisciplinary perspectives. Again, such analysis is, in essence, the study of persuasion; its chief goal, according to Judy Segal (2005), "is a greater understanding of human action. Rhetorical theory, as a whole, has considerable explanatory power in a world in which we act upon each other by influence" (2). This sort of explanatory power can illuminate a group's norms and values, or what rhetorical scholars would call the values of a discourse community. The analytical focus of rhetorical criticism, then, is not just a specific text but rather "discourse as a whole" (Segal 2005, 5).

Additionally, according to Kenneth Burke (1969), such analysis takes a special interest in the realm of social action and public discourse to identify "the use of words by human agents to form attitudes or induce actions in other human agents" (41). Rhetorical analysis can shed light on how language not only enables but also limits power. With these ideas in mind, then, we explore how the public discourses and textual artifacts surrounding the MSOP debates and conflicts and the use of the LAP questionnaire in domestic violence investigations may lead to systemic change and secondarily to theories about systemic opportunities and barriers to helping the victims of sexual assault and domestic violence. In doing so, we hope to identify not only when and how rhetorical practices might change a system, but also when those systemic changes have the potential to make a profound difference in the lives of victims and the treatment of offenders of domestic violence and sexual assault. We offer below a brief review of some of the theories we explore, apply, and extend in upcoming chapters.

Genre Theory and Systemic Change

Scholars of rhetoric have long studied discursive catalysts for systemic change in organizational cultures by way of the study of genres. Early on, Carolyn Miller (1984) defined genre as a set of "typified rhetorical actions based on recurrent situations" (156). Clay Spinuzzi (2003), in his study of genres in organizations, went on to propose: "One way to change a genre ecology [or 'an interrelated group of genres'] is to introduce new genres to mediate activities differently" (65). Moreover, as we have argued elsewhere (Schuster and Propen 2010), the introduction of a new genre, such as a victim impact statement, into the domestic violence courtroom can not only influence the conditions of an offender's sentence but also lead to collective understanding of the victim's plight and the "potential for systemic change" (27). In subsequent chapters in this book, we consider the LAP as a catalyst for change in legal and judicial systems by capturing, through interviews with stakeholders, the experiences of those now using LAP and by analyzing the changes that came from LAP and help elicit cooperation among agencies. In particular, we look at the persuasive elements in the LAP questionnaire as administered to domestic violence victims, often at the scene of an assault. In doing so, we explore the intersections of genre theory and legal studies to help illuminate the need for more understanding of systemic change in scholarly and activist work.

That is, work in genre studies has explored how documents might reflect ideologies of systems and organizations and how new genres might disrupt these systems, but emerging scholarly work has explored how a genre might work to so change perceptions, behaviors, and even core beliefs. In *Conceiving Normalcy*, for example, Elizabeth Britt (2001) considers how a Massachusetts statute mandating insurance coverage for infertility works as a "technology of normalization" that is actually "most successful when it sustains, rather than resolves, the tension between the normal and the abnormal," or the fertile and the infertile (2). Along similar lines, Emily Martin (1998) argues that women adjust and adapt to the language and cultural assumptions of biological science, which are very "real in their effects on the way doctors and patients act in the world" (125). Martin (1998) notes, for example, that "standard medical accounts of a woman's body going through menstruation, birth, and menopause depict her as engaged in various forms of industrial production: when she menstruates instead of getting pregnant, it is interpreted as failed production" (125). This and related work have often struggled with two disparate possibilities: the idea that the inclusion of more women in the system can help initiate change; or the idea that women eventually adjust to the cultural assumptions underpinning a system that does not change. Through rhetorical perspectives, we explore how women's voices and women's bodies are addressed in domestic violence and sexual assault cases in legal and judicial systems that may be on the brink of changing perception and behavior, and how the introduction of a new genre affects women's sense of agency.

Kairos, *Moral Panic, and Perceptions of Risk*

Systemic changes within organizational cultures and discourse communities are not only reflected through genres, but also often rely on and reflect the rhetorical concept of *kairos*. As Sharon Crowley and Debra Hawhee (2008) point out, "*Kairos* draws attention to the mutability of rhetoric, to the ever-changing arguments that can be found in connection with a particular issue," and so people "can become deeply interested in issues and then they grow disinterested" (48; see also Benedikt 2002; Smith 2002). While the concept of *kairos* does not assume exact causality between events, or causal analysis per se, our analysis of civil commitment debates in Minnesota, for example, traces how kairotic forces led media, public, and political interests to increase at the time of highly publicized sex offenses, and how these interests became so combative that they eventually left MSOP vulnerable to the constitutional challenge and an order for reform. Moreover, as we describe in Chapter 1, we extend Crowley and Hawhee's notion of stakeholders becoming interested and then disinterested in an issue by recognizing how these moments might repeat, forming kairotic cycles in which resolution of an issue might become impossible, particularly when perceptions of risk lead to moral panic. The debate about Shiue's potential release, for instance, is just one example of many recent conflicts about the possible release of sex offenders back into communities, which have caused moral panic within these communities.

Where *kairos* is an opportunity that a rhetor can occupy for advantage in responding to a social or political controversy, the sociological concept of moral panic necessarily complicates kairotic rhetoric. Moral panic, according to Phillip Jenkins (1998), results in "a wave of irrational public fear" that occurs "when the official reaction to a person, groups of persons or a series of events is out of all proportion to the actual threat offered" (6). As we describe in more detail later in this book, sex offenders illicit a public response of fear and anger, for example, or a kind of moral panic seen in kairotic cycles, because the public lacks the knowledge or resources to engage in the sort of dialogue that can lead to effective systemic change. In the case of the kairotic moments pertaining to civil commitment in Minnesota, then, moral panic seems to initiate a chain reaction: the media describe risk to public safety, the public believes that the risk is real and immediate, and policymakers, particularly elected officials, respond with extreme action.

For a moral panic to continue, current regulation is perceived to be a failure, and the panic might end only when citizens are reassured that "officials have vanquished the folk devils through new repressive policies" or when the public moves on to another cause (Irvine 2008, 29; see also Jenkins 1998; Kappeler and Potter 2005; Leon 2001). For example, in the case of Shiue's potential release, Mary Stauffer and concerned publics were satisfied with the outcome of the case only after it became clear that he would not be released. In a moral panic, isolated incidents become social concerns, which then become criminal issues through politicization. And so, as Chas Critcher (2002) summarizes the relationship between the public, the media, and the official response,

> to acquire significance, an issue must assume prominence in all three arenas, often passing from one agenda to another. The media agenda emerges as pivotal. It mediates between policy and public agendas, constructs the public agenda and seeks to influence policy agendas. (529–530)

With these ideas in mind, we examine later in this book the possible factors that may influence the functioning of *kairos* in a rhetorical situation that involves moral panic and that may be shaped by perceptions of risk.

Complicating the phenomenon of moral panic in the kairotic moments, then, are perceptions of risk, or as J. Blake Scott (2006) has proposed, *kairos* "is about the management of future risk" because a rhetor will claim to "successfully discern and assess, strategically intervene in, and control risk based on the probable" (116). On the one hand, arguing on the basis of a certain perception of personal risk can involve propositional thinking and, what Robert Gordon (1980) defines as fear-motived action rather than action done out of fear. Using Gordon's work, Michael Pfau (2007) goes on to suggest that fear-motived action can involve "a rational and strategic response to danger," rather than an "irrational and counterproductive action" (219). On the other hand, as we see often in high-profile sexual assaults, during periods of moral panic, as Ulrich Beck (2002) describes, perceptions of probable risk are often distorted and seen as more extreme than they really are, because of the public's insecurities over the ability to control the perceived risk (35). The rhetorical analysis we use throughout this book, then, relies on identifying the cultural norms and values through a rhetorical study of persuasive strategies and genres as well as kairotic cycles, moral panic, and perceptions of risk.

Cultural Perspectives on Domestic Violence and Sexual Assault

In this book, we combine cultural perspectives on domestic violence and sexual assault with the results of empirical research. Scholars of professional communication have identified examination of the cultural context of professional communication as essential in understanding the content and effect of that communication (see, for example, Longo 2000). These perspectives allow us to take a critical and speculative look at the current problems of domestic violence and sexual assault, adding, when appropriate, a historical context, as well as offering, when possible, different ways to imagine the future. Our perspectives on culture echo that of Catherine West-Newman (2005), in that culture "defines both the qualities of individual identity and the constitution of social groups with distinctive values and practices" (305). These perspectives also follow that of Madelaine Adelman, Hillary Haldane, and Jennifer Wies (2012), in that culture is "a way of thinking, moving, and being that shapes and is shaped by the way an individual sees and experiences the world" (692). In turn, empirical research, such as interviews and observations, provides us with a concrete way to determine how people process and document experiences with these violent acts and how agencies and officials propose solutions to such violence. Empirical research can reveal how people talk about these acts in personal interviews, public forums, and courtrooms and how they write about the acts in legislative reports and judicial decisions.

Persistent Gender Roles

Important aspects of these cultural opinions pertain to gender roles, particularly in any study involving domestic violence and sexual assault. In a patriarchal and hierarchical culture, men and women are perceived and empowered differently, not so much based on biological distinctions but on ways in which they are expected to perform. Put quite simply by Leah Daigle and Sadie Mummert (2014), gender roles are based on "the degree to which a person has adopted the cultural roles ascribed to a given sex" (257). Daigle and Mummert allow for degrees of individual conformity to gender roles; however, historically and currently men and women as a group are often expected to follow different cultural rules.

Elizabeth Pleck (2004), for example, examines the historical notion of the so-called "Family Ideal," established during the colonial periods in the United States and England, a concept that supported "distinct ideas about family privacy, conjugal and parental rights, and family stability" (7). Fathers had the right to control and discipline their wives and children so that marriage and the family could be preserved at almost any cost; wives were expected to raise the children and to keep a clean and orderly home in accordance with their husbands' rules. Domestic violence was a private family affair, beyond the boundaries, scrutiny, and intervention of the state. Rape statutes, as created in Massachusetts in 1642, for example, defined "carnal copulation" or rape as an act that "forcibly and without consent ravished any maid or woman that is lawfully married or contracted" (qtd. in Reddington 2009, 319). Moreover, juries in rape cases were often given cautionary instructions that favored the defendant, such as those offered by Lord Chief Justice Matthew Hale in the 17th century:

> (1) rape is a charge that is easily made by the victim, (2) rape is a charge that is difficult for the defendant to disprove, and (3) the testimony of the victim requires more careful scrutiny by the jury than the testimony of the other witnesses in the trial.
>
> (Qtd. in Morris 1988, 154–155)

Over the last few decades, domestic violence and rape reform laws have been examined and revised to address how gender roles might still disadvantage such victims. The no-contact orders obtained by Teri Lee and the civil commitment ordered for Ming Sen Shiue, for example, work to protect the victim as well as society from the perpetrator. However, scholars such as Kathleen Basile, Jeffery Hall, and Mikel Walters (2013), still see the need to apply a feminist perspective to domestic violence and sexual assault: "Abuse of partners is understood by examining the social context. In a patriarchal society, men have more political, economic, and social power than women; therefore men can use violence as a way to subordinate women" (851). And so, critiques of gender roles and the hierarchy maintained by a patriarchal system offer perspective when encountering an offender such as Steven Van Keuren, who assumed that his relationship role in regard to Lee was to "straighten her out."

Rape and Domestic Violence Myths

Despite reform to avoid gender discrimination that affects how sexual assault and domestic violence victims are treated, certain myths prevail. These cultural myths, according to Kimberly Lonsway and Louise Fitzgerald (1994), are "attitudes and beliefs that are generally false but are widely and persistently held, and that serve to deny and justify male sexual aggression against women" (134). These myths include "The Majority of Rape Claims Are False"; "Rape Only Happens to 'Bad' Women"; "The Majority of Rapes Are Committed by a Stranger"; "Rape Is a Black-on-White Crime"; "Women Secretly Wish to be Raped"; and "When a Woman Says 'No' to Sex, She Really Means 'Yes'" (Garland 2009, 14–19). In addition, according to Eric Janus (2006), rape myths "portray men as unable to control their sexual urges when they reach some point of sexual arousal" and so generally "shift responsibility for sexual violence onto women, minimizing not only the harm to the women but also the responsibility of both the male perpetrator and the larger society" (79–80).

Officials within law enforcement and the judicial system, however, are becoming more aware of these myths and refute them in sexual assault and domestic violence cases. Judge Amy Holmes Hehn (2014), a Multnomah County, Oregon circuit court judge, for example, reflected on a domestic homicide committed by Ian Ellis, whose actions were similar to Van Keuren's, and offered such perspectives as the following: "With rare exceptions, domestic abusers, including those who murder their partners, aren't 'crazy'"; although Ellis suffered from anxiety and depression, as did Van Keuren, "he wasn't insane; he was arrogant, entitled, abusive, selfish and controlling" (n.p.). And so Judge Hehn (2014) argued,

> Domestic abusers don't have "anger management problems." They are generally able to manage their anger just fine outside the home. An abuser uses his anger as a tactic to punish, control, terrorize and coerce his partner to achieve specific goals—to shut her up, to isolate her, to prevent her from spending money, to keep her from complaining about his infidelity, to keep her from asserting her independence. (n.p.)

Similarly, Van Keuren's new house rules isolated and controlled Lee and her children. In such cases, however, we cannot look at gender roles without looking at the place of violence within our culture.

Violence as a Cultural Construct

In both the Shiue and the Van Keuren cases, the sexual assault and domestic violence offenders were motivated to maintain control over their victims through violence. Shiue abducted Stauffer's daughter to control his victim, and Van Keuren violated his no-contact orders to prove his easy access to Lee's children and so terrify her in threatening potential violence. Kathryn Gallagher and Dominic Parrott (2011) speculate that even though progress has been made to foster egalitarian relationships between men and women, "men who still believe in the dominance of the male gender may harbor hostile attitudes toward women because they feel their control over women is declining" (578). Two perspectives at either end of the continuum on violence as a cultural construct, women's defensive violence and men's hypermasculinity, illustrate the challenge in altering the relationship between violence and gender roles.

On the one hand, cultural acceptance of gender violence is potentially but usually unsuccessfully disrupted by women's use of force to defend themselves against their abusers. Mary Anne Franks (2013–2014), for example, contrasts Stand Your Ground laws, which she believes grant men immunity in some cases of deadly violence, to the Battered Women's Syndrome, which she describes as forcing abused women who strike back in self-defense to plead for mercy, requiring them to defend any aggression against their abusers by subjecting "their behavior to extensive scrutiny and evaluation by experts, lawyers, and juries" (1102). Sally Engle Merry (2009) calls this dichotomy a two-track system of self-defense, which carries the message that although men can advance upon a stranger, women should retreat back into their homes to be protected. In other words, according to Merry, the Stand Your Ground/Battered Women's Syndrome axis "offers more power to the already powerful, immunity to the already protected, and reproach for any woman who tries to act like a man" (1127).

On the other hand, the propensity that some men show for violence may be enhanced hypermasculinity, or as Megan Vokey, Bruce Tefft, and Chris Tysiaczny (2013) define the condition, an "extreme form of masculine gender ideology" that is "comprised of a cluster of beliefs that includes toughness, violence, dangerousness, and calloused attitudes toward women and sex" (562). In particular, this extreme masculine toughness marks anger as the legitimate male emotion and other expressions of emotion as suspect, feminine, and a sign of weakness. Perhaps most important, batterers argue that their female partners are responsible for their violent responses, because these partners attempt to dominate their men, and the batterers further claim that they are victimized by a criminal justice system that constructs all men as villains and all women as victims. Thus, Kristin Anderson and Debra Umberson (2001) found that the batterers they studied constructed masculinity through gendered violence: "By gendering violence, these batterers not only performed masculinity but reproduced gender as dominance. Thus, they naturalized a binary and hierarchical gender system" (375). Violence, then, is culturally constructed along gender lines.

Marginalized or Silenced Voices

Finally, another outcome of trying to account for or understand the complications of violence and cultural gender roles is the way in which involved individuals might be stereotyped or marginalized; this marginalization casts the abuser as a "monster" or the victim as lacking courage and common sense—and both as characterized as abnormal or other than the accepted norm. Here, we borrow from Joy Johnson et al.'s (2004) definition of "Othering," which they see as "a process that identifies those that are thought to be different from oneself or the mainstream [in ways that can] reinforce and reproduce positions of domination and subordination" (255). This reinforcing of dominant discourses then produces an "Other," or, in Sara Ahmed's (2000) words, a stranger who is always "out of place" (15).

As Jennifer Dunn and Melissa Powell-Williams (2007) found in their interviews with victim advocates, when people create images of victims that deny their agency, "not only do these images fail to capture the complex experience of real battered women, but they also produce a new kind of deviance in the form of pathetic victims" (983). R. Emerson Dobash and Russell Dobash (2011), for example, found that the abuser would often perceive the victim as at fault

> because of her "flaws" as an intimate partner, mother, and/or housekeeper. Accounts about the flaws of the woman that justify the violent response of the man are, at base, reflections of his beliefs about the appropriate behaviors for women and men in intimate relationships.
>
> (130)

These rigid standards extend to the children, as with the Lee children who were not allowed to walk barefoot in their home.

Perpetrators, then, may be "Othered" in the context of both domestic violence and sexual assault. In the first place, lack of understanding about the abuser's motivation might cast the abuser into the role of Other, disregarding any mental illness, childhood abuse, and other stressors that may underlie the violence—in an act of Othering, the Lee family's attorney, Bill Harpen, stated at Van Keuren's sentencing hearing that the Lee children were "relieved to know that that *malignant soul* will not be walking the streets any more" (Kathman 2007, n.p., emphasis added). In the second place, during the time of Ming Sen Shiue's parole hearing, Stauffer, in expressing her opinion that sex offenders will reoffend if released, concluded that "the reality is this won't be over until he's dead" (Chanen 2010, September 29, n.p.). In attempting to allay the public's fears about sex offenders, politicians may in effect reinforce those fears by echoing the media's portrayal of all sex offenders as deserving of the same extreme sentence, as not belonging in any community ever, or as incapable of rehabilitation. In turn, the media both constructs certain types of knowledge about sex offenders and limits the production of certain types of new knowledge that may allow for more nuanced conversations about sex offender policy and ultimately help effect systemic changes.

Legal Perspectives on Domestic Violence and Sexual Assault

Rhetorical and professional communication scholars have turned to the legal arena not only as an essential part of cultural analysis but also as a context in which complicated persuasive artifacts emerge (e.g., Andrus 2015). As in the Shiue and Van Keuren cases, the law attempts to safeguard the public from harm, including those domestic violence incidents that might end in injury or homicide and those sex offenders whose histories make civil commitment appropriate. To do so, the law "establishes jurisdictional boundaries within which its authority prevails," to use the words of Austin Sarat et al. (1998, 3). Within the law, for example, sexual assault and domestic violence cases are classified by degrees of severity, standard penalties are meant to ensure consistency, and first responders are directed to follow policies such as when to detain the offender.

Often perceived to be static and hegemonic in setting and maintaining these boundaries, the law actually reflects and responds to or even controls social change. Early on, James Boyd White (1990) proposed that the function of legal discourse, "which purports to be neutral, to seek only public good, to be concerned with justice, and so on, is actually to mask or obscure" an exercise of power (xiii). In doing so, legal discourse, continues White, might do so "accidently or unconsciously, perhaps more malevolently, with the aim of inducing the most injured by the political process to acquiesce in it" (xiii). Sarat and Thomas Kearns (2000) continue this perspective: "Focusing on the production, interpretation, consumption, and circulation of legal meaning suggests that law is inseparable from the interests, goals, and understandings that deeply shape or comprise social life" (6). Such legal perspectives, then, are constituted in an effort "to shift the location at which we study law from the opinions of the appellate courts to the expressions of ordinary people carrying out the tasks of everyday life" (Kahn 2003, 155). Moreover, the law operates through influencing modes of thought or requiring people to normalize or self-monitor their actions. Some meanings and opinions, moreover, are "privileged while others are delegitimated or denied voice—practices in which unity is forged from difference by exclusion, marginalization, and silencing of alternative visions and oppositional understanding" (Combe 2000, 33).

These theoretical perspectives, applied throughout this book, lead to investigations of how the law responds to and reflects social and systemic change and demand, while attempting to apply seemingly objectified standards; how the law may reflect cultural bias while promoting public safety; and how the law identifies and disciplines abnormalities while working to curtail crime. A brief review of that legal system, as it affects and was affected by the Shiue and Van Keuren cases, confirms the importance of these investigations.

The Judicial System

The judicial system is responsible for interpreting and applying the law, in other words, considering those boundaries of authority that ensure equal justice for all citizens. In terms of civil commitment for additional confinement and treatment after the completion of a prison sentence, as in Shiue's case, the judicial system may be asked to consider whether an empowered majority has passed a law that could harm or take undue advantage of a marginalized minority. Thus, the judicial system has had to decide whether sex offenders, such as Shiue, may be deprived of equal protection of the law because their actions are so appalling that we are willing, to use the words of Janus (2006), to create a "reduced-rights zone" for this group (23).

The first such challenge to the constitutionality of civil commitment laws, for example, came in the landmark case *Kansas v. Hendricks* (1997). Here the U.S. Supreme Court tackled the question of whether the civil commitment of Leroy Hendricks after he completed his prison term for committing several sexual acts with children constituted additional punishment and a second prosecution. Writing for the U.S. Supreme Court in the *Hendricks* (1997), Justice Thomas opined, "There are manifold restraints to which every person is necessarily subject for the common good. On any other basis organized society could not exist with safety to its members" (n.p.). Therefore, this Court sustained civil commitment statutes whenever there was proof of both dangerousness and some mental incapacity to control behavior, thus upholding the goal of public safety. Moreover, at this time, the Court found that civil commitment was not punishment but instead treatment designed "to hold the person until his mental abnormality no longer causes him to be a threat to others" (n.p; see also LaFond 2000).

Legislative Bodies

State legislators get involved in writing laws that set boundaries of authority as well as respond to and reflect social concerns. Moreover, because legislators are elected officials, they may be particularly sensitive to the reactions of their constituents, who might express dismay, for example, if their representatives appear "soft on crime."

Under pressure, the Minnesota Legislature has more than once extended the duration of imprisonment for criminal sexual conduct. At the time of the Shiue case, Minnesota sex offender sentencing guidelines set a presumed sentence of 144 months in prison for first-degree sexual conduct for an offender with no criminal history and no aggravating circumstances as opposed to 360 months or higher for a repeat offender who acts with extreme violence and disregard for the victim (Minnesota Sex Offender Grid 2014, 1). Shiue not only was sentenced to 30 years to life on a federal kidnapping case, but he also was sentenced concurrently to 40 years on state murder charges, the highest possible term according to the sentencing guidelines (Minnesota Sentencing Guidelines Grid 2014; see also Martinez 2010, n.p.). These sentencing guidelines reflect such firm boundaries that a judge who departs from them must submit a justification to the Sentencing Guidelines Commission, and so the guidelines represent an attempt to protect the public from offenders such as Shiue.

Law Enforcement

The primary task of law enforcement is to discover, detain, and deter persons who might violate the boundaries and norms of the law. In other words, if individuals cannot self-monitor or normalize their actions, law enforcement steps in. Mandatory arrest of offenders constitutes one way in which law enforcement responds to domestic violence cases.

Law enforcement officers in many states, including Minnesota, have the liberty to arrest a domestic abuser even in a "he said/she said" situation. In the past, police officers and sheriff deputies would have to witness an incident of domestic violence or have a corroborating witness in order to arrest an offender, most likely a carryover from the rape statutes in English Common Law. Now, if the victim has visible injuries or if the officer is convinced by other evidence that abuse has taken place, the officer can arrest the offender without a warrant (Pirius 2012, 17; see also Minnesota Statutes 2014, 629.343). In the Van Keuren case, for example, if the initial charge against Van Keuren had been domestic abuse rather than a violation of a no-contact order when he was found armed with butchers knives at Lee's house, the arresting officers could have arrested Van Keuren without a warrant even if Van Keuren had fled the scene or if Lee had been the only witness. Law enforcement, thus executing the laws that enable them to arrest a domestic abuser without a warrant, in essence, re-sets legal boundaries by granting additional credibility to law enforcement and perhaps the victim.

Prosecution, Probation, and Parole

Prosecution, probation, and parole officials enforce the consequences of violating the law and supervise the actions of domestic violence and sexual assault offenders based on the assumption that these offenders have forfeited the right to live in the community until they demonstrate that they can successfully self-monitor their actions. The efforts of prosecution, parole, and probation departments to identify and correct abnormal behavior are exemplified by the "no-drop" policies followed by prosecution in domestic violence cases.

If a victim of domestic violence does not appear in court to testify against her abuser, the case is not dropped despite the constitutional guarantee within the Sixth Amendment that the accused has the right to confront any witnesses against him or her. Simply put, often victims of domestic violence do not behave like victims of other violence crimes. They may recant their account of the incident because they fear retaliation by their abusers, want the violence to stop but not the relationship, or depend on the abuser for financial support of themselves and their children. Prosecution may take so long that the victim has moved on with her life, so a trial seems unnecessary and a strain on her fragility and security. Given no-drop policies, prosecution moves forward to base a case on other evidence, perhaps relying on expert testimony to explain the typical reasons a domestic violence victim may be absent from a proceeding. In a way, the no-drop prosecution policies may protect the victims from the abusers trying to intimidate a victim, abusers who think that a case rests solely on their victims' testimony. However, such policies may also deny victims the option of withdrawing a complaint once formal charges have been filed, marking this option as abnormal in the public's mind and potentially reducing her personal sense of agency and voice (Corsilles 1994; Davis, Smith, and Davies 2001; Smith and Davis 2004).

Advocacy Groups

Finally, community-based advocacy organizations often started as refuges for women and children escaping abusive situations. In fact, the first such shelter nationally, Women's Advocates, Inc., which started in St. Paul, MN, in 1974, now serves an average of 45 women and children daily (Women's Advocates 2014). These organizations usually allow victims to choose whether to report and cooperate with law enforcement and prosecution, a choice that affirms a victim's sense of agency and voice. The groups also offer therapeutic support for emotional trauma, safety plans for victims who wish to remain at home, guidance for those seeking orders for protection, and coaching for those writing victim impact statements for sentencing hearings.

Alexandra House, in Anoka County, for example, offers resources to victims of sexual violence, violence that includes everything from sexual harassment to criminal sexual conduct in the first degree. A checklist of "What To Do If You've Just Been Sexually Assaulted," for example, which appears on Alexandra House's web site, begins with advising the victim to call 911 or go to a safe place and ends with directing the victim to preserve evidence (Alexandra House 2014). The language used to guide the victim through these steps is crafted to stress the victim's options; for example, "Make a police report if you choose. This can be done at any time"; "You may feel physically OK, but it is still a good idea to talk to a health care provider." And, at the other end of the victim's journey through the legal and judicial systems, such advocacy groups will help a victim prepare an impact statement, sometimes the only opportunity a victim has to describe for the judge the effect of the assault on her physically, emotionally, and financially. Shiue's victims and their families, for example, spoke not only during his trial for kidnapping and murder but offered their reactions at the hearing for his civil commitment. Moreover, Teri Lee's sister gave an impact statement at Van Keuren's sentencing hearing, stressing the post-traumatic stress treatment needed for Lee's children (Kathman 2007, n.p). Victims may feel less marginalized as they walk through the process with a victim advocate at their side.

Within the legal and judicial systems, voices can be silenced or empowered, and agreement or resistance may emerge as the law responds to social change, phenomena that we explore throughout this book as a reflection of the cultural context of professional communication as well as a site for scholarly study of persuasive and complex communications.

Preview of the Book

Throughout this book, we rely on secondary research as well as observations of public events and hearings and face-to-face interviews with those directly involved in managing sexual and domestic violence offenders, setting policy in the legislatures, prosecuting offenders and rendering decisions in courtrooms, overseeing conditions of release from prison and discharge from MSOP, providing advocacy services to victims, and responding first to an incident. We explain our data collection and analysis methods more thoroughly in the Appendix to the book.

We have arranged this book to alternate chapters between our analysis of the controversies surrounding civil commitment of sex offenders (e.g., Chapters 1 and 3) and the implementation and administration of the lethality assessment protocol (e.g., Chapters 2 and 4) for two reasons. First, we believe that this method of presentation establishes thematic counterpoints in that we move from misstep to progress in our first two chapters, from stakeholder stagnation in terms of effectively countering sexual assault to stakeholder cooperation in attempting to curtail domestic homicide. Second, in these chapters we begin with a precise, even micro-examination of the discourse surrounding each challenge, beginning with the policies and protocol supporting the Minnesota Sex Offender Program and the attempts to identify and support high-risk domestic violence victims. In the chapters that follow, we offer a broad rhetorical and cultural analysis of how such aspects as "Othering" a marginal group and enforcing or resisting gender roles complicates any attempt to solve the problems associated with sexual assault and domestic violence. We do so to illustrate and emphasize the contributions we believe such a multidisciplinary analysis can add to rhetoric theory and understanding.

In Chapter 1, we identify what we define as kairotic cycles in which the responses of the public and policymakers rise and then fade based, in part, on media coverage of particularly frightening sexual assaults. Additionally, we analyze the moral panic and misperceptions of risk and recidivism that tend to follow such incidents. We begin the chapter with a description of the 2012 public and political reactions to a proposed new facility for low-risk civilly committed sex offenders in Cambridge, MN, and to the possible provision discharge from MSOP of Thomas Duvall. Both efforts were derailed due to unfavorable public and political response.

Then to examine in depth the kairotic cycles within the history of MSOP, we explore three kairotic moments: the Dennis Darol Linehan case in the late 1990s; the 2003 kidnapping and murder of Dru Sjodin by Alphonso Rodriguez, Jr., shortly after his release from prison; and the provisional discharge from MSOP of Clarence Opheim in Spring 2012. The Linehan case began the public rhetoric about what to do with dangerous sex offenders upon their release from prison and initiated the legislative response to widen the net to civilly commit such offenders. The public and political reaction to the Rodriguez case led, in essence, to two decades during which no civilly committed offenders were discharged from MSOP. And, finally, the second provisional discharge since the creation of MSOP, that of Opheim, stirred up again responses by policymakers, the media, and the public, even though Opheim is now living safely in the community. Throughout this analysis, we find that such kairotic moments can become kairotic cycles, in which the solutions to a problem can be stymied by competing perceptions and entrenched positions that reoccur over time, often without resolution.

In Chapter 2, we begin with the story of how the administration of a lethality assessment tool most likely saved the life of a pregnant

19-year-old victim of domestic violence in York County, PA, in 2012. We then describe the risk assessment protocol developed at Johns Hopkins University, which then became the LAP through the efforts of the Maryland Network Against Domestic Violence. We focus on LAP as a new and potentially disrupting genre that reveals and perhaps revises the efforts and values within a system, such as the law enforcement, prosecution, probation, and judicial agencies in Washington and Anoka Counties, MN.

In this chapter, we focus on the risk assessment questionnaire itself, an 11-question tool to elicit "yes" or "no" responses from a domestic violence victim on the scene of the incident. A scoring of high risk leads to a statement from the first responder that "people in your situation have been killed by their abusers" and an immediate phone conversation with a victim advocacy group. Through our interviews, we discover the tension within the administration of LAP between systemically changing approaches to domestic violence and increasing the efficiency of existing resources. In our close examination of the implementation of LAP, we discover how the questionnaire was designed to be a catalyst for changing the mind of the victim about her situation so that she would immediately cooperate in accepting services, such as leaving the abuser to take refuge in a shelter. We conclude this chapter by looking at the ways in which a domestic violence victim is asked, throughout the LAP process, to substitute one fear for another, to be persuaded that it is safer for her to leave her abuser, even though she rightly fears violent reprisal for taking the steps to do so. Within this chapter, we extend our knowledge of the rhetoric of fear appeals as they work to persuade the domestic violence victim to participate in LAP.

In Chapter 3, we continue to complicate public discourses about the civil commitment debate but focus even more specifically on the identity politics and discursive practices of Othering surrounding the civil commitment of sex offenders. We do so to comment on the challenge of civil commitment to make effective system change. We argue that sex offenders are often essentialized and uncritically grouped or categorized through a complex set of discourses rooted in the public's fears and in elected policymakers' perceived need to allay those fears for their constituents. Thus, we add a new layer of complexity to the intersection of rhetoric, public discourse, and identity theory by complicating the ways in which stakeholders inadvertently assign a kind of power to the Other through discourses of fear and punishment.

We begin this chapter by analyzing in more detail the public perception of Clarence Opheim on the eve of his provisional discharge from MSOP, recalling and extending Burke's theory of identification and Krista Ratcliffe's (2005) refinement of that theory and her own "rhetorical listening." We also extend Sara Ahmed's (2000) account of the discourse of "stranger danger" and other scholars' perceptions of the motivations and results of Othering. We return to the expectations that the sex offender must be "cured," as assured through risk assessment tools, before being discharged into the community. It is from this vantage point that we complicate the category of sex offender and what we contend are overly determined and insufficiently critiqued categorizations of this group. This categorization, we contend, contributes to the failure of Minnesota policymakers to make sufficient changes in MSOP. In particular, the fear and power imbalance that comes from Othering the sex offender prevents efforts to move offenders who have successfully completed treatment to provisional discharge, to ensure public safety, to address the constitutional rights of offenders, and to allocate sufficient state funds to domestic violence and sexual assault programs in a budget now strained in sustaining the civil commitment program.

In Chapter 4, we return to the Van Keuren case as well as introduce the court decision in *Town of Castle Rock, Colorado v. Gonzales* (2005) to further our analysis of cultural gender roles and related expectations about violence as they pertain to the law. In the *Gonzales* case, we explore a violation of a no-contact order to see how, at times, notions of proprietariness, a form of hypermasculinity, as well as Othering, essentialization, and dichotomization complicate attempts to curtail domestic violence. Also, we explore discursive perspectives on a kind of verbal violence that distinguishes the seemingly mistaken beliefs of the domestic violence victim from the beliefs of those who persuade and manage her within the legal and judicial systems.

We also explore how LAP has served as a catalyst for systemic changes in the two Minnesota Counties. The Anoka County Department of Corrections began, in conjunction with LAP, an Intensive Domestic Assault Pre-trial Program (IDAPP), which includes electronic monitoring, alcohol and chemical testing, and counseling for offenders who volunteer to participate in the program. The city or county attorney and the judge then take this participation into account when setting bail and imposing a sentence. And, in both counties, those advocacy groups cooperating in LAP extended their safety planning to take, for example, an individual approach to victims' needs based on their responses in the LAP questionnaire. We also balance the optimism among Minnesota first responders that LAP will change minds about domestic violence with a recent study in Oklahoma about how often high-risk women, as identified in risk assessment protocols, do elect to seek formal advocacy help for separation. In doing so, we explore how LAP-related programs face the challenge of honoring a victim's sense of agency as they may change her behavior and beliefs. We end the chapter by speculating about the ultimate challenges of making broad cultural changes regarding gender and violence within the legal and judicial systems.

Finally, in Chapter 5, our concluding chapter, we review how rhetorical and professional communication analysis, in conjunction with gender, legal, and cultural analysis, can help us understand the complexities of domestic violence and sexual assault as well as how this study extends theory. In this chapter, we also update the reader on the current status of MSOP and LAP. We describe the 2014 Othering of Robert Jeno, the second successful provisional discharge from MSOP, in a community notification hearing in Le Center, MN, and we relate the political response after Judge Frank rendered his decision that the statutes that establish and govern MSOP were unconstitutional in the *Karsjens* trial. We also review two protocols that were developed in Minnesota in conjunction with LAP: an Expedited Domestic Violence Case Program and a Threat Assessment Advisory Group. We also endorse a public health approach to domestic violence and sexual assault as well as a hope that this book will contribute to the scholarly and activist dialogues about these crimes.

1 Perspectives on Public and Political Controversy

Kairos, Moral Panic, and Risk

In the fall of 2013, a plan to open a new regional facility in Cambridge, MN, for low-risk civilly committed sex offenders was suspended when media coverage escalated, the community protested, and political figures reacted. The plan by the Minnesota Sex Offender Program (MSOP) was to move 12 offenders currently residing in its St. Peter facility to Cambridge. Six offenders were from the assisted living unit, which houses offenders who are aged or medically compromised and thus need specialized care, and six were from the alternative unit, which houses offenders with learning disabilities, cognitive impairments, or traumatic brain injuries. These offenders, called "clients" throughout MSOP, in order to stress individual responsibility for change, but referred to in the media as the Cambridge 12, had reached "maximum treatment effect," as Dr. Nicole Elsen, a treatment psychologist at St. Peter, testified in the *Karsjens et al. v. Jesson et al.* trial (Elsen 2015, February 18, n.p.). In other words, the so-called Cambridge 12 would not benefit from further treatment and could function in a less restrictive environment. However, despite the fact that those in the new facility would be closely supervised, one local resident expressed the fear generated within the Cambridge community in saying, "I am not going to sleep well with those *beasts* over there" (Browning 2013, n.p., emphasis added).

The Cambridge proposal came around the same time that MSOP supported the petition to provisionally discharge Thomas Duvall, a convicted rapist who had been in civil commitment treatment since 1991. Although MSOP felt that Duvall could be safely transferred to a secure halfway house, Minnesota State Attorney General Lori Swanson opposed the discharge and requested an evidentiary hearing to determine Duvall's fitness for discharge. That fall, the Cambridge proposal and the Duvall discharge combined to create what Democratic-Farmer-Labor (DFL) Minnesota Governor Mark Dayton called a "political circus," as policymakers such as GOP state Representative Kurt Zellers considered Duvall's possible discharge to be "outrageous, offensive and an affront to public safety" (Bierschbach 2013, n. p.). In reaction, the governor sent a letter to Lucinda Jesson, the Commissioner of the Department of Human Services, the department that oversees MSOP, directing her to "oppose any future petitions by sexual offenders for provisional releases" and to "suspend your department's plans to transfer sexual offenders to other tightly supervised facilities, such as in Cambridge" (Dayton 2013, n.p.). The governor wanted Jesson to wait until the state legislature had the opportunity to review and/or revise existing civil commitment statutes to ensure the public's safety, and to agree to and provide funding for additional less restrictive facilities—actions that the legislature failed to take in 2013, 2014, 2015, and thus far in 2016. Dayton closed his letter with a frank statement about where he stood on provisionally discharging MSOP clients such as Duvall:

> By way of background, as you know, for many years the State of Minnesota has kept its most serious criminal sexual offenders locked away with virtually no chance of release. That is where most Minnesotans would prefer to keep them, and I agree. As a father and a grandfather, I believe the risks are too high to allow them to walk freely.
>
> (Dayton 2013, n.p.)

But he also alluded to the necessity for change should the federal court find MSOP unconstitutional, particularly in violating due process rights as guaranteed in the Fourteenth Amendment, in what became the *Karsjens* class action civil suit.

The governor's decision was applauded by local politicians who had cautioned the governor about the Cambridge plan. Brian Johnson, representing Cambridge in the state legislature, said he was "pleased" that Governor Dayton had "finally agreed" to Johnson's own position on "the dangerous transfer of sexual offenders to less secure facilities" and cautioned the governor to consult more with lawmakers about such actions in the future (Kytonen 2013, n.p.). Also, the mayor of Cambridge commented that in making his decision the governor had "truly listened to our concerns" (Kytonen 2013, n.p.). And, so when Commissioner Jesson was cross-examined by the Defense in the *Karsjens trial*, she admitted that in terms of the Cambridge proposal, "The community reaction was more than anticipated" (Jesson 2015, n.p.). The result, testified Nancy Johnston (2015), the Executive Director of MSOP, was that although the Cambridge 12 had reached MSOP's ultimate goal "to treat sex offenders in order to render future treatment unnecessary," at the moment there was "no place to put them" other than leaving them in the existing facility in St. Peter (n.p.).

We begin this chapter with the Cambridge and Duvall stories to demonstrate how policy solutions can be derailed by media coverage, public fear, and partisanship sustained in professional communication and public discourse. When fear is out of balance with needs and risks, attempts at reform and intervention tend not to succeed. At the same time that the public may perceive risk about, say, the discharge of a sex offender back into the community, policymakers and legal experts may also be working to act in the best interests of public safety. Thus, discourses about risk perception often simultaneously reflect the public's and policymakers' perceptions about public safety and the necessary treatment and confinement of sex offenders after they have completed their prison sentences and before their reentry into the community. In the rest of this chapter, through rhetorical and professional communication perspectives we examine more closely the civil commitment of sex offenders as a case study illuminated specifically by theories of *kairos*, moral panic, and risk perception.

Our purpose is twofold: to point out how the examination of such kairotic contexts must often include the dimension of moral panic and perceptions of risk among all stakeholders when professional communication and rhetorical scholars examine extensive and controversial public issues or policy decisions; and in doing so, to enhance our theoretical understanding of *kairos* in the public and legal arenas by identifying how kairotic moments in such situations may become kairotic cycles, condemned to repeat without resolution. In this case, these kairotic cycles help us understand the failure to thus far resolve the fiscal problems and constitutional challenges that MSOP, in particular, faces. In our goal of extending theoretical perspectives as well as the potential relationship between scholarship and advocacy, we explore whether the rhetorical concept of *kairos* always represents the right choice at the right time, or whether *kairos* may become so heavily influenced by moral panic, and in particular, perceptions of risk, that the right choice may not be persuasive or even obtainable.

Again, 20 states and the federal government have civil commitment laws to deal with sex offenders, those "criminals we have come to call 'sexual predators,'" or "the worst of the worst," who appear so dangerous that they "seem to be pathologically different from the rest of us" (Janus 2006, 2). We focus on MSOP because although Minnesota's standards for civil commitment are similar to other states (see, for example, Abracen and Looman 2006; Jackson and Hess 2007; Sreenivasan, Weinberger, and Garrick 2003), in 2015 Minnesota had over 720 offenders in civil confinement at a cost of $129,000 per head, per year, as opposed to about $29,565 per year for a prison inmate, and thus MSOP had an annual operating budget of over $76 million (Tice 2014, n.p.). Moreover, until the spring of 2012, MSOP had not successfully provisionally discharged a sex offender from the secure treatment facilities at Moose Lake and St. Peter. That is, the first person ever to be conditionally discharged violated a condition of his discharge (although he did not reoffend sexually) and was returned to MSOP where he eventually died. By August 2015, only two MSOP clients were back in the community. Minnesota is not alone in these challenges. In September 2015, U.S.

District Judge Audrey Fleissig ruled that although Missouri's sexually violent predator law was constitutional as written, it was not constitutional as applied. By April 2015, no one in Missouri's Sex Offender Rehabilitation and Treatment Services (SORTS) had been released, and Judge Fleissig ruled the SORTS program "suffers from systemic failures regarding risk assessment and release that have resulted in the continued confinement of individuals who no longer meet the criteria for commitment, in violation of the Due Process Clause" (Berman 2015, n.p.; *Van Orden et al. v. Schafer et al.* 2015).

These challenges are not inevitable, however. By the end of 2014, for example, Wisconsin, which shares a similar demographic population with Minnesota, had 362 civilly confined clients in their Sand Ridge Secure Treatment Center, and since 1994 had placed 129 clients back into communities throughout the state, with about a third of those completely discharged and no longer needing supervision (Freeman et al. 2014, 89–90). Minnesota's situation, however, made MSOP vulnerable to that mandate by Chief U.S. Magistrate Arthur Boylan, who, in the summer of 2013, ordered Lucinda Jesson to convene a task force to recommend ways to reform MSOP or face a take-over by the federal courts (Oakes 2011, n.p.). This mandate then led the way to the direct constitutional challenges to the state civil commitment program in 2015. With these ideas in mind, we consider how Minnesota's situation can be illuminated through the theoretical perspectives of *kairos*, moral panic, and risk perception and can also contribute to our scholarly use of these perspectives.

The Concept of Kairotic Cycles

To extend rhetorical notions of *kairos*, particularly when affecting public policy decisions, we use Minnesota as an example to trace the controversies over civil commitment as they emerged within three kairotic moments: the Dennis Darol Linehan case in the late 1990s, which generated the first public rhetoric about civil commitment in Minnesota; the November 2003 kidnapping and murder of 22-year-old female college student Dru Sjodin by Alfonso Rodriguez, Jr., which in essence prevented Moose Lake and St. Peter from discharging even those offenders who had participated fully in their treatment programs; and, finally, the provisional discharge of the sex offender Clarence Opheim in spring 2012, which again stirred up responses by policymakers, the media, and the general public.

This last kairotic moment was initiated by a particular document or artifact—the Minnesota Legislature Auditor's (2011) report on the problems of and necessary reforms to MSOP—which became evidence in the *Karsjens* federal trial in early 2015. We examine the political, public, and media response to these three kairotic moments and provide observations of legislative hearings, public symposia, media response, and the *Karsjens* case, as well as the results of 21 interviews with stakeholders. (See the Appendix for a description of our data collection and analysis.) In doing so, we illustrate how moral panic and risk perception can so influence what seems the right choice at the right time that stakeholders may get caught in what we call kairotic cycles, where solutions to a problem are stymied by competing perceptions and by entrenched positions that reoccur over time and without resolution.

The Rhetorical Notion of Kairos

John Poulakos (1999) defines rhetoric as "*the art which seeks to capture in opportune moments that which is appropriate and attempts to suggest that which is possible*" (26, emphasis in original). The ancient Greeks proposed that persuasive rhetors must be aware of recent events that make an issue urgent at the moment, the arguments that various groups seem to favor, the power dynamics or hierarchies involved, the prevailing values of the audience, and any other challenges bound up with the particular issue. *Kairos* identifies situational time to make a point through exigence or persuasive communication. Exigence, according to Lloyd Bitzer (1999), is "an imperfection marked by urgency" and must be capable of being changed by rhetoric to be rhetorical (221). Many rhetorical scholars combine these two highly related concepts of *kairos* and exigence within "the rhetorical situation," or what we consider as kairotic moments.

Moreover, the most persuasive solutions are usually produced by the cultural and political elements of a situation rather than by transcendent and unchanging laws (Bizzell and Herzberg 2000). Carolyn Miller (1992), for example, concludes that *kairos* indicates that situations are also created by rhetors and can foster a "dynamic interplay between objective and subjective, between opportunity as discerned and opportunity as defined" (312; see also Miller 1994). *Kairos* then becomes not only a critical opening but also a constructive power to fill an existing gap or create a new rhetorical void, which the rhetor can then occupy for advantage. In this chapter, we extend Crowley and Hawhee's (2008) ideas about the "mutability of rhetoric" and the notion that stakeholders may become interested and then disinterested in an issue, as we consider how these moments may form cycles in which the resolution of an issue might become stymied or even impossible, especially when perceptions of risk lead to moral panic within the public arena (48).

The Problem of Moral Panic

If we see *kairos* as an opportunity that a rhetor can occupy for advantage in responding to a social or political controversy, the sociological concept of moral panic necessarily complicates kairotic rhetoric. The functioning of moral panic in a rhetorical situation that involves the creation and implementation of laws governing the civil commitment of sex offenders allows us to speculate as to how the interplay between confinement and treatment as well as between public safety and constitutional rights for sex offenders stymies resolution by state policymakers within kairotic cycles.

We recognize that, in some situations, extreme panic might seem reasonable, such as in response to a natural disaster or a radical threat. Moreover, to many stakeholders—in particular, the general public—moral panic might constitute an expected response, for example, to the possible release of a notorious sex offender from prison or the discharge of this offender from MSOP. In this book, however, we distinguish between such fear and even disgust on the one hand, which might prove reasonable and even productive to effective systemic change given the presence of a sex offender among the general population, and moral panic on the other hand, which becomes so extreme, disruptive, and costly that it becomes counterproductive to such systemic change. We rely on the thoughts of the many sociological scholars who provide perspectives on so-called irrational moral panic—or who likewise define moral panic itself as so extreme as to prevent reasonable solutions. We do so in light of the low recidivism rate of sex offenders and the close supervision and continued treatment of such discharged sex offenders—factors we add to our argument within this chapter. We are particularly interested, then, in how *kairos* functions in the context of the sort of chain reactions, such as those that seem to be happening in Minnesota. Here, the media communicate a perceived risk to public safety, the public perceives that risk as legitimate and immediate, and policymakers respond with extreme action. Thus, we examine the possible factors that may influence the functioning of *kairos* in a rhetorical situation that involves moral panic and that may be shaped by perceptions of risk.

British sociologist Stanley Cohen (1980) defines the stages and complications of moral panic as follows:

> A condition, episode, person or group of persons emerges to become defined as a threat to societal values and interests; its nature is presented in a stylized and stereotypical fashion by the mass media; the moral barricades are manned by editors, bishops, politicians and other right-thinking people; socially accredited experts pronounce their diagnoses and solutions; ways of coping are evolved or (more often) resorted to ... Sometimes the panic passes over and is forgotten, except in folklore and collective memory; at other times it has more serious and long-lasting repercussions and might produce such changes as those in legal and social policy and even in the way the society conceives itself.
>
> (9)

Others have gone on to interpret what Cohen meant by the very phrase "moral panic." David Garland (2008), for example, speculates that by "panic," Cohen meant a "sudden and excessive feeling of alarm and fear ... leading to extravagant or injudicious efforts to secure safety" (10). By "moral," deep emotional dimensions as well as transient feelings, according to Janice Irvine (2008), map "specific features of the historical movement, institutional agents and practices, cultural and discursive strategies, media representations, dynamics of specific political movements and their activists as a way to understand the eruption of feeling" (4). According to these scholars, moral panic can represent emotional and extreme, even irrational, responses to a perceived and unsettling threat.

Again, in instigating and perpetuating a moral panic in cases such as the one we studied, three groups of rhetors often play a key role: the media, the public, and the professionals involved in the decision-making process. Daniel Filler (2003) and others recognize and describe the rhetorical moves made by such groups: claim makers use melodramatic language to demonize offenders and to contrast the deviants from the rest of society; they emphasize that because the crimes are random, anyone can become the next victim (Best 1987; Vess 2009). Moreover, Garland (2008), responding to the work of Erich Goode and Nachman Ben-Yehuda (2006), states that these rhetors engage in concerns that spark anxiety; hostility toward the deviants; consensus about the negative social reaction; disproportionality or exaggerations about events and risk; volatility, particularly given media reporting; and perhaps eventually introspective soul-searching throughout society to identify the deviant event as a result of systemic problems (11). This last effort, examining systemic problems, is particularly challenging. In reforming MSOP, Chief U.S. Magistrate Judge Boylan, in essence, asked the task force to move beyond both the extreme public fear of sexual predators, often exaggerated through media coverage, and the insecurity of elected officials should they appear "soft on crime" to their constituents. Boylan called for systemic changes to ensure that at least some sex offenders could safely reenter the community upon successfully completing treatment.

Media coverage, then, plays an important role in our study because, through the very nature of the business, media often serve as the catalyst for a moral panic and thus have the power to influence or curtail systemic change. Stuart Hall et al. (1978), early on in their study of moral panic about mugging in Britain, for example, recognized that novelty was a conventional news value and that the media often categorize not only crime but also ideological frames within society to catch the public's attention. And so, Marjorie Zatz (1987), in her study of Chicano youth gangs in the United States, concluded that it was the business of the media "to create images and structure ideas in thematic ways ... to produce a particular ideology" (131). Even when the statistics do not support beliefs about rising crime in any one category, the media often stigmatize those who break the law and threaten the social order. As Michael Welch, Eric Price, and Nana Yankey (2002) later assert, in the moral panic over the 1989 "wilding" attack on a New York City jogger, the media contributed to a widespread public belief that the singular attack posed a social threat and that some action must be taken to stop such a threat (10).

For the media to contribute to a moral panic, however, "there must be some latent potential on the part of the public to react to a given issue to begin with"; the media must "touch something of a responsive chord in general public," according to Goode and Ben-Yehuda (2006, 24–25). The common fear of stranger rape, for example, overshadows the fact that most sexual assaults are committed by someone with whom the victim is acquainted. Civilly committed sex offenders vary widely, in terms of being found guilty of statutory rape, familial sexual assault, stranger rape, and/or pedophilia, and their history of crime differs just as widely; for example, this population in Minnesota ranges from those who committed their crimes only as juvenile offenders to repeat adult offenders, and their ages range from 19 to 92 (Minnesota Department of Human Services 2014).

The public, however, according to Sean Hier (2002), participates in interpolating from media coverage that sexual assault outside one's family or social circle is the real danger. Subsequently, as Anna Barvir (2007) says, once the public finds out about an abduction, rape, or murder, "everyone jumps on the first bandwagon to city hall" (705). Furthermore, perceptions of risk contribute to moral panic, particularly in contrast to the low recidivism rates among sex offenders.

The Effects of Risk Perception

Assessing risk of recidivism proves quite difficult and must be balanced against public safety and the constitutional rights of the offender. In appealing his civil commitment order in 2010, Ming Sen Shiue, for example, argued that his crime was a single incident, and that because it happened thirty years ago and he was now sixty years old, violence was no longer a relevant issue. In fact, although the results of recidivism or reconviction studies vary, most indicate that sexual offenders, including child molesters and rapists, have a reconviction rate of between 6 and 19 percent, much lower than for other kinds of crimes (see, for example, Center for Sex Offender Management 2000). Also, according to Janus (2006), "The vast majority of sexual violence is most likely not committed by released sex offenders. In fact, of the most serious offenders (those who receive prison sentences) only one in seven had a prior conviction for a sex offence" (50).

Those who manage sex offenders assess the probability of risk or recidivism in two primary ways: the clinical approach method, which relies on a professional who, based on information gathered through such sources as interviews and records, assesses the dangerousness of each offender; and the actuarial method, in which factors that indicate the risk of re-offense are combined with empirical research into a formula used to weigh those factors and to produce a risk score for each individual (Janus 2006, 55–56). These assessments lead to both categorizing a sex offender (with Level 1 being considered the least likely to reoffend and Level 3 being the most likely to reoffend), a system common nationwide, and then judging whether the petition to civilly commit a Level 3 offender should be granted. Level 3 sex offenders in Minnesota, such as Shiue, if released back into the community after finishing their prison sentences, must register as sex offenders for at least ten years or the duration of probation, whichever is longer. The penalties for those who fail to register or update any changes in their profiles reflect the investment that society makes in following such offenders to protect the public; for example, conviction for failure to register adds five years to the registration period, and convictions are then subject to a prison sentence (Minnesota Bureau of Criminal Apprehension 2010, n.p.; see also Minnesota Statutes 244.052, 2014). As in other states, Minnesota state legislature shares the belief that

> if members of the public are provided adequate notice and information about a sex offender who has been or is about to be released from custody and who lives in or near their neighborhood, the community can develop constructive plans to prepare themselves and their children for the offender's release.
>
> ("Sex Offender Notification" 2014, n.p.)

Those legislators who create risk management systems assume that identifying and labeling the most dangerous offenders will protect the public—or help the public protect itself.

For those Level 3 sex offenders, for example, law enforcement notifies schools and daycares, organizations that serve individuals most likely to be victimized by the sex offender, and members of the community whom the offender is likely to encounter. This action means that neighbors find notices placed in their mailbox stating that a Level 3 sex offender has moved close by. A website available to any member of the public contains a photo and demographic information for each offender, including current address and offense information (see, for example, Minnesota Department of Corrections 2014). In 1996, the Minnesota Legislature passed a law requiring every law enforcement agency to have such policies for disseminating information about the location of certain sex offenders to the public. In addition, in 1999, the U.S. Court of Appeals for the Third Circuit confirmed that notification did not violate double jeopardy and *ex post facto* constitutional rights because notification did not constitute additional punishment (*E.B. v. Verniero* 1997), and that sex offender registration and notification laws did not violate fundamental privacy rights (*Paul P. v. Verniero* 1999). The often limited resources of law enforcement and the increasing homelessness of sex offenders who must follow restrictions on where they may live challenge these protective measures; the public, however, is still reassured that the most dangerous offenders will be monitored.

Despite these careful tactics created by legislators, implemented by law enforcement, and sustained by the judicial system, misunderstandings about the probability of recidivism contribute largely to public and political impressions of the risk of having sex offenders free in the community. As Scott (2006) has described, a rhetor will attempt to "control risk based on the probable" (116). However, a risk society, according to Beck (2002), occurs when the "speeding up of modernization has produced a gulf between the world of quantifiable risk in which we think and act, and the world of non-quantifiable insecurities" (40). This insecurity, according to Beck (1999), is a reflection of being out of control and unable to measure and predict risk. Scott (2006) summarizes this perspective in relation to *kairos* as follows: "[K]airos and rhetoric might be viewed less as seizing an advantage—whether created or inherited—than as adjusting, with no clearly foreseeable effects, to ongoing and projected knowledge-power relations that are continuously circulating, mutating, and affecting" (138). During periods of moral panic, perceptions of risk are particularly distorted, and seen as more extreme than they really are, because of these insecurities over the ability to control risk.

Perceptions of risk are also highly influenced by cultural perceptions; in other words, people must believe in risk for that risk to have any real effects. Again, despite statistical reassurances about the rarity of stranger rape, the cultural perception is that we are all in danger of becoming victims of this predator (Wilcox, Jordan, and Pritchard 2006). According to a study by the U.S. Department of Justice (2005), however, incidents of domestic violence and acquaintance sexual attack far outnumber incidents of sexual assault by strangers (9; see also Becker et al. 2003). And again, risk of recidivism among sex offenders, whether known or unknown to the victim, is much lower than in other violent crimes, such as homicide or assault and battery. The issue of recidivism becomes even more complicated when examining whether re-offense is reduced more by treatment while confined to a secure facility or by treatment within the community, with some studies concluding there is no statistical difference between the two populations (Freeman et al. 2014, 60–61). But as Lisa Anne Zilney and Laura Zilney (2009) state, "[R]egardless of what academic studies reveal, the general public believes that sexual offenders have a very high re-offense rate" (124).

Again, the media play a role in unsettling the public, who then demand official reaction to perceived risk from stranger assault, particularly after a highly publicized and violent sex crime. With extensive media coverage in a risk society, fear of crime then becomes a "mistaken impression" about the probability of becoming victimized (Tullock 1999, 36). And so, through media coverage, Beck (2007) asserts, "We all know that *the face of tragedy could have been our own*" (70, emphasis in original). The "truth" about risk is also a product of disputes within the public arena, in which experts make a bid for citizen approval (Grabill and Simmons 1998, 423). Some elected officials may attempt to appeal to their constituents by exaggerating risk and then proposing more rigid guidelines for containing these risky individuals.

Certainly we recognize that even one instance of sexual assault is tragic. However, the focus on civilly confined sex offenders, fueled by misperceptions about risk and recidivism, also draws attention away from the greater problem of domestic violence and familial or acquaintance sexual assault and draws funding away from educational, prevention, and intervention attempts to address these issues. The Domestic Abuse Project (DAP) (2013), for example, reported that its 2013 annual budget was $1.8 million, with just 11 percent of that funding coming from the state of Minnesota, but it still provided 2,043 victims of domestic violence with 32,352 services during that year; those services range from providing support and safety plans for victims, to accompanying victims to court hearings (1). This budget contrasts greatly to the funding devoted to MSOP. Moreover, DAP's (2013) therapy program provided help to 381 men, 151 women, and 68 youth to help substitute positive behaviors to overcome learned behaviors of abuse and violence (2). Also, Minnesota's largest center devoted to preventing family violence, one that provides crisis shelters, legal advocacy, and counseling services, received $3,758,576 in 2014 from the Minnesota Department of Public Safety, Office of Justice Programs, but supported 25,254 unduplicated victims of domestic violence as well as several thousand more who did not identify as victims (Personal Correspondence 2014). Finally, as we show later in this chapter, risk can be carefully managed once a sex offender is provisionally discharged from MSOP—a discharge that could end in a return to a civil commitment facility if *any* provision is violated.

In this chapter, then, we illuminate the public and legislative demand for controlling perceived risks during three kairotic cycles of debate about civil commitment. In doing so, we intend our work not only to contribute to rhetorical and professional communication theories, particularly about *kairos* but also to continue the scholarly conversations begun by rhetorical scholars about risk in general. Such conversations include that of Leah Ceccarelli (2001), who examined manufactured scientific controversies designed to promote or delay public policy, and Huiling Ding (2013), who studied transcultural risk communication to discern how key players such as global agencies, local communities, and the media, responded to concerns about the spread of the H1N1 flu virus, for instance.

Kairotic Rhetoric About Civil Commitment of Sex Offenders: The Dennis Darol Linehan Case

Certainly in the history of civil commitment of sex offenders, *kairos* plays an essential part in determining whether public safety concerns or whether fundamental liberty rights of sex offenders to be treated in the least restrictive environment possible emerge as more persuasive in creating and implementing the law. As Miller (1994) notes, *kairos* "points both towards the way in which opportunities may be perceived and responded to and towards the ways in which they may be defined or constructed" (83). *Kairos* affects not only how successful a persuasive strategy might be but also if action is taken at all. As Beck (2000) reminds us, when kairotic rhetoric is based on fear, and when that fear extends into moral panic fueled by perceptions of risk, extensive media coverage, and strong legislative response, risk can characterize an intermediate state between security and destruction, where the perception of threatening risks determines thought and action.

Decisions in Florida and Wisconsin

State legislatures and agencies, for example, might resist ways to reintegrate sex offenders back into the community after the shock of a high-profile sexual assault, or they might invite that community to engage in discourse about community reintegration to ease fears and avoid moral panic. In the first instance, the Florida state legislature as of 2014 avoided developing post-release supervision and step-down procedures for those sex offenders civilly committed—procedures made by both the Department of Children and Families and the Office of Public Policy Analysis and Government Accountability that would better ensure the successful reintegration of offenders back into the community (Freeman et al. 2014, 88). Some speculate that this inaction resulted from the case of 8-year-old Cherish Perrywinkle, who was raped and murdered by registered sex offender Donald James Smith in June 2013. Earlier, Smith had pled guilty to a misdemeanor for stalking Cherish and her family and had been released from the county jail where inmates are not subject to review for civil commitment. In reaction to the Perrywinkle tragedy, Florida doubled the mandatory minimum sentence for rapists who attacked children younger than 12 years old and extended civil commitment laws to offenders serving jail sentences. According to Florida state

Representative Matt Gaetz, "'We know one certain fact ... No one has ever raped a child while sitting in state prison'" (Salzhauer and Gordon 2014, n.p.). In the second instance, sex offender programs provide education and information in community notification processes when an offender is released. The Wisconsin civil commitment program, for example, has taken the common position that "it is responsible for providing education and information whenever the opportunity arises in order to dispel myths and provide accurate information about safety measures that can be employed to reduce vulnerability to sexual assault" (Freeman et al. 2014, 98). Wisconsin's program goes farther, however, in responding to the media through a public information office and participating in media educational series about civil commitment in the state. In addition, communities are assured that they will not inherit released sex offenders from other counties but are involved in helping "their own" readjust to life outside of confinement, a process that is designed to promote "a sense of fairness" in discharging offenders (Freeman at al. 2014, 98). Resistance by legislatures or involvement by the community depends on the rhetorical situation, as we see next in the Dennis Darol Linehan case.

Legislative Response to Linehan's Crimes

In Minnesota, the Linehan case generated what we consider the first public kairotic rhetoric about civil commitment of sex offenders and illustrates in more depth how *kairos*, moral panic, and perceptions of risk complicate public and political controversies. Although the state had had a civil commitment law since the 1930s pertaining to the mentally ill and dangerous, the statutes were revised in response to the *Linehan* case. Linehan was imprisoned for killing 14-year-old Barbara Iversen during an attempted rape, and then, after he escaped from prison in 1975, he tried to assault a 12-year-old girl. In 1992, when Linehan was due to be released from prison, authorities attempted to civilly commit him as a "psychopathic personality." The Minnesota Supreme Court overturned this decision. A requirement of the existing statute was that before being civilly commuted, an offender had to have "utter lack of control" over his sexual impulses. The Court heard convincing testimony that Linehan did have such control. In response, the Legislature passed the Sexually Dangerous Persons Act, and because he met the new and broader criteria, Linehan was civilly committed (*In re Linehan* 1997, n.p.). Linehan himself recognized that he was the "poster child" for civil commitment, and according to local media coverage, his history was "a parent's worst nightmare" (Oakes 2008, n.p.). Policymakers revised the laws in response to the possibility that Linehan and other high-risk offenders, who at the time received very little or no treatment while in prison, might reenter society after completing their sentences, and the media celebrated this legislative action in stories such as "Dangerous Folks: Linehan Stays Where He Belongs" (*StarTribune* 1999, n.p.).

The opposing argument that such laws violated specific constitutional rights, such as due process, double jeopardy, and *ex post facto* protection, did not prevail at this point for two main reasons (see *Kansas v. Hendricks* 1997; *In re Blodgett* 1994; Zonana et al. 1999). First, according to the courts, if a civilly confined offender was indeed offered treatment during civil commitment, then the time spent civilly committed for the same crime was not additional punishment per se and therefore was not unconstitutional. Second, to protect public safety, policymakers as well as the public seemed to accept what Janus (2006) identifies again as that reduced rights zone: "Most fundamentally, they [civil commitment cases] take away a person's liberty not as a punishment for a past act but to protect against a feared, but uncertain, future act" (33). Future court decisions seemed to continue in the some direction. In *Kansas v. Crane* (2002), for example, the U.S. Supreme Court, consistent with its stance in *Kansas v. Hendricks*, upheld the constitutionality of the Kansas Sexually Violent Predator Act, and in *US v. Comstock* (2009), the courts affirmed that the federal government could also civilly commit sex offenders. With this affirmation in mind, in 2010 the Association for the Treatment of Sexual Abusers took the following stance: "Such civil commitment programs should develop steps for a sex offender to be conditionally released to a less restrictive setting, if and when appropriate [upon completion of treatment], while taking into account community safety consideration" (2010, 2).

Thus, the subsequent system in response to the Linehan situation was created to handle future so-perceived high-risk offenders. A sexual predator could now be civilly committed either as a Sexually Dangerous Person (SDP) or as having a Sexual Psychopathic Personality (SPP), the requirements for which we explained in our Introduction. The legislature went on to refine these requirements to include that an offender "had *likelihood* of causing serious physical harm to another person," and a second option, which increased the number of offenders identified as SDPs or SPPs—that of causing "*emotional* harm" (Ombudsman 2010, 1, emphasis added). To reenter the community, the SDP or SPP had to convince first a special review board and then a Supreme Court appeal panel that he or she could adjust to society and no longer needed treatment or supervision in a secure setting and that a personalized provisional discharge plan offered protection to the community. And so, in 1995, Minnesota opened a new 20-million-dollar, 100-bed facility to accommodate the growing number of civilly committed sex offenders.

The "Linehan Factors"

Subsequently then, deciding the civil commitment appeal in the Shiue case, for example, Mary Stauffer and the public would essentially rely on the post-Linehan definitions of SDP and SPP. Indeed on September 29,

2010, the district court found that Shiue met the criteria to be civilly committed as an SDP. The district court stated that the course of harmful sexual conduct was evidenced by the rapes of Stauffer and by Shiue's sexually motivated conduct, including "the burglary; stalking; murdering the child witness; kidnapping M.S. and E.S.; threatening to kill M.S. and her family to gain her compliance; and assaulting M.S. while she testified" (*In re the Civil Commitment of Ming Sen Shiue* 2011, n.p.). Moreover, the district court found that Shiue suffered from "a sexual, personality, or other mental disorder or dysfunction and that he is 'highly likely' to engage in acts of harmful sexual conduct"; the court also agreed with the diagnosis that the appellant suffered from "paraphilia sexual sadism and a personality disorder" (*In re the Civil Commitment of Ming Sen Shiue* 2011, n.p.). Because the court found no evidence that there was a less restrictive alternative that would meet Shiue's treatment needs and the requirements of public safety, it determined that MSOP would be the most appropriate program for Shiue should he ever leave prison.

Moreover, Shiue met the "Linehan factors," as they were now called. In examining the likelihood of re-offense, the Linehan factors determined that the following six aspects must be considered in a civil commitment case:

> (1) the offender's demographic characteristics; (2) the offender's history of violent behavior; (3) the base-rate statistics for violent behavior among individuals with the offender's background; (4) the sources of stress in the offender's environment; (5) the similarity of the present or future context to those contexts in which the offender used violence in the past; and (6) the offender's record of participation in sex-therapy programs.
>
> (*In re the Civil Commitment of Ming Sen Shiue* 2011, n.p.)

The district court then considered these factors and found that they supported the conclusion that Shiue would be likely to reoffend if he were ever released.

Success of any civil commitment system, however, depends on accurate assessment of risk. Legal scholars, such as Wendy Larcombe (2012), seem confident that an "expanding body of criminological and psychological research into recidivism and risk assessment now informs the design of actuarial tools used in a range of corrections settings to assess the ongoing risk that convicted sex offenders pose to the community" (483). According to a risk assessor at the Minnesota Department of Corrections, however, such assessment "has a certain rate of false positives and false negatives," a fact that such officials accept but that the public does not tolerate (A-5; see the Appendix for information on interview citation style). The aftermath of cases such as that of Linehan influence the public to expect "no risk" from sex offenders, "an unreasonable expectation" (A-5). Moreover, on the one hand, recidivism had been "dropping significantly in the last 15 years," and one can "safely assume that civil commitment plays a part" in this decrease, attests this risk assessor (A-5). On the other hand, spending money on "educating parents" about "who [the] biggest threat is against their children," the family member or the acquaintance, could have a similar effect, but this official also notes, "it's a lot easier to fund something that has that concrete presence than something as nebulous as prevention" (A-5).

That is, as Stephen Morse (1998) has asked, "Who can object to increased public safety in the abstract?" (265). However, Morse also expresses concern that any "pure preventative detention" or non-treatment measures potentially involved in endorsing civil commitment constitute a "morally, politically, and practically frightening prospect" (266–267; see also Carlsmith et al. 2007; Morgan 2006). Equally frightening, then, are the images of sex offenders loose within the community and the violations of the constitutional rights of those civilly committed possibly without adequate treatment. The first fear reflects the concerns of the public, once made aware of the presence of such offenders; the second fear involves the upheaval by state legislatures of protected rights for all citizens, marginalizing and silencing those who disgust us or terrify us, the monstrous "Others," so that treatment steps are so ill-defined as to constitute an indefinite sentence. According to Franklin Wilson (2004), "It is safe to say that society finds violent and sexual offenses intolerable. The knowledge that such offenses have occurred numerous times only serves to amplify society's disdain for the acts and their perpetrators" (379; see also Stern 2000).

This insistence on controlled risk through assessment and treatment during confinement, in essence, silences not only those stakeholders raising constitutional challenges to civil commitment but also those who recognized that the systemic changes did not address the issue of fiscal commitment at the expense of broader educational, prevention, and intervention efforts to curtail both domestic violence and sexual assault. These factors were still in place during the next kairotic moment we trace in Minnesota, when college student Dru Sjodin was abducted and murdered by Alfonso Rodriguez, Jr., a moment that signaled the difficulty of escaping what was becoming kairotic cycles of the civil commitment controversy.

Moral Panic About Sexual Predators: The Alfonso Rodriquez, Jr., Case

If the Linehan case represents the initial kairotic rhetoric about civil commitment, that is, when public safety concerns overrode constitutional rights, low recidivism rates for sex offenders, and the need for more balanced fiscal allocations, then the Alfonso Rodriguez, Jr., case was the catalyst for another wave of moral panic over the perceived risk of sex offenders. The legislative solution to civilly confine dangerous sex offenders did seem to reassure the Minnesota public alarmed by the prospect of an offender such as Dennis Linehan walking free, that is, until November 22, 2003, when 22-year-old female college student Dru Sjodin was abducted and murdered by Rodriguez.

In between the time of the Linehan and the Rodriguez cases, debate over the fate of sex offenders did not receive much public attention although the issue certainly arose in courtrooms. In the case *In Re the Matter of Leon James Preston* (2001), for example, Minnesota plaintiff Preston argued that he did not meet the requirements for civil commitment: he not only protested that there was insufficient evidence that he would engage in harmful sexual conduct in the future but also argued, in a strange twist of logic, that because "he was able to plan his assaults, groom victims, and wait for an opportune time to offend," he could actually control his impulses (n.p.). Psychologist James Alsdurf testified that Preston's behavior "was substantially likely to result in serious emotional harm to the victims" (n.p.). But it was psychologist John Austin who summed up Preston in the language that evoked not only fear but also disgust: Preston, Austin testified, was a "manipulative pedophile" (n.p.). The Court agreed, and the civil commitment of Preston stood.

Moreover, although even harsher condemnation of such offenders based on disgust and fear might be outside the norm in the judicial arena, concerned legal observers note that such condemnation still appears. In Montgomery County, Texas, for example, District Judge Michael Seiler was well known among the parties for calling all offenders under consideration for civil commitment "psychopaths" and once suggesting that the best way to curtail their potential for re-offense was castration "at neck level" (Hassan and Ward 2014, n.p.). Business-as-usual in the legal arena at times might include such examples of disgust and fear, but it was the Rodriguez case that once more served as a catalyst for moral panic among the public and policymakers—panic so high that it required drastic long-term systemic response, a response that not only sustained this kairotic moment in Minnesota but confirmed the kairotic cycles still evidenced in the debate over civil commitment in the state.

The Legacy of Rodriguez

Rodriguez had recently been released from prison after completing a 23-year prison term for stabbing and attempting to kidnap a woman. Although he was assessed by the Department of Corrections to be a Level 3 sex offender and had refused sex offender treatment while in prison, he was not civilly committed upon completing his sentence. On December 1, 2003, Rodriguez was arrested in connection with Sjodin's disappearance. His arrest was based on evidence ranging from his presence in the Columbia, ND, shopping mall the night Sjodin disappeared after completing her shift at a Victoria's Secret store, to the presence of weapons in his car. Sjodin's body was recovered on April 17, 2004, in Crookston, MN, after the winter's snow drifts melted. Because she was brought across state lines, the trial was held in federal court where Rodriquez was found guilty and sentenced to prison and death in a U.S. penitentiary in Indiana.

The Linehan case provided the means to civilly confine sex offenders but not a fail-safe way to identify those who should be civilly committed. Moreover, as a result of the murder of Sjodin by Rodriguez, one of our interview participants said,

> I will tell you that since 2003, sex offenders' civil commitment in terms of being on the radar screen went from here [gestures about waist high] up to here [gestures above the head]. And it hasn't come back down, and it never will.
>
> (A-1)

Moreover, during her testimony in the *Karsjens* (2015) trial, Deborah McCulloch, Director of Wisconsin's Sand Ridge Secure Treatment Center, one of the experts appointed by the court to evaluate MSOP, identified the "sweep" or jump in petitions for civil commitment after the Rodriguez case as a result of the "clear political influence on the process" (McCulloch 2015, n.p.). The kairotic moment created during the Linehan case, then, led to what was initially considered by some to be the right choice at the right time in strengthening the ability to civilly confine sex offenders on the premise of additional treatment. The kairotic moment created by the Rodriguez case, however, involved public fear and a resulting political response, and the moral panic that ensued revealed additional perceived imperfections in the system.

As what typically happens at the time of moral panic, the media alerted the public to a deterioration in public safety, and policymakers looked for ultimate solutions. Local and national news coverage, for example, contained such outcries as "Feelings of anger, fear and pain fueled call for justice in Dru Sjodin's hometown after the body of the University of North Dakota student was discovered in a ravine Saturday, making a heartbreaking end of a five-month search" (Cosgrove-Mather 2007, n.p.). One local resident was quoted as saying, "They should bring back public hangings" (Cosgrove-Mather 2007, n.p.). In response to such public outcry, the Department of Corrections Commissioner decided to forward the files of *all* Level 3 offenders to the appropriate 87 county attorneys in Minnesota for review for possible petition for civil commitment.

Minnesota Governor Tim Pawlenty became the flag person for reform, and the local partisan politics exaggerated the rhetorical situation. Although Rodriguez had not been civilly committed, Pawlenty quickly discouraged any future discharges from civil commitment facilities at Moose Lake and St. Peter, MN. His response, according to one newspaper story, "stripped the Human Services Department of the power to grant offenders supervised release [from prison]," thus overloading MSOP (McEnroe 2001, n.p.). Once Pawlenty stepped in, the kairotic rhetoric focused on whom to blame for any failures in the system. Policymakers, particularly elected officials, sought someone to accuse as being responsible for not seeing how dangerous Rodriguez was—for not controlling the risk to public safety. Minnesota Attorney General Mike Hatch, regarded as Pawlenty's likely opponent for the position of state governor in 2006, suggested the Pawlenty administration's previous budget cuts had compromised the state's ability to assess and confine dangerous sex offenders such as Rodriguez (Robson 2004). In response, Pawlenty used the media widely to talk about reinstating the death penalty for sex offenders when sexual assaults led to murder (see, for example, ABC News: Good Morning America 2003; CBS News: The Early Show 2004; Minnesota Public Radio 2004). And so, as one interview participant summed up the effect of Pawlenty's revision of how sex offenders were handled in Minnesota, "We wouldn't be here if it hadn't been for Dru Sjodin. I mean the whole system would probably still be functioning the way it was" (A-3). Another interview participant commented: "It's not that the discussions [about civil commitment] aren't occurring at these levels, but all of a sudden that [Rodriguez case] puts it into the spotlight" (A-6). Again, the kairotic rhetoric implicit in Pawlenty's public statements, Hatch's critique of the effect of Pawlenty's budget cuts for sex offender risk assessment, and Pawlenty's response to Hatch's accusation, all raised perceptions of high risk and subsequently led to major expansion of the number of civil commitments in the state.

Calls for Further MSOP Reform

For some, overall reform of MSOP at this time was absolutely necessary. Dennis Benson (2015), who became the Executive Director of MSOP in 2008, noted in his deposition for the Plaintiffs in the *Karsjens* case that indeed the Dru Sjodin murder was "the turning point" for how the state would manage sex offenders. Up to that time, Benson testified, MSOP was like the world of Dr. Seuss: "What I would do if I ran the zoo!" (Benson 2015, n.p.). Before the escalation of civilly committed sex offenders after the Rodriguez case, MSOP was a smaller, "wide-open" system where at times the staff feared for their personal safety as well as that of their clients (Benson 2015, n.p). After the reaction to Rodriguez's crimes, new treatment procedures and new security measures were put in place. For some, however, the reform that came after the Rodriguez case was questionable. According to one of our interview participants,

> I think that the program has been extremely successful in its mission of confining people. I don't think of it as the legitimate treatment program; I don't think that mission is to rehabilitate sex offenders. I think it's just about providing extended confinement for people whom decision makers are scared of.
>
> (C-3)

At any rate, after the kidnapping and murder of Dru Sjodin, the media, the Legislature, and public continued to work in "tandem," according to one interview participant, to "drive public policy decisions" in well-publicized sexual assault cases (T-1). The attention drawn by the Rodriguez case is not unusual, but this case in particular captured the public's attention and contributed to a push for stricter regulation as a solution to the problem of sex offenders (Zander 2008). In reaction to the Rodriguez case, we see evidence not only of moral panic but reactions by those who feared for their political careers should they oppose these stricter regulations. As Jenkins (1998) proposed, "[C]laims about danger are rather like commodities in a competitive marketplace, items that gain or lose a following depending on how well retailers strike a chord among the consumers whom they wish to attract" (216). Our interview participants seemed to agree with this analysis: "There's somewhat a symbiotic relationship between the media and legislature and criminal justice authorities" (C-3), because "public officials are responsible to their constituency and, depending on how strongly their constituency feels about certain things, that's going to drive public policy decisions" (T-1).

Moreover, despite statistics that deny the frequency of stranger sexual assault and that provide evidence of low recidivism rates among sex offenders, the kairotic rhetoric surrounding the Rodriguez case stressed personal risk. Best (1987) explains that when the media focuses on events in the lives of individuals, people respond by identifying with them: "Selecting horrific examples gives a sense of the problem's frightening, harmful dimensions" (106). Of course, some stakeholders resist these perceptions. As one interview participant said,

> I have got two kids, a daughter and a son, both at least as exposed to that kind of awful kind of conduct as is anybody … but if you look at the broader perspective, where does the real danger lie?
>
> (J-2)

Another interview participant similarly concluded: "In actuality, the real danger is probably in their home by a babysitter that they trust, an uncle, a grandfather, and so I think that that's hard for the public to wrap their heads around" (C-1). But Pawlenty himself defended his executive order by identifying personally with the details of the Rodriguez case:

> I look at my little daughters and try to imagine what it would feel like or be like to be in their [Sjodin family members'] shoes ... it gives you just a taste of—of the trauma and the tragedy that they're going through and the heartache and—and it just brings it home in a very different way.
>
> (CBS News: The Early Show 2004, n.p.)

In the kairotic moments of the Linehan and Rodriguez cases, media coverage and public perception of risk from sex offenders put pressure on policymakers to ensure public safety. But this requirement is, as one interview participant characterized it, "an unrealistic expectation," one resulting in "absolutist statements like 'It will never happen again'" (A-5). Although sympathetic to everyone wanting "to be entirely safe" (E-1), those having to administer the ever more complicated civil commitment procedures know that "all it takes is one nasty case, and the whole community is up in arms" (A-4). Civil commitment, however, which increased scrutiny of sex offenders judged most likely to reoffend, provided additional treatment and confinement facilities, and set extremely high barriers for discharge; thus, civil commitment seemed to many the right choice at the right time, that is, until the events of 2011 through 2014 raised alarm about the MSOP budget and once more about the constitutional rights of those civilly confined.

Assessing Risk for Recidivism: The Clarence Opheim Provisional Discharge

The third kairotic moment in the debates over civil commitment in Minnesota reveals the cycles that such rhetorical moments may form, cycles in which measures might be tightened to address a concern or threat, but cycles in which the same arguments are raised, and eventually progress may be limited. Certainly, the Linehan case served as a catalyst for a seemingly necessary extension in the law to include SDPs or SPPs as candidates for civil commitment. Although extreme in terms of increasing the population and costs of MSOP, the Rodriguez case widened the net to catch Level 3 sex offenders who might need additional treatment before reentering the community. The systemic changes resulting from the Linehan case were justified on the basis of risk perception, which became a public, media, and policy concern, silencing any objections based on violation of constitutional rights and the anomaly of such extremely violent offenders as Linehan. The changes resulting from the Rodriguez case demonstrated the effect of moral panic, when melodramatic language so demonizes offenders that the media, public, and policymakers may not be willing or able to participate in creative discussion and change, even when that language is countered by an extensive document to the contrary, in this third kairotic cycle a report from the state legislative auditor that condemned some aspects of MSOP.

The Legislative Auditor's Report on MSOP

The third moment in the kairotic cycle of the MSOP debates began not with a violent crime but with an attempt to reopen discussion about civil commitment. During a January 2012 symposium held at Mitchell Hamline School of Law, Eric Janus, then Dean and President of the school, warned that unless those offenders who had successfully completed treatment through MSOP were provisionally discharged into the community, the program was "approaching a potential train wreck"; this wreck would be caused, Janus said, by constitutional challenges, the extreme cost of housing and treating so many offenders, and the increasing scrutiny by decision makers inside and outside the state ("Sex Offender Civil Commitment in Minnesota: Challenges and Opportunities" 2012, n.p.).

Janus' prediction seemed to come true even before Chief U.S. Magistrate Boylan's mandate to reform MSOP. In June 2012, for example, the UK denied extradition to Minnesota of a sexual assault suspect because he faced possible civil commitment; Lord Justice Alan Moses and Justice David Eady of London's High Court concluded that civilly committing the perpetrator, charged with assaulting three young girls, would be a "flagrant denial" of his human rights under Article 5 of the European Convention of Human Rights (Evans 2012, n.p.). Then, that July, U.S. District Judge Donovan Frank decided that the *Karsjens* case could proceed as a class action suit; it appeared that the Plaintiffs' attorney had thus far argued persuasively that "'being committed under the Minnesota sex offender program is a life sentence'" (Smith and Hage 2012, n.p.).

At this time, the public seemed to have reached a phase of disinterest while the Minnesota Legislature, the attorney general, and the Department of Corrections continued to consider changing the way sex offenders were handled, but they ultimately rejected most changes that would identify, as one interview participant commented, a "clearer pathway out" of civil commitment (S-3). Then two task forces were assigned to review and revise the state's handling of civil commitment. One recommended a blended determinate–indeterminate sentencing system for sex offenders to allow judges more options and a specially configured commitment review board to be "insulated from political pressure" (Tomljanovich 2005, 3). But these recommendations were not implemented. Moreover, after the governor received the report for the second task force, according to one group member, "Pawlenty just took the most extreme features" of the report, ones that raised again the potential threats to public safety from sex offenders, and "that became his legislative initiative" (T-3). The Pawlenty administration and the Legislature maintained their response to the moral panic set off by the Rodriguez case and the resulting political and public pressure to maintain public safety over constitutional rights. Then the Legislative Auditor's report appeared three months after Governor Dayton assumed his post. The report awoke both the public and the media.

The audience of the Auditor's report was meant to be internal to a great degree, an artifact of professional communication, consisting of a narrow group of internal stakeholders, particularly MSOP officials and legislators. As one interview participant summed up the initial effect of the report, most problems with MSOP were in the report, but the report did not need to "discover" these, instead it "kind of articulated" them (C-2). Stakeholders began to interpret the report as a warning, however, in that: "We are reaching a huge bubble or a cliff and that we are going to have to expend so much money pretty soon because we are committing people and not letting them out" (S-1). The 111-page civil commitment report contained 16 recommendations, including alternative housing, such as the housing eventually suggested for the Cambridge-12 or a stay of commitment for certain sex offenders. Moreover, the Auditor identified the problematic binary in terms of the "all-or-nothing outcome" for civilly committed offenders within the district courts. One interview participant confirmed this dilemma in his own courtroom:

> There are some close cases [for civil commitment] or maybe even some marginal cases that have got a risk to them, but you are not super-excited about your only other alternative, and that, at least today, is pretty much a lifetime sentence, you know, in MSOP.
>
> (J-2)

And, implicitly invoking the idea of moral panic, MSOP clinicians reported to the Auditor, who included these opinions in his report: "[I]t was difficult for any individual to take the risk to release a sex offender because sex offenders are so reviled in the community and because there is always some risk that the sex offender will reoffend" (Minnesota Legislative Auditor 2011, 87). Nonetheless, the Legislative Auditor's report seemed to be well poised to lead to quiet and perhaps thorough revision by MSOP officials and legislators.

However, an external audience soon became aware of the Legislative Auditor's report—the media and the general public—and thus a kairotic moment ensued that once more included perceptions of risk and instances of moral panic. At this time, however, the right choice seemed to be to avoid that potential "train wreck" of constitutional challenges and wider judicial scrutiny of MSOP. Hennepin County (Minneapolis)

District Judge Peter Albrecht, for example, resisted making civil commitment decisions: "Nobody involved at our level wants this to be a system where we are actually locking people up for life under the pretext of treating them" (Oakes 2008, n.p.). Retired District Judge Linn Slattengren worried early on that MSOP "is so restricted by political pressures that some offenders are effectively imprisoned for life" (Oakes 2011, n.p.). However, a Minnesota Public Radio news story's interpretation of the Auditor's report served as an example of a familiar catalyst for moral panic and the possibility of another unproductive kairotic cycle: "The [Auditor's] report warns Minnesota may not be protecting the public from the most dangerous sex offenders" (Shenoy 2011).

The Right Time to Open MSOP's Doors

Despite the re-emerging moral panic about public safety, and in light of the crippling effect of the MSOP budget on state funds and growing concern that MSOP was unconstitutional, the right choice to avoid a federal takeover rested in part on the provisional discharge of sex offender Clarence Opheim. It seemed the right time to many stakeholders to demonstrate that the treatment programs at Moose Lake and St. Peter could lead to safe reentry into the community. Opheim's discharge became an opportunity to respond to constitutional challenges and budgetary concerns. The public pressure on MSOP was still "burdened with unrealistic expectations" in terms of "fixing" the sex offender "overnight" (A-5). Many of those decision-makers, however, joined MSOP staff in pushing for the Opheim provisional discharge.

One thing that helped in this argument for reform was that civil commitment programs could now rely on what seemed to be more accurate forensic risk assessment tools. The Stable-2007 actuarial tool, for example, measured dynamic factors that might lead to sexual violence, such as hostility toward women and lack of concern for others, and the Static 99R tool measured static factors, such as prior sex offences and relationship of offender to victim. These two tools used in combination purported to ensure more exact prediction of recidivism. Moreover, in MSOP, the forensic risk assessment unit as well as the treatment team offered recommendations as to whether a client should be considered for full discharge, provisional discharge, or transfer in custody to the MSOP community preparation services at St. Peter, MN. In the last stage before discharge, the client would submit to a polygraph to ensure that all prior offenses had been disclosed and a penile plethysmograph to measure physical response to visual and auditory stimuli linked to the client's once preferred victims.

However, in the *Karsjens* case, the plaintiffs revealed that forensic risk assessments were done only at the time a client petitioned for discharge or transfer in custody. Annual risk assessments were needed to measure progress in treatment and could correct not only for the great increases in civil commitments after the Rodriguez case but also the lack of any full discharges and the extremely low number of provisional discharges. According to one expert testifying for the plaintiffs in *Karsjens*, these more accurate assessment tools might reveal that a number of clients confined to MSOP might not indeed "meet the statutory requirements for confinement" (Miner 2015, n.p.). Moreover, a senior staff psychologist from the secure juvenile treatment facility in Wisconsin testified that "a fresh set of eyes" was very important to "rule out a lot of people who should have never been committed" (Caldwell 2015, n.p.). Finally, the criteria for discharge had been reinterpreted by the state court to eliminate the need to prove that the client was "capable of making an acceptable adjustment to open society," an out-of-date standard still used by some MSOP staff to opine on discharge petitions (Minnesota Statutes 253B.18, 2014, subd. 15; *Call v. Gomez* 1995). The two remaining criteria focused on the MSOP client no longer needing inpatient treatment and supervision and being no longer dangerous to the public, criteria about which the treatment team and risk assessors should be qualified to measure.

The kairotic opportunity to garner support for the Opheim provisional discharge, as the way to respond to constitutional and fiscal scrutiny of MSOP, came when the Minnesota House Health and Human Services Reform Committee asked to hear MSOP representatives on the upcoming discharge of Opheim. Executive Director Benson made clear in his opening presentation that discharge from MSOP was provisional discharge, not complete release from the program, and included continued outpatient treatment and supervision. Opheim's discharge contained 32 provisions such as GPS tracking, covert observations, daily contact, no contact with victims, sex offender registration, escorted outings, and residence in a secure living facility. Violation of any of these 32 provisions would send Opheim back to the MSOP facility in Moose Lake. Representing those charged with screening all petitions for civil commitment, Assistant Hennepin County Attorney George Widseth testified that he had originally opposed Opheim's discharge because his record was "more severe than I have ever seen," but Widseth was convinced that the public could be kept safe from Opheim (Minnesota House, Health and Human Services Reform Committee 2012, n.p.). Finally, Representative James Abeler reassured the committee members: "It's a scary time, but it's time" for a discharge from MSOP; after all, the state "believes in rehabilitation" (Minnesota House, Health and Human Services Reform Committee 2012, n.p.). The rhetoric of the hearing tapped into and reflected the *kairos* of that moment by stressing that public safety could be managed, which was clearly the primary concern of those who were alarmed at the idea of Opheim reentering the community.

The persuasive strategies of Abler, Benson, and Widseth were not completely successful, however, in silencing the opposition, or those who felt the right choice was to keep the doors of Moose Lake and St. Peter locked. The session ended, for example, with Representative Gruenhagen recommending that sex offenders be "locked up for life, no chance of parole and/or the death penalty" (Minnesota House, Health and Human Services Reform Committee 2012, n.p.). Gruenhagen's proposal represents what Lisa Sample and Colleen Kadleck (2008) suggest some public officials imagine when considering a sex offender: "A 'sick' male who is afflicted with some biological or psychological irregularity that causes him to be unusually persistent in his offending. Unless some intervention occurs, he will never stop his behavior" (50). Indeed, Opheim had assaulted 29 victims in approximately 100 separate incidences of sex offenses (*In the Matter of Clarence Joseph Opheim* 2011, 1). This was the offender who provoked a letter to Governor Dayton from Speaker of the House Kurt Zellers and House Majority Leader Matt Dean—a letter in which they warned Governor Dayton: "Releasing a dangerous child sex offender into a densely populated urban area is reckless, and runs counter to your stated goal of making public safety the top priority for state government" (Zellers and Dean 2012, 1). Moreover, Gruenhagen's comment reflected once more the politicization of the civil commitment issue, as the majority of media reporting on the hearing repeated or focused almost exclusively on his comment (see, for example, Forliti 2012, February 15; NBC News, KARE 11 2012; Wolfe 2012, February 15).

In reflecting on the *kairos* of this moment, our interview participants attributed a certain courage to those who supported the Opheim discharge:

> I often have said to legislators, "I understand the difficult position that you are put in. You don't have tons of time or opportunity to educate all of your constituency, but if you take a vote that even remotely appears that you [were] 'soft on sex offenders, you might lose your job.'"
>
> (T-1)

"But sometimes you have to do something; you have to be politically courageous" (T-2). As one interview participant put it, politicization of the issue can create "an easy dichotomy, [where] you are either for the victim or for the offender" (C-4). Certainly, weeks later, the media coverage when Opheim was indeed provisionally discharged seemed designed to alarm readers and influence policymakers. One article began by describing how "convicted child molester Clarence Opheim will walk off the campus at the Minnesota Security Hospital in St. Peter and into a cauldron of politics and community apprehension" (Wolfe 2012, February 19, n.p.). The writer of another news story stated that in a public meeting about the Opheim discharge, nearly 300 people were reassured about the restrictions on Opheim, but noted that some "questioned why—if the restrictions are really necessary—the convicted molester was being allowed to move into the community in the first place?" (Forliti 2012, March 5, n.p.).

Just a few months after Opheim's provisional discharge, however, Opheim moved from his initial placement to "the next stage of his rehabilitation," demonstrating, according to one media source, that "the system worked," and according to the mayor of the suburb where Opheim first resided, that "ongoing monitoring and social services have succeeded" (*StarTribune* 2012, November 30, n.p.). Moreover, on December 2, 2013, the task force that reviewed MSOP in response to Chief US Magistrate Boylan's mandate delivered its report. Included in the recommendations were less restrictive options for placement of sex offenders and additional processes to reduce the number of civilly committed offenders in a more "objective" review. The task force also argued that its recommendations would "eliminate to the greatest possible extent the influence of politics" on commitment decisions and better protect "the rights of those persons subject to civil commitment proceedings and the interests of the public" (Magnuson 2013, n.p.).

The Minnesota Legislature, however, failed to respond to the task force recommendation. Legislators, such as Senator Warren Limmer, warned, "Inaction is not an option. There is a consequence to inaction. It may create a [sex offender] program that no one may like if the federal court is the instrument" (Serres 2014, January 15, n.p.). But others expressed pessimism: "'[T]here was no appetite in the Legislature for letting anyone out. They'd rather spend millions of dollars keeping people locked up than take the chance of something bad happening'" (Oakes 2012, n.p.). Indeed, the Legislature had showed "no appetite" for change by the time the federal court heard the *Karsjens* case.

Risk Perceptions, Moral Panic, and Kairotic Cycles

Analyzing the events, texts, and debates that emerged in the three kairotic moments concerning civil commitment in Minnesota—the Linehan case, the Sjodin kidnapping and murder, and the Opheim provisional discharge—reveals how the public, the media, the Legislature, and other policymakers and stakeholders argued for effective treatment and the constitutional rights of sex offenders, or for public safety and confinement, or a balance of the two. Such kairotic rhetoric raised issues about risk, particularly socially constructed perceptions of risk, and led to moral panic about sexual predators, which ultimately seemed to instigate and exaggerate public fear and lead to stricter and perhaps ineffective regulations. The juxtaposition of these various public discourses about the civil commitment of sex offenders in Minnesota, and the often-incendiary debates that they have fueled and continue to fuel, illustrate the effect that *kairos* can have in the public sphere and the ways in which *kairos* can serve as a catalyst for policymaking and legislative change.

Our understanding of *kairos* in such rhetorical situations, however, can be greatly enhanced when we recognize that perceptions of risk and the reach of moral panic can influence or derail what seems the right choice at the right time. Although we cannot capture the "truth" of the general public's response to such a situation, only perceptions from stakeholders willing to express those perceptions, this understanding should help illuminate the rhetorical effects on public policy controversies and decisions within the field of professional communication. And so, as we discovered, the addition of new stakeholders and concerns at any particular kairotic moment can shift the balance in an ongoing debate. However, we also found that such kairotic moments can lead to kairotic cycles, in which the solutions to a problem can be stymied by competing perceptions and entrenched positions that reoccur over time, often without resolution. We believe that this recognition of kairotic cycles adds to our theoretical perceptions, particularly in the area of rhetoric and professional communication.

Again, in the Linehan case, the Legislature responded to public safety issues by changing the laws governing confinement of sex offenders. With the Rodriguez case, the politicization of the issues, the moral panic and fear experienced by the public, and the demands to control risk led to an either/or kairotic situation. A stakeholder or decision maker was either for absolute confinement and protection of potential victims or must accept that risk cannot be assessed to the extent demanded by the public. To take the latter position could alienate constituents upon whom elected officials depended to secure their jobs. And so, the Rodriguez case widened the net to catch Level 3 sex offenders who might need additional treatment before reentering the community but also caught others who could have safely gone back into the community on supervised release directly from prison. But with the Opheim case, the threatened "train wreck," a wreck that would be initiated within the courts, came closer and closer as the arguments that emerged in the two previous kairotic moments were recycled, too often without change or reflection. The Opheim provisional discharge, the pressure from the federal courts, and the constitutional challenges of those civilly confined within the *Karsjens* civil suit did create enough support to test the system, in an attempt to demonstrate that treatment and reentry into the community could be successful.

With Judge Frank's opinion in the *Karsjens* case that the statutes that govern MSOP were unconstitutional as written and as applied, however, another kairotic cycle may emerge. After Judge Frank's opinion was published, the Plaintiffs had argued that the state should be given the opportunity to "correct the constitutional deficiencies" in MSOP, and if there were different ways to correct those deficiencies, "given that the State has continually touted its own expertise in operating its own programs, the State should propose such remedies" (Gustafson et al. 2015, 7). However, the Defendants' brief on those remedies continues to argue that there is no constitutional need to change the MSOP treatment program. Moreover, the burden of proof for such a change would have to be quite high: "There is no Fourteenth Amendment right to sex offender treatment, unless state law requires such treatment, in which case a state's administration of the treatment program is only unconstitutional if it 'shocks the conscience'" (Brennaman et al. 2015, 13). An amicus memorandum submitted on behalf of Hennepin County Attorney, representing the largest county in Minnesota, does seem to propose a necessary balance of interests and a recognition of the effects of moral panic:

> Protecting public safety while assuring the rights of those subject to [civil] commitment proceedings involves unique considerations that may be sometimes difficult for members of the public to understand ... When civilly committed, the person must be provided such treatment as is reasonably available so that he need not be confined longer than necessary. If he needs to be held in a very secure treatment facility, then that is where he should be held. But if public safety can be sufficiently protected by placing the individual in a less-restrictive setting, then that is what should occur.
>
> (Freeman et al. 2015, 3)

In fact, after the *Karsjens* trial, MSOP in just over a year conditionally discharged six sex offenders, as one reporter noted, "an unprecedented pace for a program with a history of confining rapists and other violent offenders indefinitely, sometimes for decades, with little opportunity for release" (Serres 2016, February 10, n.p.). Warren Maas, the president of the Minnesota chapter of the Association for the Treatment of Sexual Abusers, asked about the lack of public outcry given this latest conditional discharge: "Where is the drama? Where is the political hue and cry?" (Serres 2016, February 10, n.p.).

The drama, the hue and cry, may have appeared during the community notification meeting about the sixth recent MSOP discharge, that of Oliver Dority, who was moving to a halfway house in St. Paul. One media source described the event as follows: "Anxious-looking residents, many huddled in their parkas, began showing up for Wednesday's hearing half an hour before the program, filling nearly every seat ... Most asked pointed security-related questions" (Serres 2016, February 11, n.p.). One woman who attended the meeting was quoted as saying, "I don't feel comfortable about this at all," even though the MSOP officials "tried to assuage fears by emphasizing that offenders who go through years of treatment like

Dority are far less likely to commit sexual crimes again than those who go untreated and undetected" (Serres 2016, February 11, n.p.).

Our interview participants implicitly described the dynamic interplay between competing perceptions of confinement ensuring public safety, and treatment leading to provisional discharge, that are perpetuated and sustained through these overall kairotic cycles. As one interview participant noted, the reality may be that the majority of sex offenders are some of the easiest people to supervise "because they are so compliant" (L-3). But media coverage often is "histrionic," as another interview participant shared: "If they [the media] put every one of those stories in perspective, maybe they could help be part of a more thoughtful conversation" (T-4).

In this chapter we offer some ideas for scholars of professional communication and rhetoric about how rhetorical concepts such as *kairos* and how interdisciplinary concepts such as moral panic and risk perception operate both in theory and in practice in a rhetorical situation. We also suggest how the kairotic moment may be viewed as an opportunity for reframing any public policy issue. If the reframing lapses into repeating kairotic cycles, however, little progress may be made. In the next chapter, we explore how a new genre called the Lethality Assessment Protocol (LAP) operates in legal and judicial systems with regard to domestic violence, to change not only behavior but core beliefs. If the kairotic cycles in civil commitment controversies illustrate missteps in policymaking, then LAP exemplifies some progress in addressing the equally complex problem of intervening in domestic violence situations.

2 Disrupting Genres
Influencing Behavior and Belief

In 2012, in York County, PA, a police officer administered a lethality assessment questionnaire to a pregnant 19-year-old female victim of domestic violence. Because her boyfriend had strangled her and then thrown her to the floor, the victim screened in at high risk for being murdered by her boyfriend. In following the assessment protocol, the officer convinced the victim to speak immediately with a Safe Home advocate who could help her file an order for protection and find somewhere else to stay. A Hanover Hospital nurse, involved in monitoring the victim overnight, also contacted the advocate to express concern because the victim feared going to a homeless shelter. And so, Still Waters, the YWCA's ACCESS-York Victim Assistance Center, sheltered the victim once the advocate transported her from the hospital and eventually sent the victim out of state to live with her mother. According to a York County spokesperson, the case "illustrates the success of connecting a victim at high risk of lethality with an advocate through the program's hotline and, eventually, to lifesaving services" (Qtd. Bureau of Justice Assistance 2012, n.p.). This lethality assessment questionnaire served as a tool, in that the questionnaire compared the victim's situation to certain features and outcomes of domestic violence victims as a group in order to measure her degree of risk. But such questionnaires also serve as a genre, as defined by Amy Devitt (2004), to not only "help people do things in the world" but also to serve as "both social and rhetorical actions, operating as people interact with others in purposeful ways" (13–14). It is this new and emerging genre, set within an extensive protocol, which we explore throughout this chapter.

Specifically, we focus on the lethality assessment tool and accompanying protocol adopted in Washington and Anoka Counties, MN, after the Van Keuren case. This Lethality Assessment Protocol (LAP) was created by the Maryland Network Against Domestic Violence not only to identify high-risk cases but also to alert the victim to the potential lethality of her situation, provide her with services immediately, and better monitor her abuser. In hindsight, it is impossible to know whether LAP would have saved the life of Teri Lee; certainly she had already identified the risks that Van Keuren posed, but LAP might have affirmed her instincts about this danger and provided her with an even broader and more collaborative support system.

Unlike the confinement and therapy required of the sex offender through MSOP, as explored in the last chapter, LAP directs attention to changing the behavior and even the core beliefs of the victim. The domestic violence victim may suffer from what has been called the Battered Women's Syndrome, often used in court to justify a victim's killing her abuser (Savage 2006), or post-traumatic stress disorder, identified as the catalyst for such victims to develop coping skills such as dissociation and compliance (Walker 1991). These two categories, of course, do not capture all the reasons why women remain in abusive relationships; Sarah Buel (1999), for example, lists 50 such obstacles, ranging from guilt and the belief that "but for the victims' incompetent and faulty behavior, the violence would not occur" (22) to cultural and racial defenses when the victim believes that "battered women's shelters and batterer intervention programs' staff fail to reflect the diversity of the communities they serve" (20).

The LAP approach to gender violence is also unique in two other ways. First, LAP, in essence, works to persuade the domestic violence victim to take immediate steps, asking the victim to exchange one type of personal fear for another, in essence to change her behavior and her beliefs. Such a victim fears the violence that might ensue if she confronts the power and control of her abuser and attempts to leave that abuser; however, those who administer and score the risk assessment tool try to persuade the domestic violence victim that it is best to leave her abuser based on the newly aroused fear of being killed should she stay. Second, rather than misperceptions of risk that plague public discourse about sex offenders, those administering LAP have more grounded perceptions of risk of lethality to offer the victim.

In the York County incident, for example, law enforcement, medical caregivers, and advocacy groups all collaborated to protect the victim from what was a dangerous situation, made potentially lethal because the assault involved strangulation. According to the Minnesota Coalition for Battered Women (2005), within 30 seconds strangulation can cause brain damage or death, and about 43 percent of domestic homicide victims had been strangled by their abusers within 12 months prior to their deaths (n.p.). Indeed, in Minnesota, strangulation of a family or household member is now a felony-level crime (Minnesota Statutes 2014, 609.2247). In praising the state's new domestic abuse strangulation statute, Kelly Francis of *Bench & Bar of Minnesota* (2008) reminded attorneys and judges, "Whether by use of an electrical cord, an article of clothing, an abuser's bare hands or even a plastic bag, strangulation is a red flag that violence is escalating and homicide is possible" (n.p.). Other states also understand the lethality risk involved in strangulation. The Executive Director of the National District

Attorneys Association in Virginia, Scott Burns, for example, noted that the "education and a new heightened concern" for the criminal act of strangulation now meant possible charges of aggravated assault or attempt to cause death or serious bodily injury (Training Institute on Strangulation Prevention 2013, n.p.). Risk of death from strangulation is well documented and appraised.

Strangulation is just one of many acts now identified as signaling that domestic abuse could escalate to domestic homicide. Threatening to kill the victim and/or to commit suicide, unemployment, stalking, or intense jealousy, among other traits, certainly mark high risk in a domestic violence situation as validated by the developers of LAP. Steven Van Keuran, for example, was fired from his job as a pharmaceutical technologist at 3M Company as a result of assault and battery charges against Teri Lee and became so depressed that he had trouble sleeping and eating, an early indication of possible escalation. And indeed, he began to stalk Lee. At Van Keuren's bail hearing, Lee testified: "I do feel physically threatened ... There's no doubt in my mind that he will come back to my home. He's stated ... that he had nothing left to live for" (Vainik 2006–2007, 1113). In turn, Van Keuren left a voicemail message for a friend before leaving for the Lee home on the day he murdered her: "I want to take Teri's life and my life because she doesn't deserve to live" (*State of Minnesota, Respondent v. Steven Van Keuren* 2008, n.p.). Even while Lee was dying, Van Keuren was ultimately unable to release her, as he used a box cutter knife to slit both their wrists so he could press them together in a "blood bond" (Kathman 2007, n.p.). Identifying these lethality risk factors is a task best shared among many responders with the expertise and resources to intervene early into domestic violence incidents.

We believe that our exploration of the LAP questionnaire reveals how, according to Anis Bawarshi and Mary Jo Reiff (2010), rhetorical and professional communication analysis can extend our knowledge of how genres "enable their users to carry out situated symbolic actions and relations, enact social roles, and frame social realities," such as labeling the victim's situation as potentially lethal (59). Moreover, approaching such genres as social actions, illuminate, say Bawarshi and Reiff (2010), how "genres participate in the construction of the situations to which they respond" (69). Detective Sergeant Randy McAlister, for example, the first officer on the scene of the Lee and Hawkinson shooting, concluded that the murders "got Washington County thinking about how we can do things differently ... One of the key questions: was it possible to proactively identify those most at risk of being killed by an intimate partner?" (Adame 2014, n.p.). Thus, through the lens of genre theory, the assessment questionnaire defines domestic violence in new ways, such as high or low risk for lethality, to create new roles for those who experience that violence and those who must respond to the victims and manage the offenders. Moreover, we believe that our exploration of LAP and its attempt to persuade the victim that she must leave her abuser to avoid further injury or death, adds a new dimension to genre study, in terms of how a new genre might not only change the behaviors but also the beliefs of the participants. Perceptions of risk are used to validate the persuasive strategies used in administering the LAP questionnaire.

Genre Theory on Systemic Disruption and Enlightenment

To illuminate the effects of introducing and implementing LAP in legal and judicial systems, we therefore use genre theory, or the study of how typified rhetorical actions not only reflect but also can disrupt systemic behaviors within an organizational culture, in such a way as to change and even enlighten or advance that culture. The introduction of new genres, such as LAP and the artifacts associated with it, often occur in a moment of *kairos*, when those members of an organizational or social group take advantage of an opportune moment to pursue systemic change, such as with the Van Keuren case in Washington County. Specifically, those administering LAP hope that by identifying risk, they can more effectively engage appropriate agencies and advocacy groups as well as change a domestic violence victim's perceptions and actions to better ensure her safety. Moreover, as opposed to the belief held by some that sex offenders cannot be rehabilitated, as we saw in Chapter 1, efforts such as LAP focus on both management and anticipated rehabilitation of domestic violence offenders. Finally, although new genres such as LAP can provoke some internal resistance, risk assessment tools and procedures regarding domestic violence do not attract the sort of negative political and public attention, as do those involved in the potential discharge of civilly committed sex offenders. There is little moral panic manifested by media coverage of domestic violence, perhaps an indication that many in the general public do not imagine themselves in a similar situation.

At the scene of a domestic violence incident and with the cooperation of the victim, a first responder, usually a police officer or sheriff's deputy, fills out a lethality assessment questionnaire and then scores the victim's answers. (See Figure 2.1 for the standard version of the LAP questionnaire.) If the victim answers "yes" to any of the first three questions and/or "yes" to at least four of the remaining eight questions, the responder is trained to tell the victim, "People in your situation have been killed." The responder may also trigger the protocol based on anything else the victim shares or on the responder's belief that the victim is in a potentially lethal situation despite her score elsewhere on the questionnaire. For those identified as high-risk victims, the responder immediately calls a victim advocate and gets the victim's permission to hand the phone over to the victim. The advocate offers the victim shelter, helps her with a safety plan, and suggests legal and counseling services, all the time reaffirming the victim's high level of risk. Thereafter, others get involved in the case. A community corrections officer, for example, gets a copy of the completed LAP questionnaire along with the police incident report. A high-risk score is shared with the judge who might then set a higher bail and stricter conditions for the offender's release and with the prosecutor who can expedite the case. Probation staff and prosecutors might persuade the offender to enter domestic violence or anger management programming even before a trial or a plea agreement in felony-level cases. In this way, the lethality assessment questionnaire serves not just as a form to be completed at the scene but as a part of a "genre repertoire," as Devitt's study (2004) calls it, or "the set of genres that a group owns, acting through which a group achieves all of its purposes, not just those connected to a particular activity," or all the purposes involved in managing and curtailing domestic violence (57).

To understand the potential for LAP, particularly the questionnaire itself, as a new genre and as a catalyst for individual and systemic change, we interviewed those in Minnesota involved in the selection, administration, and application of LAP and LAP-related initiatives. We spoke directly with judges, police chiefs and officers, sheriffs' deputies, corrections and probation officers, city and county attorneys, and victim advocates. (See the Appendix for more detail on our research design, data collection method, analytical perspectives, and interview citation style.) In this chapter, we begin our analysis with the goals and the genre features of the assessment questionnaire itself, a tool whose creators and users anticipated would not only better secure the safety of the domestic violence victim but also contribute to wider contribution from and cooperation among agencies. In this analysis, we reveal the ways in which risk assessment is conducted and communicated to the victim, the tensions that arise between either changing or supporting the existing system as a result of this new genre, and the persuasive strategies used to urge the victim to leave her abuser via potentially intimidating questions. Later, in Chapter 4, we extend our exploration to study how LAP, as well as the resulting systemic changes for which LAP serves as a catalyst, might affect or be affected by broader cultural values.

Early on, linguist John Swales (1990) identified a genre as a typified rhetorical action to include a "class of communicative events" bound by "some shared set of communicative purposes," which appears in a recognizable pattern identifiable to the members of the discourse community who make use of the genre (58). When rhetorical scholars began to challenge the narrow view of genres as communicative patterns that stabilized discourse communities, they recognized that genres were not only reflective of communal values but also dynamic within systems. Carol Berkenkotter (2008), for example, described how genres reflect systemic beliefs within organizational cultures in her work on

Maryland Network Against Domestic Violence

LETHALITY SCREEN FOR LAW ENFORCEMENT

Officer:	Date:	Case #:
Victim:	Offender:	

Check here if victim did not answer __any__ of the questions. ☐

A "Yes" response to any of Questions #1-3 automatically triggers the protocol referral.

1. Has he/she ever used a weapon against you or threatened you with a weapon? Yes ☐ No ☐ Not Ans. ☐

2. Has he/she threatened to kill you or your children? Yes ☐ No ☐ Not Ans. ☐

3. Do you think he/she might try to kill you? Yes ☐ No ☐ Not Ans. ☐

Negative responses to Questions #1-3, but positive responses to at least four of Questions #4-11, trigger the protocol referral.

4. Does he/she have a gun or can he/she get one easily? Yes ☐ No ☐ Not Ans. ☐

5. Has he/she ever tried to choke you? Yes ☐ No ☐ Not Ans. ☐

6.Is he/she violently or constantly jealous or does he/she control most of your daily activities? Yes☐ No ☐ Not Ans. ☐

7. Have you left him/her or separated after living together or being married? Yes ☐ No ☐ Not Ans. ☐

8. Is he/she unemployed? Yes ☐ No ☐ Not Ans. ☐

9. Has he/she ever tried to kill himself/herself? Yes ☐ No ☐ Not Ans. ☐

10. Do you have a child that he/she knows is not his/hers? Yes ☐ No ☐ Not Ans. ☐

11. Does he/she follow or spy on you or leave threatening messages? Yes ☐ No ☐ Not Ans. ☐

An officer may trigger the protocol referral, if not already triggered above, as a result of the victim's response to the below question, or whenever the officer believes the victim is in a potentially lethal situation.

Is there anything else that worries you about your safety? (*If "yes"*) What worries you?

Check one: Victim screened in according to the protocol ☐
Victim screened in based on belief of officer☐
Victim did not screen in ☐

If victim screened in: After advising her/him of a high danger assessment did the victim speak with the hotline counselor? Yes ☐ No ☐

Note: *The questions above and the criteria for determining the level of risk a person faces is based on the best available research on factors associated with lethal violence by a current or former intimatepartner. However, each situation may present unique factors tha influence risk for lethal violence that are not captured by this screen. Although most victims who screen "positive" or "high danger" would not be expected to be killed, these victims face much higher risk than that of other victims of intimate partner violence.*

Figure 2.1 Followed by this notice: ©Maryland Network Against Domestic Violence, 2014. All rights reserved. Used with permission.

early psychiatry: "It is in the history of the genre of the psychiatric case history that we can see the tensions at work between two rival 'thought-styles' ... with regard to mental illness" (3). As we see later in this chapter, viewing LAP as a disrupting genre reflects the tensions between two systemic choices: revising the organizational and cultural response to domestic violence versus better allocating limited resources within existing legal and judicial systems.

Thus, this application of genre theory is particularly important to our analysis of LAP. Bawarshi and Reiff (2010), for example, expanded the connections among genre, situation, action, and ideology to define genre as a "powerful, ideologically active, and historically changing shaper of texts, meanings, and social actions … [as well as] forms of cultural knowledge that conceptually frame and mediate how we understand and typically act within various situations" (4). However, for a situation to be considered a rhetorical exigence or a kairotic opportunity, that situation must be capable of being modified. In particular, individuals must be "capable of being acted upon by the discourse as to modify the exigence" (Bawarshi and Reiff 2010, 63; see also Bawarshi 2000; Bazerman 2003; Bitzer 1999; Miller 1994). The call for change in assessing and managing domestic violence cases after the Van Keuren case, for example, came directly from those who were involved. Thus, the introduction and implementation of LAP as of 2013 into jurisdictions in 30 states, but particularly into the Minnesota counties we studied, provides an opportunity to understand, apply, and even expand genre perspectives.

Activity theory also enhances these perspectives on the potential of genres to reflect and mediate cultural knowledge and values. Activity theory was initially understood as needs-based and as taking place within a system in which groups of workers make use of tools or artifacts to work toward a particular goal or outcome. As Spinuzzi (2003) suggests, genres, such as the lethality assessment questionnaire, become "tools-in-use" as they contain "the traces of an ongoing activity, represent problem solving in that activity, and thus tend to stabilize the activity in which they are used" (39; see also Spinuzzi 1996). These tools or artifacts, however, do not merely help make connections between groups and the objects with which these groups might work. Rather, as Spinuzzi (2003) proposes, through their acts of mediation, such artifacts and tools qualitatively change the types of activities in which subjects engage. In essence, the assessment questionnaire associated with LAP has the potential to become a mediating tool meant to accomplish meaningful advocacy work for domestic violence victims, for example, and successful collaboration among victims, first responders, advocacy groups, and others. "Change the process," concludes Jeffrey Grabill (2000), "and one changes the institution" (36). Also, if systemic cultural change is to take place, perhaps stimulated by the introduction of a disrupting genre, an internal genre might become a catalyst for policy dialogues between the public and the internal agency. As Michael Knievel (2008) finds, a disrupting genre might influence the intentions of and relationships among these groups. In fact, some policy scholars propose, "Public policy probably does not exist until it is instantiated by and through genres" (Gerston 1997, 343: see also McCool 1995).

Again, the perspectives we bring to our analysis of LAP continue to push the current boundaries of genre theory by asking not only to what extent LAP changes current domestic violence policies but also if the protocol and accompanying artifacts can alter the domestic violence victim's actions as well as her perceptions and beliefs. Up to this point, genre scholars have focused primarily on how writers become acculturated through learning the genres of a specific organizational culture. Carol Berkenkotter and Thomas Huckin (1995), for example, studied how a new graduate student or a beginning researcher might achieve success by following the conventions of the genres within a new discourse community, such as learning to stress novelty in his or her research and writing. In examining how a domestic violence victim's actions and beliefs are often set within cultural gender roles that keep her with her abuser, despite the legal and judicial system's messages that she must leave that abuser, we hope to contribute to what Devitt (2004), for example, identifies as her primary thesis: "My view here is *not* that the genre determines how its users view the world; rather, I would argue the use of a genre privileges one way of viewing the world, the view of the group from which it stems" (61, emphasis in original). In a way, this view matches Aviva Freedman and Peter Medway's (1994) call to fill their perceived gap in genre research, the possibilities that generic activities might not only "do violence" to the writers of the communication but also "harm" the recipients of a communication (13). Finally, we depart somewhat from the practice of scholars who analyze the linguistic features that mark a specific genre; instead we pinpoint, through a close reading of the assessment questionnaire, and by way of the perceptions shared with us by its creators, the persuasive features meant to encourage the victim to exchange fear of reprisal for fear of death.

Risk Assessment for Domestic Violence Victims

Right around the time of the Van Keuren case, concern over domestic homicide escalated on global, national, and local levels, setting the stage for the creation and endorsement of risk assessment screening for victims. As Devitt (2004) mentions, "Situation and genre are so tightly interwoven as to be interlocked. People construct situations through genres, but they also construct genres through situations" (22). A report on the results from the first global review of violence against women, for example, found that about a third of all women have been assaulted by a former or current partner, and 40 percent of women killed worldwide were murdered by an intimate partner. According to the head of the World Health Organization, Dr. Margaret Chan, this phenomenon is a "global health problem of epidemic proportions" (Cheng 2013, n.p.). Moreover, the Minnesota Department of Public Safety and the Coalition for Battered Women speculated that although about 63,000 victims sought services from advocates in 2012, "thousands more suffer in silence" (*StarTribune* 2013, October 5, n.p.). More specifically, in 2011, Anoka County, MN, experienced more domestic homicides per capita than anywhere else in the Twin Cities, nearly double that of nearby Washington County where the Van Keuren case took place. Paul Young, Chief of the Anoka County Attorney's Violent Crime Division, offered that "some women simply weren't asking for help" and that others might be relying exclusively on the no-contact orders that come with felony-level domestic violence cases (Baca 2011, n.p.).

A criminal court issues a no-contact order against a defendant in a criminal proceeding, such as that which resulted from the July 2007 incident when Van Keuren, armed with butchers knives entered Lee's house. Victims are also encouraged by law enforcement and advocacy services to seek orders for protection, often called restraining orders, within civil court. Under Minnesota law, for example, an order for protection requires that the victim submit a petition for relief alleging the existence of domestic violence. If granted, the abusing party is excluded from the residence of the petitioner and from any work, church, shopping, or school areas and must not contact the petitioners by any means, including third-party communication or email. The court will also order the abusing party to surrender any firearms and to participate in treatment or counseling services (Minnesota Statutes 2014, 518B.01, Subd. 4). But, as many involved in domestic violence and sexual assault cases note, the no-contact order and the order for protection are "just pieces of paper" to a determined offender. On a more positive note, however, five years after the Lee and Hawkinson murders, when LAP was in place in Anoka County, the four law enforcement agencies participating thus far in the protocol had responded to 132 domestic violence cases, completed 92 risk assessments, and deemed 63 victims at high risk for lethality. More than half of these high-risk victims worked with Alexandra House, the local advocacy organization. Still, despite these numbers, Connie Moore, Alexandra House's executive director, cautioned: "What it shows is that domestic violence—no matter where you are—is a key issue" (Baca 2011, n.p.).

The Creation of the Danger Assessment Tool

Before Washington and Anoka Counties, MN, went looking for better ways to intervene in domestic violence and curtail domestic homicides, scholars and practitioners were already developing and validating risk assessment tools to help officials make more effective decisions about sentencing, probation, and release for offenders and to assist in victim empowerment, safety planning, and domestic violence prevention and education. Included in these tools were the Domestic Violence Screening Inventory (DVSI), the Kingston Screening Instrument for Domestic Violence (K-SID), the Spousal Assault Risk Assessment (SARA), the Ontario Domestic Assault Risk Assessment (ODARA), and the Danger

Assessment. For all of these tools, "Predictive validity, the correct prediction of future events" was the "most important measurement of the efficacy of a risk assessment instrument" (Messing and Thaller 2013, 1539). Much as with the risk assessment tools involved in civil commitment of sex offenders, the tools to assess risk for lethality among domestic violence victims were measured according to their perceived ability to preserve public safety and predict recidivism. These assessment tools were also based on the actuarial method, which identifies and combines the most important factors for risk to produce a formula that is then applied to a large sample of individuals, in this case domestic violence victims. The resulting formulas produce a score for each individual based on combined risk factors. As Detective Sergeant McAlister noted in the Lee and Hawkinson murders, "Van Keuren had no criminal record two months before the September 2006 shooting. But there were already telltale signs of menacing behavior that authorities had ignored" (Adame 2014, n.p.). These menacing actions would be evaluated in a risk assessment tool such as LAP.

Among all the early lethality assessment tools, it was the Danger Assessment (DA) created by Dr. Jacquelyn Campbell, from the School of Nursing at Johns Hopkins University, which seemed most predictive that an abused woman might be killed by her current or past intimate partner. This 20-item questionnaire was developed in consultation with advocacy, law enforcement, and clinical experts, and it was validated by studies conducted by Campbell and her colleagues (Campbell 2003, n.p.). According to Campbell (2005), lethality risk assessment was important for at least four reasons: Abused women themselves want to know "how much risk their situation presents, even if the assessment is imperfect, so they can act accordingly"; advocates and first responders wanted to be able to assess risk for those women they were supposed to protect; judges and probation officers wanted to do more than guess the level of risk in domestic violence cases based on their own professional experience; and all agencies needed to distinguish the factors involved in cases of domestic abuse from the factors present in cases of domestic homicide (1207–1208). Moreover, Campbell, working with Maryland Network Against Domestic Violence (2014), had found that "only four percent of abused victims of domestic homicide had used a domestic violence hotline or shelter within the year prior to being killed by an intimate partner" (2), and Campbell (2004) interpreted this statistic to mean that "women who actually took advantage of these services were almost never the victim of murder or attempted murder" (1471; see also Sharps et al. 2001). Campbell also tested the validity of each of her 20 questions asked of a domestic violence victim. She found, for example, that having a child living in the home who was not the abusive partner's biological child more than doubled the risk of domestic homicide and that the strongest risk factor for domestic homicide was the abuser's lack of employment (Campbell et al. 2003). Finally, Campbell (2005) determined that a coordinated community response was needed to make the best use of any risk assessment tool. Thus, unlike the perceptions of risk that we saw in Chapter 1, those that contributed to unproductive kairotic cycles of moral panic, the risk assessment connected to lethality assessment tools were validated and therefore could be a persuasive element in any claim that the victim needed to leave her abuser.

Campbell's DA questionnaire was originally accompanied by a calendar, on which the domestic violence victim was asked to mark the approximate number of days when abusive incidents occurred and to rank the severity of the abuse. When Washington and Anoka Counties adopted a lethality assessment tool based on Campbell's DA, this calendar was not included—but the purpose and assumptions behind it remained. The calendar was meant to be a way "to raise the consciousness of the woman and reduce the normal minimization of IPV [intimate partner violence]" (Campbell, Webster, and Glass 2006, 658). Campbell (2004) had found, "Women are unlikely to overestimate; however, many will underestimate the severity of the situation" (1462). As one domestic violence practitioner remarked, "I think because of typical victim behavior it's not that they don't know; it's that they don't want to see" (Cattaneo and Chapman 2011, 1294). A lethality risk assessment tool was meant not just to identify high-risk victims and to provide services to them but also to help victims accurately determine their own risk—and to persuade them to separate from the abuser, the route to safety commonly mapped out by that coordinated community poised to respond to a domestic violence incident. "The process of risk assessment with a survivor of intimate partner violence gives the service provider access to the gold standard of information about the violence in the relationship," Campbell (2004) claimed, but it also "makes the survivors a partner in that assessment so that they assess for themselves the extent of their danger" (1475). This partnership was a persuasive strategy used to convince victims to take advantage of services and to eventually leave their abusers. And so, as Devitt (2004) reminds us, "For genre to be a tool alone is to reduce its force ... to limit the nature of genre to formulae, a preexisting, static material object that people can pickup and use or just as easily set aside" (48).

Again, one potential result of administering this risk assessment questionnaire was to so change the beliefs and actions of the domestic violence victim that she might be empowered to separate from her abuser, even though Campbell et al. (2003) recognized that "having been separated from an abusive partner after living together was associated with a higher risk of femicide" (1090). Other scholars have long noted not only this higher risk to the victim after a decision to separate from the abuser but also how the victim may be misunderstood if they do not separate. As Katharine Baker (2005) proposed, a victim who decides not to leave her abuser appears as one "who is helpless, not one who is struggling" (459). Kathleen Ferraro (2006) further speculated that because such victims are "viewed as voluntarily choosing to be in those relationships, their situation is analogous to people who choose to belong to criminal gangs": they cannot claim duress if they are voluntary members of a "relationship known to involve violence" (81). Women sense that it is dangerous to leave their abusers but are considered sick and foolish when they do not. The force of the risk assessment questionnaire is reflected within the complete protocol, to change the behavior and beliefs of the victim so that she takes advantage of a support system that will help her leave her abuser—or protect herself if they have already separated.

The Creation of the Lethality Assessment Protocol

Unlike the creation of MSOP, which was a result of political and public alarm over notorious sexual assaults, LAP was the invention of scholars. Soon after Campbell introduced the DA, the Maryland Network Against Domestic Violence created LAP from "an opportunity born" from the research of Campbell that, among other findings, determined that officers had previously responded to a call to the scene for 50 percent of domestic homicides and that re-assault of high-risk victims was reduced by 60 percent if these victims went into a shelter (Maryland Network Against Domestic Violence n.d.b, n.p.). LAP, as defined by the Maryland Network, was a two-pronged process that featured both the "research-based lethality screening tool" and the referral to advocacy and other groups that enabled first responders to take appropriate action based on the results of what was now an 11-question risk assessment tool. When other states adopted LAP, they did so on the basis of these possible benefits (see, for example, Virginia Department of Criminal Justice Services 2013).

Moreover, when the media reported on the introduction of LAP into Anoka and Washington Counties, the message was even more confident. "It seems simple, really, but saves lives," the largest newspaper in the state asserted, and then quoted from the Washington County Attorney that LAP was "one of the greatest things we've seen in domestic abuse in a long time" (Giles 2012, n.p.). Also, the Anoka County Chief Deputy Sheriff distinguished LAP by its thoroughness and predictive features: "With the assessment, we look at the total history of what has happened before and what is likely to happen in the future" (Sakry 2012, April 19, n.p.). Finally, in Anoka County's first successful grant application to the Office on Violence Against Women, the County's criminal justice professionals admitted that the number of domestic homicides in the county had served as "a wake-up call regarding the need to triage the services provided in domestic violence cases," and in the response the county requested and received $400,000 to strengthen advocacy services, further educate judges, implement LAP, and develop a specialized unit to provide intense supervision and monitoring of offenders (Criminal Justice Professionals 2010, 1 of "Project Narrative"). "One-size-fits-all services [previously relied upon] do not provide enhanced safety and services for victims at the greatest risk of serious harm or death at the hands of an intimate partner," the County concluded (1 of "Project Narrative"; see also Criminal Justice Professionals 2012 for the second round of the grant application, which was awarded an additional $300,000). Given the perspective of those in Anoka and Washington Counties, soon followed by Chisago and parts of Ramsey Counties, MN, the introduction and implementation of LAP, a research-based product, to replace previous "one-size-fits-all" approach seemed poised for success.

Potential Systemic Tensions in the New Genre

With these national and local goals set for LAP, those who introduced, implemented, and now administer the assessment tool in Minnesota endorsed but at times complicated the articulated goals of the protocol. A close look at the strategies and effects of introducing a new genre into an organizational culture often disrupts and reveals tension or possible underlying conflict within that system. As Berkenkotter and Huckin (1995) have taught us, "Furthermore, individual actors have their own uniquely formed knowledge of the world; and socially induced perceptions of commonality do not eradicate subjective perceptions of difference. Genres, therefore, are always sites of contention between stability and change" (6). In particular, our interviews about LAP reveal a potential tension between the use of the protocol to better support and empower the victim and the use of the protocol to more effectively deal with the offender—in other words, a precarious balance between a potentially welcomed systemic change to deal with domestic violence and an ongoing need for increased efficiency and effectiveness of the established mission and familiar responses of the legal and judicial systems, a complication of genre theory that we illustrate in our study. Moreover, such a tension represents unresolved reactions to domestic violence. After all, the state of Minnesota has dedicated seemingly unlimited financial support to MSOP, support that could be allocated to domestic violence programs.

We consider these tensions as we relate the responses of those involved in administering and implementing LAP when they were asked about allocating resources, cooperating with the protocol, influencing judges and prosecutors, and persuading victims.

Allocating Limited Resources

The introduction of LAP as a new genre immediately revealed some tensions between limited resources within law enforcement, prosecution, and probation and the need for systemic change in dealing with domestic violence cases. For some interview participants, the new genre was seen as potentially solving that resource problem rather than disrupting or advancing the legal and judicial systems. A judge, for example, expressed how victim safety might be weighed against the efficient uses of resources:

> Well, right, overall I am saying that this [goal] is victim safety, avoiding repeat [incidents and police calls], avoiding an exacerbation of the incident. But I think that it [LAP] also, now I am thinking in terms of secondary benefits, certainly it alerts the advocate to the people [high-risk victims], where if they are spread thin, where do you put the most of your energy.
>
> (W-25; again see the Appendix for our interview citation style)

A first responder also revealed these somewhat competing goals in implementing LAP:

> Well, obviously the overarching goal is violence reduction and specifically femicide ... within that, I mean sort of the sub-goals are to get them [domestic violence victims] hooked up with the advocates right away, and that's key. Probably number two would be to really help the police department really prioritize their domestic violence cases, because obviously we have limited resources as well.
>
> (W-1)

The interview participants quoted above did label resource allocation as a "secondary" goal, and some participants excluded such resource allocation when they expressed the primary goals of LAP. Another first responder, for example, said the goal of LAP was

> to get the victim to services. It wasn't that the intention was better prosecution or any of those things. Those have been good consequences, but we have always said that our goal is to identify those victims and get them into services.
>
> (K-10)

However, the realities of the sustaining need to distribute effectively the limited resources of the legal and judicial systems are still reflected in these perceived goals of LAP. And, the question remains: why are such resources directed toward domestic violence limited while those directed toward confining and treating sex offenders unlimited? Could it be that sex offenders are still seen as disturbing overall society while domestic abusers are viewed as individuals out of control within a specific private place?

Moreover, when asked about more specific benefits of LAP, police officers and deputy sheriffs, in particular, continued to reveal that potential tension between helping the high-risk victims get services and making better decisions about how to manage the offender and therefore channel the resources of those who do that management. A first responder, for example, summed up that tension as follows:

> I think that the goal of this [LAP] is to protect women … there are other actions that happen, like we identify potential abusers or maybe a chronic abuser who has some issues, and I suppose that that information could be used somewhere down the line by the judicial system.
>
> (R-16)

When another first responder identified the benefits of LAP, he pointed out how using the assessment protocol eased the burden on police:

> That's always been a frustration of police officers is that "Oh, it's the battling Brunos again." It's a vicious cycle, and so they had taken some ownership to be able to say, "Gee, I have got to do this thing [administer the risk assessment questionnaire] because it would be great if we didn't have to keep coming back here on a weekly or monthly basis." And, actually see that there is progress in helping these women who seem to be in an absolute vortex.
>
> (K-22)

To disrupt the system via LAP beneficially, these ongoing challenges by first responders needed to be addressed within the introduction and implementation of the genre itself.

Enlisting the Cooperation of First Responders

One method of addressing the challenges faced by first responders upon arriving at a domestic violence incident was to stress how LAP would better ensure the safety of these responders. A law enforcement officer, for example, described how the LAP risk assessment questionnaire "took a lot of the weight off the officer's shoulders" by giving them "a little bit more influence in their ability to talk victims or survivors and family members into taking the situation a little bit more seriously." Rather than encountering the challenge of "what are you doing messing in my family's life?" officers would present the questionnaire in terms of gathering "just the facts" (R-15). Another first responder indicated that if officers know that they are returning to a location where the victim has previously screened in at high risk, they might say, "OK, this is probably a more dangerous situation I am going to than I realized" (R-13) and thus officers have a heightened awareness of ensuring their own safety.

These safety and efficiency concerns among first responders are not unique to Minnesota. Angela Gover, Dagmar Pudrzynska Paul, and

Mary Dodge (2011), for example, surveyed 309 police officers on their attitudes about and perceptions of domestic violence. Eighty-four percent of the officers felt that domestic violence calls took up too much time and effort and "showed a high level of frustration with repeat calls to the same address (93%), and believed that too many domestic violence calls are for verbal arguments (93%)" (626). Additionally, 75 percent of the officers felt that they were more likely to be injured during a domestic violence call, but 61 percent of officers agreed with the statement: "Arresting someone at a DV [domestic violence] call seldom helps reduce future DV incidents" (626). Although LAP was designed to save the lives of domestic violence victims by getting them to accept advocacy services, Minnesota law enforcement reflected the same reactions as captured in the Gover, Paul, and Dodge survey: first responders seemed most likely to administer the assessment questionnaire if they believed that it was effective in screening for high risk, reduced the number of times they might be called to a location, alerted them to the personal danger at a location, and gave them the tools to act effectively at the scene of a domestic violence case, all of which were absolute requirements to complete the mission of law enforcement and to introduce the new genre successfully into the system. And so, as Bawarshi and Reiff (2010) concluded, "Within any socio-historically bounded structure or system of activity there exist competing demands and goals, contradictions, tensions, and power relations that shape which ideologies and actions are reproduced" (81). Without the cooperation of first responders, who often tire of repeat domestic violence calls to a residence without seeing any results or change, LAP would certainly fail. Perhaps, then, both benefits, effective management of limited resources and changes in the victim's behavior and belief, are needed for systemic change regarding domestic violence.

Influencing Judges and Prosecutors

Along with agreeing that the risk assessment tool could enhance the challenge of law enforcement, many judges, corrections and probations officers, and city and county attorneys emphasized that the "protocol" side of LAP could improve legal and judicial systemic responses to domestic violence. A member of a county attorney's office defined this systemic responsibility as follows:

> The Lethality Assessment in its purest form and what it has been validated for is to assess risk right then and there. What we are trying to do is to say, "OK, if a person screens in, are there other things the system can do to help?"
>
> (K-27)

Again, the first effects of assessing high-risk cases within the broader legal and judicial systems are often higher bail and stricter release conditions after an abuser has been arrested. As one judge summed up the importance of LAP in her job, "This is important at that bail setting, that very first juncture when that individual is about to be released from custody, and you are talking about release conditions" (K-23).

Given a high-risk score on the assessment tool, obligatory concern for public safety also drove a city attorney often to say to himself, "It's, you know, kind of a severe incident. Yeah, I am going to ask for much higher bail" (K-21). Also a community corrections officer admitted that sending the LAP results to the judge puts a "little bit different spin that most people use this tool [for]," but community corrections wants to get risk scores to the court: "We wanted to be able to somehow share that with the court, and again try to get to our root question of, 'If you have five abusers in jail overnight ... how do you know where to focus'" (W-3). Thus, the use of risk assessment not only alerts the victim and perhaps persuades her to make use of advocacy services, but it also helps eliminate what one judge calls "a crap shoot as to who you are believing and do they have a persuasive counsel and you let someone very violent out versus someone who is really going to never do it again" (W-25). To this judge "this is data" that helps her decide whether to lift a no-contact order, require higher bail, or set other conditions for release (W-25). These collaborators engaged with LAP in the hope that the protocol will support the system by performing triage among not only victims but also offenders, but perhaps more important, they see that LAP helps them do their jobs with more ease and confidence, even though they might bend the primary purpose of the new genre to suit those goals.

Persuading Victims

Finally, our interview participants stressed that one ultimate purpose of LAP was not only to get services to the victim but also to persuade her to leave her abuser, a significant challenge, best expressed by Suruchi Thapar-Björkert and Karen Morgan (2010): "Often women are expected to adhere to a dominant cultural script that directs them to get away and stay away from their abusers" (45). Thapar-Björkert and Morgan found that even advocacy volunteers have a dilemma in working with victims as they try to support victims' choices but also want women to avoid violent situations. Again, this responsibility can be placed almost exclusively upon the victims once they absorb the message from a high-risk LAP score: "This means that the victims are considered to be the ones who have to change their lives and adapt themselves to the domestic situation, the ones who have to look for a solution to their problem" (Thapar-Björkert and Morgan 2010, 47). Melissa Dichter and Richard

Gelles (2012) summed up this victim dilemma as follows: "Individual risk perception is important not only because it may be an accurate predictor of future victimization but also because the perception of risk is associated with taking action toward protective or risk-avoidance behaviors" (45). An important goal of LAP, according to our interview participants, is persuading the victim to undertake such behaviors.

The introduction and implementation of LAP nationwide and within Minnesota reveals tension between supporting the victim and efficiently dealing with domestic violence as a crime that necessitates triaging cases, distributing resources, and managing and rehabilitating the offender. To be successful in both these goals, even resolving these tensions, LAP also requires changes in perception—of those first responders who must increase the time they stay with a victim to administer the questionnaire and contact advocacy services; of the victim who must see herself as at risk for being killed if she continues to stay with her abuser; and of the groups who provide the victim with support as she goes through this most dangerous stage. In part, these goals are accomplished by so illuminating the potential lethality to that victim that she replaces her ongoing fear of alienating her abuser with that fear of being killed by that abuser. To understand how genres reveal and/or disrupt behaviors and beliefs inherent in an existing system, we examine next the challenge of such enlightenment and change, an area of genre theory not as yet fully explored.

The Persuasive Features of LAP

Rhetorical criticism, as we explored in our Introduction to this book, is the study of persuasion or the attempt to identify the norms and values of a discourse community and to identify which strategies are designed to influence human action. More specifically, genre theory focuses on how a new genre might disrupt a system to change processes and procedures and even values and beliefs. In this section, we reveal how the questionnaire associated with LAP might also work to change not only processes and procedures but also actions and perceptions involved in domestic violence. To do so, we identify the features of the LAP questionnaire that specifically act to persuade victims of domestic violence to take the advice and embrace the resources available system-wide: the ways in which the questionnaire is validated and formatted, the content and word choices within the questions, and the controversy over adding a twelfth question to the original eleven.

In a way, we are adapting or extending the concept of "uptake" within genre theory. According to Bawarshi and Reiff (2010) and based on the work of Anne Freadman (1994, 2002), "The ability to know how to negotiate genres and how to apply and turn genre strategies (rules for play) into textual practices (actual performances) involves knowledge of what Freadman refers to as *uptake*" (85, emphasis in original). Although

Bawarshi and Reiff (2010) consider uptake in the context of organizational players knowing how to produce artifacts according to genre and situation, we take the liberty to extend some of these concepts to the persuasive effect of the genre, in this case the anticipated effect of the lethality assessment screening on the high-risk victim. Carol Berkenkotter and Cristina Hanganu-Bresch (2011) considered uptake an important concept in examining "the work that genres ... accomplish for the institutions in which they appear," particularly setting off a "series of genres flows" (222). We recognize that LAP affects such a series of presentencing investigations, bail stipulations, release agreements, judicial decisions, and such, but we believe that a close analysis of a genre such as LAP, perhaps through the recognition of persuasive strategies, also reveals the anticipated response or the "uptake" of the domestic violence victim. Moreover, we identify strategies designed to avoid a "misfire," our liberal adaptation of what John Austin (1962) would consider a failed uptake when a speech act is not performed at all (165). Throughout this analysis, we reveal how the LAP questionnaire potentially limits the victim's choices and agency—silences her resistance to the persuasive elements of the genre.

Validity and Format

Perhaps the most persuasive aspect of the LAP questionnaire, both for those who administer and those domestic violence victims who encounter it, comes not from any distinctive feature but from the overall perceived validity of the assessment tool.

This claim of validity enhances the *ethos* or the perceived character of those administering the questionnaire as well as supporting the "truth" claims of the questionnaire itself. As Lawrence Prelli (1989) has explained, such scientific ethos is rhetorically established through certain norms, including unbiased research, and certain persuasive strategies, including boundary work to distinguish what is claimed to be scientific work from that of outsiders, or what is considered fact-based from what is suspect.

The LAP questionnaire is presented to the victim and believed by those implementing it as consisting of "evidence-based questions," commented one judge (K-23), or as "backed up by science and by research," according to a first responder (W-1). Therefore, as a victim advocate concluded, it is important to "maintain the integrity" of Campbell's research as reflected in the LAP questionnaire, in other words, conserve "its research focus," in order for not only advocacy groups but also for the courts "to take it seriously and find it to be a legitimate assessment" (K-18). For some first responders, the LAP questionnaire is "the best tool that we have got" to identify high-risk victims (K-22). More specifically, however, as a community corrections officer concluded, the questionnaire functions as a risk assessment tool: "So I think that when you look at these questions, it enhances knowledge within the system of what creates risk" (K-20). Finally, a first responder commented that when victims see their scores on the assessment tool "in black and white, when you tell them, 'Heh, this is research based' ... when they see that other people smarter than myself have come up with this," the assessment tool does "have an impact on them" (W-1). Thus, the perceived scientific validity of the LAP questionnaire by the victim and throughout the legal and judicial systems makes it a persuasive instrument in and of itself.

Overall, the endorsement of LAP's validity matches the overall pursuit of the legal and judicial systems to ensure fairness and uniformity in response. The Minnesota Sentencing Guidelines Commission, for example, was established by Minnesota Statutes 244.09 (2014) and sets such boundaries "to establish rational and consistent sentencing standards that reduce sentencing disparity and ensure that the sanctions imposed for felony convictions are proportional to the severity of the conviction offense and the offender's criminal history" (Minnesota Sentencing Guidelines and Commentary 2013, 1; see also Minnesota Court Rules 2014). The presumed sentences for all felonies, from murder to the sale of a controlled substance, appear on the Minnesota Sentencing Guidelines Grid (2014, 1). The validity claims associated with LAP match these system-wide values and function as persuasive elements in working with a victim. As Devitt (2004) would say, "I would describe genre as reflecting especially and commonly a group's values, epistemology, and power relationships—its ideology" (59–60). But with LAP, the genre perpetuates the cultural values that determine that the best way to end domestic violence is for victims to leave their abusers. Regardless of the services offered to help victims do so, victims defy scientific prediction, even proof, if they fail to take that action.

The format of the assessment tool is also important for law enforcement as well as victim acceptance. Again, as Gover, Paul, and Dodge (2011) discovered, for example, some first responders still have misconceptions about the dynamics of domestic violence. Of the over 300 officers whom Gover, Paul, and Dodge surveyed, only 28 percent disagreed with the statement, "Many domestic violence victims could easily leave their relationships, but don't," although the majority of officers did recognize the abusers' need for power and control (628). In the context of possible conflicting perceptions about domestic violence, extra effort was made in the Minnesota counties to persuade first responders to administer the assessment tool based on the ease of its format and its eventual effect. A county attorney staff member, for example, admitted that to get first responders to cooperate with administering the assessment tool, the LAP collaborative group in the county "had to defer to what law enforcement was telling us would be the most likely to be used and the easiest for officers to use quite literally in the middle of the night in a potentially hostile situation" (K-27). A victim advocate also acknowledged that the "biggest feedback" her organization had received from officers was that they preferred to "just ask the questions; they don't get creative … get all 'social-worky'" (W-4). The assessment tool has to be "a short question and answer, with yes or no answers," commented another county attorney staff member; otherwise, "it's difficult to get buy-in" from first responders (W-5). In addition to ease of use, however, first responders were most likely to cooperate with administering the risk assessment tool if they could see the results of their efforts. "Cops by their nature need information, they are curious, and if they don't get information, they think that what they are doing is not doing any good," concluded one law enforcement specialist. "When the cop sees that, 'Oh, you mean I filled this form out and the judge actually doubled or tripled the bail,' then the officer remains engaged with LAP" (S-1).

Not all first responders, however, agreed with the virtues of the questionnaire, even given its easy application. One first responder, for example, commented that going through the questionnaire with the victim destroyed the personal rapport that she tried to establish with the person, sending the victim the message: "Oh, well, you [the officer] are just doing your job. You don't really care about me" (W-7). Other first responders recognized that for victims to cooperate in answering the assessment questions, officers were best trained to use the tool "as just continuing their interview questions, and not to make it seem as if they are doing a simple form … to make it not seem so cold" (K-10). However, the majority of those we interviewed endorsed the questionnaire format without reservation. As a county attorney staff member offered,

> I think with the victim too, it's easier if you ask the "yes" or "no" question than elaborate [in asking] "tell me about your past; tell me about your history," especially on the scene. A lot of them [victims] are so emotional they are not willing to participate in that.
>
> (K-24)

The LAP questionnaire, then, continues to be introduced as an easy-to-use, scientifically validated, and evidence-based assessment tool.

Content and Word Choice

Although the format and validity of the assessment tool are of importance generally to first responders administering the tool as well as the victims responding to it, the content of particular questions reveals specific fear-based persuasive strategies aimed toward changing the perceptions and actions of the victim. Here it becomes important to remember what Devitt (2004) stressed: "Genres have the power to help or hurt human interaction, to ease communication or to deceive, to enable someone to speak or to discourage someone from saying something different" (1). In capturing the perceptions of those who designed and those who now use the risk assessment questionnaire, we see that both content and word choice encourages some actions and responses and discourages others.

Question 3 ("Do you think he/she might try to kill you?"), for example, is a "key one," according to a first responder, because "the alarm bell goes off" (G-14; see Figure 2.1 again). This question almost seems "anti-scientific because you are asking for someone's opinion," offered another first responder, "but the actual research has shown that's probably the most actual predictor of violence" (W-1). Question 1 ("Has he/she ever used a weapon against you or threatened you with a weapon?") is also an "eye-opener," according to another first responder (R-16). And, a victim advocate relies on question 6 ("Is he/she violently or constantly jealous or does he/she control most of your daily activities?") to tell if a victim is "minimizing things" (W-4). If a victim answers "no" to the first three questions in the assessment tool, says this advocate, a "yes" to question 6 "is a pretty big flag in my opinion" and can be used to persuade the victim to realize the history of her abusive relationship. Thus, the function of these specific questions seems to be not only to assess the risk to the victim but also to change the perceptions held by the victim—to make her aware of the danger she faces of being killed and thus to encourage the separation process.

The word choice used in question 5 ("Has he/she ever tried to choke you?") reflects further the persuasive mission of the assessment questionnaire. The word "choke," rather than "strangle," was deliberately chosen. Put simply by a probation officer, the creators of the questionnaire found that domestic violence victims "didn't relate to strangulation. They related to the word choked" (K-3). Helping victims to recall a time when "they begin to pass out or they can't breathe" (K-26) fulfills the purpose of the assessment tool by changing the perception of the victim about lethality risk. A police officer further explained another deliberate word choice in question 5 by contrasting it to question 2 ("Has he/she threatened to kill you or your children?"):

> Anybody that's a parent can tell you that, if he threatened to kill your children, "Oh, my gosh." Then you know it's pretty serious ... But very few women who are victims of strangulation report that they are strangled. "Oh, he choked me? Yeah, he choked me; he chokes me all the time. But no, he never strangled me."
>
> (R-15)

As another probation officer explained, the designers of the assessment tool "were really specific about whether they used 'strangulation' or 'choke': the victim would be overly alarmed at the use of strangle, 'that seems more of a legal term, and so the victim would answer 'no' to that question" (W-8). The results of question 5 could also be instrumental in better managing the offender, as a county attorney staff member suggested: If an offender is educated about the dangers of strangulation, then the offender "is actually more likely to do more [in terms of rehabilitation] and not reoffend" (K-27).

As a genre, LAP aims to work against the entrenched language and cultural assumptions associated with the domestic violence victim, and thus has unusually high expectations placed upon it. At the same time, the genre strategically incorporates entrenched language, such as "choke" rather than "strangle," to maximize its rhetorical effect. Thus, LAP was certainly created to be a persuasive document as well as an assessment tool. As Devitt (2004) reminds us, the "act of constructing the genre … is also the act of constructing the situation" (21).

The Twelfth Question

Looking at the specific risk assessment questions reveals persuasive strategies by way of validity, format, content, and word choice. Examining the controversial addition of a twelfth question to the questionnaire in some counties in Minnesota and elsewhere reveals again the balance, even perhaps tension, of assessing the victim's situation by use of a validated tool at the same time increasing effectiveness of the system by collecting as much information as possible about the offender and the victim. These two purposes could be achieved in conjunction with each other, but in the minds of some stakeholders adding this twelfth question invalidates the scientific basis of LAP even though that question offers additional information useful for victim services. Although Washington County uses the 11-question assessment tool as developed by the Maryland Network Against Domestic Violence, Anoka County and some parts of Ramsey County and Chisago County have added a twelfth question to the tool: "Has he/she ever forced you to have sex when you did not wish to do so?"

On the one hand, Washington County defends its decision to use only the initial 11 questions because of the persuasive power of the perceived validity of the tool.

> My contention is that it was a research tool, that there is a reason what these questions are asked, worded the way that they are … I don't believe you can add questions to it … I just think then you have lost fidelity, concluded a community corrections officer.
>
> (W-3)

A victim advocate offered a similar defense of the 11-question version:

> You know, this is an evidence-based tool; by adding another question … then you are off doing your own thing … I like this one

> [11-question version] because we can say when we go to conferences and when we present to officers, we can say, "This is statistically what is considered," you know, "lethal."
>
> (W-4)

On the other hand, other counties in Minnesota defend the addition of that twelfth assessment question based in particular on advice from victim advocates. The inclusion, commented one judge, for example, was particularly supported by an advocacy group as "another sort of abuse/control type question" because "it provides information of a different type of physical control or physical abuse that might not be fleshed out by the others" (K-23). A police chief who was instrumental in adding the twelfth question to her precinct's version of the assessment tool argued that "from the advocates' point of view ... the majority of women who suffered at the hands of an abuser were also being forced to have sex," so if "you are going to address abuse, let's address all abuse" (R-15).

Moreover, other members of the Minnesota LAP coalition found the twelfth question informative, even though it had not been validated, because the ways in which a victim might answer that question helped them more fully understand the power and control dynamics in the abusive relationship. A member of a county attorney's staff, for example, expressed why the question might be informative: "Some people do use sex as a weapon or as a punishment ... and so that is a piece from an advocacy perspective that is significant to know" (W-5). And, a first responder dismissed any debate about the question and instead endorsed importance of the information gleaned from the question:

> Forced to have sex when you don't wish to do so, that is a definite mind set on the part of the male to exercise that dominance and control ... What all the PhDs think about in terms of why it [the twelfth question] should not have been included or what not, that debate goes on. From my perspective of a police officer, when I hear that kind of stuff ... that sparks many of our domestic quarrels.
>
> (K-22)

If the purpose is to convince the victim that she is in grave danger from her abuser, then educating the victim about the lethality and abnormality of her particular situation, according to the interview participants quoted above, should outweigh validity claims. The educational mission of LAP, in particular question 12, was thus endorsed by a city attorney, for example:

> If you put it [the twelfth question] in this kind of a questionnaire, and after asking some of the prior questions, and you get to that one ... if the victim associates that with a situation where, "Boy,

> they are asking these dangerous questions, and then they ask that one" … I think that it's a good question to ask, because I just don't think some of these victims really consider that to be part of a dangerous situation.
>
> (K-24)

Therefore, a first responder had settled in her mind the question of validity versus victim enlightenment:

> It [the twelfth question] takes away from the validity of it … [but] maybe if someone is asked that, they may believe that "well, maybe I was [forced to have sex]," realizing that just because you are the wife it doesn't mean that you have to succumb to all of the husband's wishes.
>
> (W-2)

With the inclusion of the twelfth question in the LAP questionnaire, the persuasive mission of the assessment tool is again clear, whether or not the persuasive strategies of a claim for validity or a need to educate the victim are resolved. The overall mission of LAP is to convince the high-risk victim to change her perceptions and actions so that she will leave her abuser, in other words, to direct her fear-motivated actions away from appeasing her abuser to leaving that abuser, as we explore next. Whether the introduction of the LAP screening questionnaire, as a new genre, was meant to more efficiently use existing resources or to add new ones to aid the domestic violence victim, her safety depends not only on the resources provided to her by others but also, and perhaps primarily, on her own change in behavior and belief. Thus again, we add to scholarly studies of genres within the field of professional communication, our reflections on how disrupting genres have the potential not only to direct new behavior but also to change beliefs so that behavior is accepted and, in essence, institutionalized. These disrupting genres, such as LAP, in content and presentation contain persuasive strategies designed to make those organizational and cultural changes.

Fear-based Arguments to Separate the Domestic Violence Victim from Her Abuser

As we discussed earlier, our interview participants, particularly advocates and first responders, recognized that although one benefit of the lethality assessment tool is to distinguish between high-risk and low-risk victims in order to channel resources to the victims most in danger, the inherent goal of LAP is to persuade the victim to leave her abuser. We explore the implications of this goal in the remainder of this chapter and later in the book.

Douglas Walton (2000) identifies the overall persuasive strategy that we recognize within LAP, a fear-appeal argument in which the target audience is convinced to "adopt a course of action by portraying the only alternative as some horrible disaster (usually death or severe injury) that is very fearful to that audience" (xiii). Moreover, according to Pfau (2007), "in order to feel that fear in the Aristotelian sense, one must believe that a destructive or painful event or object is likely to affect oneself, and that the object of fear is near at hand—both temporally and spatially" (221–222). This persuasive strategy is effective, because the event is contingent or capable of being altered; specifically, for example, in the case of LAP and the domestic violence victim, if she is convinced to take advantage of advocacy services so that she can leave her offender (Pfau 2007, 223; Aristotle 1991, 141). Again, however, to persuade the victim to leave her abuser, LAP and those who administer it must override the many needs that hold the victim to her abuser and, again, to exchange the fear of alienating the abuser for the fear of being killed by the abuser. Here again these strategies are different from the kairotic cycles evidenced in our analysis of civil commitment and MSOP: moral panic among the public and many stakeholders over their possible vulnerabilities to stranger sexual assault support some policymakers' endorsement of indefinite confinement and treatment of the sex offender. With LAP, the onus is put on the victim to take advantage of existing support systems.

Because LAP serves as a disrupting new genre within the judicial and legal systems, one with the potential to curtail domestic violence through the persuasive aspects of the risk assessment tool we studied above, and ultimately through fear-based appeals to the victim, we must capture a sense of why female victims of domestic abuse resist the protocol and what first responders do to counter that resistance. In a way, such resistance is a misfire of the genre—a failure of uptake. But in this case that failure of uptake, as not previously explored by rhetorical and professional communication scholars, can be a result of the victim's retaining her choice and agency, regardless of her immediate danger.

Resisting LAP

Domestic violence victims have long told the courts why they choose not to separate from their abusers. In *State v. Norman* (1989), for example, a wife, who shot her husband after he beat her for an entire day, explained, "[S]he was too afraid of her husband to press charges against him or leave him" (n.p.). In this case, forensic psychologists testified that Judy Norman suffered from "battered women's syndrome" and described how "such abuse and degradation" may lead a woman to believe she is "unable to help herself and cannot expect help from anyone else. She believes that she cannot escape the complete control of her husband and that he is invulnerable to law enforcement and other sources of help" (n.p.). From the *Norman* case, we learned that the domestic violence victim might not have the means, confidence, and courage to leave her abuser. Despite these forensic explanations, however, "a woman's 'failure' to permanently separate from a violent relationship," says Mahoney (1991), "is still widely held to be mysterious and in need of explanation, an indicator of *her* pathology rather than her batterer's" (6, emphasis in original). To avoid victim blaming and to encourage a victim-centered legal and judicial system, we must again understand and address the complexities of the victim's perceptions and actions. A staff member of a county attorney's office summed up these mysterious and complex perceptions and actions in terms of LAP as follows: "I think that it runs the gamut. It can be absolute fear. It can be absolute love" (K-27).

Today, because completing the LAP questionnaire can be the first official step into, or, for some, back into the broader legal and judicial systems, domestic violence victims "who have not had good experience with law enforcement and don't trust them are not going to answer any other questions than they have to," according to one member of a county attorney's office (W-5). A first responder agreed with that assessment: "I am finding that the victims that have had a lot of contact with police officers through domestic violence situations ... maybe have been through the court systems ... are the ones that are more hesitant or not willing to answer those [risk assessment questions]" (G-13). This reluctance is further illuminated by the research of such scholars as Carla Pajak et al. (2014), who found that in interviews domestic violence victims, the undesirable effects of using legal resources included "provider coercion, provider attitude of blaming the victim, system discord, and women's feelings of shame and stigma," all of which undermined women's trust in the system and caused some to "navigate service use by portraying themselves as a 'good victim'" (2583). Ferraro (2006) defines that good or ideal victim as follows: "Cultural imagery of victims of abuse portrays women victims as mentally ill (say, suffering post-traumatic stress disorder), damaged, and helpless. 'Ideal victims' are meek and distraught, innocent of provoking their victimization, and possessing a body that symbolizes these qualities" (19). The impetus for demanding a good or ideal victim on the part of legal and judicial officials and for the resistance of domestic violence victims to LAP comes, to a certain extent, from mutual distrust.

If Pajak, Ferraro, and others have explained why victims might not trust the system, Schneider (2000) further details why the system might not trust the victim:

> If a woman is to act on the help offered by the legal system, she must be willing to send him [her abuser] to jail, sever her relationship

> with him, and risk his violence when he is released. If she repeatedly calls the police and presses charges, then withdraws and refuses to prosecute, the courts and police become frustrated, ignore her complaints, and may also ignore the complaints of other women.
>
> (51)

A member of a county attorney's office understood how a victim's feelings about loss of control might alienate first responders:

> There are also very reluctant victims who call the police because they need an immediate response, and as soon as the police come, they don't want somebody arrested, they don't want anything to happen, and they don't want it to appear as if they are cooperating with what's about to happen, you know, somebody being arrested, that kind of thing.
>
> (W-5)

Many of these victims want the violence to stop and the relationship to heal without such extensive legal and judicial intervention.

Along with mutual distrust, victims of domestic violence might resist LAP because of the many pressures that they face. One victim advocate, for example, indicated that it was hard to pin down the reason for victim refusal

> without knowing all the dynamics that exist at the time. Was it just the crisis of the situation? Was it timing, and there are children present? Was it the way the officer presented it? ... [S]ome of them [victims] may just be wanting some information, limited information about what's going on with the system.
>
> (K-19)

A first responder indicated that such refusal might also be caused by "clouded judgment, many times they are either under the influence of drugs or alcohol," or it could be reliance on the abuser for financial support: "'Heh, if I am really going to sever, end this relationship, who is going to pay my bills, who is going to support me?' So there is that part of it, if he is father of children, for instance" (R-14). Deborah Epstein (1999) has cautioned that too often the legal and judicial systems ignore "the real-life obstacles facing women who wish to end their relationships," obstacles that include "lack of economic resources; concern for children; emotional attachment to the perpetrator; perceptions of the availability of social support; and religious and culturally-based values and norms" (39). Again, victims of domestic violence may want the violence to stop but the relationship preserved.

Moreover, race, ethnicity, cultural identity, and socio-economic status (SES) might also influence the extent to which domestic violence victims cooperate with or resist LAP. One first responder, for example, mentioned how SES seems to affect victim/offender cooperation in his community: We are

> trying to keep convincing them that there is more work that needs to be done in their relationship, even if they decide to continue on with it, fine, but what else can be done to get them to not have it blow up and have police intervention. Very difficult, very difficult, especially in, I think, this community where the socio-economic conditions are on the lower rung in our metro area.
>
> (K-22)

Recent scholars add some nuance to these factors. Yvonne Amanor-Boadu et al. (2010), for example, found, "For immigrant women, increased fear of an abuser increased their likelihood of leaving, whereas for non-immigrant women, increased feelings of being controlled by an abuser predicted a greater likelihood of leaving" (626). Moreover, Jeffrey Ackerman and Tony Love (2014), in analyzing data from the National Crime Victimization Survey, determined that "minority groups notified the police about intimate partner violence events more than non-minorities" (162) and "higher SES victims are less likely than are lower SES victims to notify the police" (177).

Many of our interview participants, however, identified emotional stress as a primary reason domestic victims might be unwilling, indeed unable, to participate in LAP at the time of the incident. One first responder described resistance to the protocol as follows:

> The emotions are running so high at some of these deals, they [victims] are going into a basic mental mode, and they don't want to talk to anyone, much less some advocate who is going to be "touchy/feely" over the phone.
>
> (K-22)

For some victims, the primary emotions, according to another first responder, are "shame and embarrassment" (W-1). For many others, that emotion is fear, particularly if the offender has not been arrested, as described by a community corrections officer: "Sometimes it's not safe because the offender is still around, or he wasn't arrested because he was gone on arrival" (W-8). At the moment of violence and attack, described a first responder, the victim "just got scared of the person [but] they just don't want to follow through and assist us with the investigation portion because of that fear" (R-13). Thus, the victim might be so fearful of her abuser's reaction to her reporting the abuse that she cannot be persuaded to leave that abuser as based on the potential lethality of a later incident. Such high emotions at the time of the incident, when the first responder is trying to get a victim to complete the LAP questionnaire and speak to an advocate, certainly set up what we are interpreting as a genre misfire—none of the subsequent actions will take place given the victim's refusal.

Finally, domestic violence victims might resist LAP because they are simply not ready to leave the abusive relationship—being ready to leave seems a matter of personal timing. A city attorney, for example, compared the victim of domestic abuse to

> in many ways like an alcoholic, which is until they hit bottom, it doesn't matter what we say or what we do. It's something that they have to realize on their own, unfortunately, and our hope and goal is maybe to help [them], I hate to say, hit bottom quicker.
>
> (K-24)

According to Jacqueline Dienemann et al. (2002), for women there are four phases of leaving an abusive relationship: bonding, enduring, disengaging, and recovering. Viveka Enander and Carin Holmberg (2008) further complicate these stages in their recent interviews with women who had left abusive relationships. They introduce the concept of a traumatic bond, to describe the abusive relationship, a bond "consisting of *entwined ties*"; some of these ties were "*emotional* ties, i.e., *love, fear, hate, compassion, guilt,* and *hope*, while others are more *composite* ties, i.e., *the desire to understand, dependency*, and *internalization*" (207, emphasis in original). Given this bond, Enander and Holmberg (2008) identify three different but overlapping processes of stages of leaving:

- "*Breaking Up* concerns the act of leaving and what precedes and initiates it. The factual leaving was often preceded by a feeling of having hit rock bottom and of being totally 'done in'" (212);
- *Breaking Free* takes place when "an abused woman no longer feels anything for the abusive man, his emotional power over her is also broken. That a battered woman has broken the abuser's internal power over her does not, however, mean that his external oppression of her has ceased" (217); and finally in
- *Understanding*, "a woman defines the relationship she lives/has lived in as abusive and herself as a battered woman. We propose that this is a process primarily occurring after (the actual) leaving. In other words, women do not leave because they realise they are abused; rather, they realise they are abused because they have left" (218, all emphases in original).

These three processes reveal that domestic violence victims might not be fully prepared to leave their abusers until, ironically, they have done just that.

Overcoming Resistance

In light of these many and complex reasons why a domestic violence victim might resist LAP, first responders, victim advocates, and others in the legal and judicial systems attempt to overcome victim resistance through what Pfau (2007) identifies as the third stage of fear appeals: after identifying the lethality danger the victim faces or a danger that must be described as near but as capable of being avoided, those administering and implementing LAP need to eventually instill courage in that victim (229). This effort often involves changing the victim's self-perception rather than fully focusing on her abuser's dangerous acts.

Our interview participants, for example, often stated that the risk assessment questionnaire had the potential to help victims take the first step in leaving their abusers when victims see not only themselves as victims but also the relationships as "abnormal." A city attorney, for example, described how the LAP assessment questionnaire might change the self-perception of a victim: "'Heh, he has done that to me in the past, and you know he has threatened me,' and sometimes that might be enough for a light bulb to go off and these victims to figure out, 'I am a victim'" (K-24). A first responder also hoped for that result:

> And, you know, quite honestly, the other thing that is really helpful is that the victims see these risk factors for themselves. I have had several victims break down in tears and say, "I never realized it was so dangerous ... I was ready to go back, and this tool kind of helped change my mind."
>
> (W-1)

> "Because we ultimately do want them to leave," concluded another first responder.
>
> (W-7)

To overcome a domestic violence victim's reluctance to complete the LAP questionnaire and to speak to a victim advocate at the time of the incident and to help instill courage in the victim, first responders employ a number of persuasive strategies. They have been taught the importance of the timing of strategies. As one Maryland first responder explained, "If you get these victims a couple of days later, their batterer will be trying to make amends and the victims will have had time to rationalize [the assault]" (Remsberg 2007, n.p.). Enander and Holmberg

(2008) define this rationalization as internalization, when "a victimized woman may internalise the abuser's concept of reality ... to regard not only herself, but the whole world, with his eyes, resulting in her questioning herself and her concept of reality" (208). These techniques also include establishing a personal rapport, one that is unique to individual officers. Some first responders "are better at establishing a rapport with victims than other officers," commented a victim advocate, "not that the officer is maybe insensitive or anything, but it just might be ... how the victim responds to them at the time" (G-11). Those first responders who have had personal experience with domestic violence in their own lives, for example, might share these perspectives with victims. As a first responder explained, "We are somewhat intimidating just by what we wear, and that's why I try to do that personal spin ... 'I have been there. You know, just let me know, let me help you'" (W-7).

First responders have also developed a similar personalized explanation for the risk assessment tool and a subsequent phone call to an advocate in high-risk cases. Maryland Network Against Domestic Violence (n.d.a) training tools direct the first responder to introduce the assessment questionnaire by saying, "This will help me better understand your situation" and to explain making the phone call to advocates as finding "better ways to help" the victim (n.p.). In an interview, David Sargent (2011), who served 21 years with the Metropolitan Police Department in Washington, DC, and is a primary trainer for Maryland Network Against Domestic Violence, relayed his approach to the reluctant victim:

> And we say, "Well, that's fine, you don't have to [participate], but I'm gonna call the domestic violence hotline to get some information to pass onto you and while I'm on the phone, I'd just like you to think about speaking to them."
>
> (n.p.)

The victim advocate on the phone hears the officer continue the conversation with the victim, for example: "Are you sure you don't want, I have got them [advocates] right here, if you want to talk to them" (W-4). And this advocate related that "it's very few and far between that they don't," and so the first responder has succeeded in convincing the victim to participate in LAP (W-4). With the first responder and the advocate articulating that the victim always has a choice to continue with LAP and that continuation will be fully supported, the victim might find the courage to deal differently with her abuser.

Moreover, first responders are trained in other persuasive techniques. The Maryland Network Against Domestic Violence (n.d.b) advises:

> When the victim chooses not to speak with the hotline counselor: The officer reviews the factors that are predictive of death so the

> victim can be on the lookout for them, encourages the victim to contact the domestic violence program, provides the victim with referral information, and may follow other protocol measures designed to address the victim's safety and well-being.
>
> (n.p.)

Washington County (n.d.) issues its first responders a laminated card to carry with them that includes the following instructions: "If victim does not wish to speak with advocates, tell victim you need to speak to advocate to seek guidance and gently ask victim to reconsider" (n.p.). If the victim still does not want to speak with the advocate, then the first responder is directed to repeat what he or she said if the victim screened in as high-risk: "Advise the victim she's in danger, that people in her situation have been killed" (n.p.). Victims might expect police officers and deputy sheriffs to tell them, "'Ah, he's a no good. You have got to leave him" (W-1). But the victim's position might change when they hear their potential for being killed; as a community corrections officer stated:

> I have heard from victims, and I have heard from law enforcement that have said that ['Women in your situation have been killed by their partners'] and got a reaction that no one thought they were going to get. Like, they have never heard someone say that directly to their face.
>
> (W-8)

Moreover, this same phrase, perhaps in slightly different form, seemed to be used in high-risk cases in all precincts that administer LAP. Southern Connecticut police officers, for example, are told, "We want you to use the phrase, 'kill'" because according to Lieutenant Jeffrey Nixon, "You do it with empathy" but "You put it right out there" (Florin 2012, n.p.). Again, these strategies for overcoming resistance on the part of the victim involve substituting one highly related fear for another: fear of leaving her abuser for fear of being killed by her abuser. Again, this substitution necessitates a certain degree of courage and change in self-identity or belief on the part of that victim.

Finally, recognizing this work on the part of the victim, the first responder, the advocate, and others involved in LAP complicates our understanding of the rhetorical nature of fear and resistance. Margareta Hyden (2005), for example, recognizes that fear within an abusive relationship

> contains the unarticulated knowledge of what she [the victim] wants and doesn't want. She wants to avoid the undesirable and to attain its opposite. She doesn't want her abuser's lack of respect or his way

> of forcing himself on her and attacking her body. She doesn't want his diminution of her.
>
> (172)

This fear, therefore, concludes Hyden, is a form of resistance to violence:

> Fear, helplessness, and resistance are closely inter-associated … fear is the resistance offered by those who are presumed to be powerless. The fact that the woman is frightened means that she rejects the man's violence, without necessarily having a well-prepared strategy for how she can avoid being re-exposed to it.
>
> (172)

This aspect of fear acknowledges the agency and even power of the victim who rejects the abuser's violence and so might welcome an escape strategy.

Overall, LAP aims to change the perception and subsequent behavior of the victim of domestic violence so that she might elect to take certain actions, such as separating from her abuser—a difficult and at times unsafe decision for the victim. LAP then has the potential to encourage the victim to leave, and the protocol itself involves providing a safety plan for the victim to do so. If LAP and the subsequent systemic changes meet expectations, if uptake indeed results, then not only will domestic homicides be reduced but also scholars and activists may recognize the mechanisms by which such changes are introduced and considered successful. In particular, we have revealed the extent of persuasive strategies used to support the genre's ability to change behavior and belief, an extension of the disruption that other rhetorical and professional communication scholars have explored.

Using LAP to Decrease Domestic Abuse

The search for and adoption of this risk assessment tool represents a moment of *kairos* within the legal and judicial systems of, first, Washington and Anoka Counties, and later, parts of Ramsey and Chisago Counties, MN, within the context of a national and global response to domestic violence, particularly domestic homicide. The implementation of the protocol in its entirety, however, must be negotiated by recognizing the need to balance change, and yet support an existing system; to respond to the needs of the victim while effectively and efficiently managing and channeling limited resources; to offer victim-centered services while managing and rehabilitating the offender; and to respect the choices of the victim while convincing her to leave her abuser. Indeed, the introduction of the LAP questionnaire as a new genre disrupts the current legal and judicial systems to reveal the ideologies that drive them. Rhetorical and professional communication scholars have previously recognized this disruption and resulting revelation; however, looking at such forces within the context of domestic violence illuminates how not only behavior but belief might be altered through the persuasive elements of the genre.

In this chapter, we focused on the perceived goals and the validity claims for the LAP questionnaire as well as the persuasive nature of its design, content, and word choice. The function of specific questions, for example, seemed not only to assess the risk to the victim but also to work to change the perception of the victim—to make her aware of the danger she faces and thus to start the separation process. Moreover, we illuminated the fear-appeal arguments within the administration of LAP by analyzing how victims resist the protocol and how first responders, advocates, and others attempt to overcome that resistance—to avoid an uptake misfire. However, to avoid victim blaming, legal and judicial systems must understand and address the causes of both the domestic violence victim's distrust of the system and the systems' distrust of that victim. We hope that we have also extended the rhetorical nature of fear-based arguments as well as the persuasive nature of genres, because to be successful, LAP, in essence, must work to substitute one fear for another. And, again, this substitution involves a certain degree of courage and change in self-perception.

If, as we said in the Introduction to this book, the Minnesota efforts regarding domestic violence and sexual assault represent the continuum of progress and misstep, then through genre analysis we see that so-called success in the area of domestic violence might be defined as persuading the victim to accept a certain action—separation from her abuser—or at least accepting victim services immediately. Although victim advocates, for example, are trained to leave that choice up to the victim, the administration and evaluation of LAP still insinuates that if the high-risk victim does not leave her abuser, she is likely to be killed. The misstep in addressing the extremes of sexual assault might be a result of isolation of the abuser due to moral panic and risk perception rather than a focus on healing and reintegrating the reformed abuser. This contrast is speculation on our part, but rhetorical analysis seems to support that speculation.

We continue our analysis of LAP within Chapter 4 by first focusing further on specific systemic changes made as a result of introducing LAP into the legal and judicial systems, and then suggesting how this new genre serves as a catalyst for broader cultural changes in gender roles and hierarchies. But first, in Chapter 3, we return to the controversies surrounding civil commitment of sex offenders by analyzing the methods and cultural results of marginalizing that offender. Those rhetorical and legal strategies of marginalization inform our perspectives on both sexual assault and domestic violence.

3 Othering Within Public Discourse

The Challenges of Power and Communication in Policymaking About a Controversial Group

In March 2012, convicted sex offender Clarence Opheim became the first person to be provisionally discharged from civil commitment under the Minnesota Sex Offender Program (MSOP) in almost a decade. Again, civil commitment is designed to extend treatment, under confinement, to those sex offenders considered too dangerous to reenter society after serving their criminal sentences. As mentioned in Chapter 1, the exit doors from Moose Lake and St. Peter, MN, where so-called sexual predators are housed and treated, had in essence closed after the highly publicized abduction and murder of Dru Sjodin in November 2003. Specifically, the public and political outcry following Sjodin's murder led Minnesota Governor Tim Pawlenty to discourage any future discharges from MSOP, to charge the state's county attorneys with reviewing an ever-increasing number of petitions for civil commitment of Level 3 sex offenders, and to use the media to talk about reinstating the death penalty when sexual assaults led to murder. As one policymaker put it, MSOP was initially intended

> for those people who really, really had done egregious assaults … with multiple victims, multiple experiences of rape, and high levels of violence … the intent was to be dealing with the worst of the worst.
>
> (C-4)

Since the escalation following the Rodriguez case, however, this policymaker cautioned, "One starts questioning whether or not that's the entire pool that they are now working [with]" (C-4). (Again, see the Appendix for a discussion of our data collection and interview methods.) And as we found, the intersections of risk perception, moral panic, and kairotic cycles prevented what might seem an effective systemic change, or a decrease of escalation in confinement, given the strain on the state budget, the constitutional challenges, and low recidivism rates for these offenders.

The news of Clarence Opheim's upcoming discharge reopened the wounds caused by the Rodriguez case. On the one hand, Opheim's record was indeed extreme: he had problems with alcoholism, he had befriended and then offended against children in his neighborhood, he had a high number of victims, and he was initially found to have a high risk for recidivism; thus, in many ways, he represented that "worst of the worst." On the other hand, Opheim had concluded his required treatment program, and his discharge was predicated on conditions of strict supervision, with return to confinement if he violated those conditions. Understandably, however, his upcoming discharge sparked public fear and outrage. The public, media, and political response matched the tenor of the Rodriguez case, reflecting and reinforcing many of the themes that are often echoed in public discourse about sex offenders—themes that we discussed in Chapter 1 and that we continue to rhetorically analyze in this chapter. These broad themes include the public and the media's tendency to characterize all sex offenders as the worst possible criminals, regardless of their specific ages, backgrounds, and offenses; public shaming of the sex offender; distorted perceptions of a high likelihood of recidivism; inaccurate perceptions about stranger versus acquaintance rape; the deterministic view that links the poor prospect of successful treatment with the very nature of sex offenders; and elected officials' discomfort with being labeled "soft on crime" if they support provisional discharge of sex offenders. Moreover, although we argue in this chapter that these generalized characterizations contribute to an Othering of sex offenders in public discourse, we understand the processes of Othering to function more broadly, certainly a useful perspective for rhetorical and professional communication scholars and activists. We also consider the ways in which victims of domestic violence are Othered through their hesitance to leave their abusers or are viewed as deviant, irrational, or uncooperative in these contexts, a theme we explore in Chapter 4. Thus, we expand upon rhetorical and professional communication theories by illuminating how such processes of marginalization close down the possibility of productive discussion and instead serve to create the framework for stereotypes, which are then perpetuated through public discourse and the media, as we discuss next.

The media coverage surrounding Opheim's provisional discharge reinforced these dominant stereotypes. At a public meeting to offer reassurance about Opheim's discharge, for example, a county attorney described the extent of Opheim's supervision:

> If he trips, does anything silly, he'll be gone ... There will be a microscope on this man all the time ... He can't go to the telephone booth without somebody with him. He can't have a cellphone. It's terrible; it's great. I've never seen a plan like this.
>
> (McEnroe 2012, n.p.)

However, the Opheim provisional discharge still raised public fear and possible political repercussions, as had the Rodriguez case. And so, a local editorial acknowledged the challenge of balancing risk and public safety with civil liberties:

> Is there risk with Opheim's release? Absolutely. While he has hit all the treatment benchmarks required for patients in Minnesota's program according to his attorney, no one can guarantee that he won't offend again ... Still, Opheim's looming release is an attempt to balance public safety with the growing concerns about the civil-commitment program's unsustainable costs and suspect constitutionality.
>
> (*StarTribune* 2012, February 8, n.p.)

The concerns voiced surrounding Opheim's discharge are commonly invoked in discussions about sex offenders more broadly, the primary focus of this chapter. Within this broad categorization of "sex offender," for example, the range of crimes and potential for rehabilitation vary widely. Of interest to this chapter, then, is not necessarily the fact of the public's concern over Opheim's provisional discharge, but rather the manner in which the public discourse about Opheim as sex offender may be read as representative of discourse about all sex offenders. For, as one policymaker noted,

> there are probably some individuals, maybe younger individuals, who may have committed certain kinds of offenses that might lend them to be treatable to the extent where at some point they are pretty much within the range of normal human experience and could probably live more or less successfully on their own or maybe under some kind of monitoring conditions. There are other people probably for which that will never be the case.
>
> (S-3)

Indeed, as we demonstrate in this chapter, the identity of the sex offender is often politicized and homogenized in the process, largely as a result of the complex set of discourses rooted in the public's fears and in policymakers' perceived need to address those fears in ways that allay them. On the one hand, as Minnesota Representative Tony Cornish has emphasized: "'[P]olitics can't be separated' from this debate because 'perception is reality' and the public's fear of sexual predators is justified as well as intense" (Tice 2013, n.p.). On the other hand, Indiana State Senator Karen Tallian (2013) warns us against so expanding the definition of sex offenders that "everyone is painted with the same brush," an aspect of looking carefully at what we fear (n.p.). We believe that in analyzing such complicated discursive contexts, in which voices might be silenced and social categories determined, rhetorical and professional communication scholars would benefit from applying and extending ideas related to identity theory, as we have done with the sex offender.

As we explain throughout this chapter, such theoretical application casts "power" in a new and more pertinent light during discursive conflict.

Again, we borrow here from Johnson et al.'s (2004) definition of Othering or a process that by identifying the so-called "different" reaffirms dominant and subordinate social positions (255). We consider also Ahmed's (2000) ideas about the discourses of stranger danger; she writes, for example:

> Strangers are not simply those who are not known in this dwelling, but those who are, in their very proximity, already recognised as not belonging, as being out of place. Such a recognition of those who are out of place allows both the demarcation and enforcement of the boundaries of "this place," as where "we" dwell.
>
> (21–22)

Indeed, as Ahmed (2000) notes, and as we will demonstrate, "the paedophile is hence represented as the ultimate stranger that communities must have the power to evict" (35). We initially apply Burke's ideas about identification but then describe the limitations of those ideas for complicating the discourses that result in the Othering of this controversial population. That is, we argue that while identification helps us understand the discursive forces that perpetuate the Othering of sex offenders, it does not bear recuperative power in helping stakeholders to think more critically about the implications of those discourses in ways that can begin to move beyond them.

To better address these discursive complexities and their implications, throughout this chapter, we move on to ideas about contemporary identity politics as we study the rhetorical complexities of working with one of the most challenging, marginalized, and stigmatized groups in society—a group that, on the one hand, has developed a negative reputation for good reason but, on the other hand, and as a result, is often essentialized uncritically in public discourses. We describe the power of this Othered group to invoke fear, despite their subordination and marginalization in society, and subsequently, the ways in which policymakers respond by validating the public's fear or anger through subtle practices of Othering sex offenders, in effect perpetuating a cycle of fear, domination, and redistribution of power, a cycle as difficult to escape as the kairotic cycles we identified in Chapter 1.

Critical, scholarly conversations about identity politics and Othering have typically been applied to groups more easily understood as marginalized. We apply some of these concepts to a rhetorical situation where it is perhaps less easy to acknowledge the Othering at work, precisely because it is also possible to recognize why that marginalization would happen in the first place (see, for example, Egumenovska 2012; Gilles et al. 2013; Van Houtum and Van Naerssen 2001). As a result, we attempt to add a new layer of complexity to this theory base by complicating the ways in which stakeholders inadvertently assign power to the Other, at the very least existing as a roadblock to progress, through discourses of fear and punishment, and so the ways in which a feared and loathed group unwittingly gains a kind of power through their marginalization. The Othered group has already been disempowered socially and culturally, but the groups with power for making decisions, lawmakers and politicians, for example, have also been disempowered as a result of their continuing to work to Other the sex offenders—there is no room for progress, no room for constructive dialogue. Thus, we offer a new way of conceptualizing how this marginalized group are Othered, through the roles that they are oftentimes assigned but that they only sometimes reinforce. Moreover, we consider how a sort of power is assigned to a group perceived as irredeemable and non-conforming, even when that group, as a whole, does not always possess such qualities and cannot directly exercise that power.

Perpetuating and Sustaining Social Categories Through Practices of Othering

Implicitly acknowledging the public's perception of the likelihood of Opheim's recidivism should he be provisionally discharged, the county attorney, quoted earlier in this chapter, cited the extreme nature of his surveillance. Burke's concepts of identification and consubstantiality help us account for how persuasion can occur, and how social groups may arrive at the sort of common ground that can serve to perpetuate and sustain persuasive acts and discourses. Thus, in this section, we illuminate the discourses that contribute to the Othering of this controversial population by applying Burke's ideas about identification and consubstantiality.

Identification and Consubstantiality

Burke notes that identification is one vantage point from which we can view how rhetoric functions; in fact, he feels that identification is logically prior to persuasion. He invokes an observation by W. C. Blum, who says: "In identification lies the source of dedications and enslavements in fact of cooperation" (Burke 1969, xiv). In considering identification as the foundation for persuasion, Burke (1969) writes: "You persuade a man only insofar as you can talk his language by speech, gesture, tonality, order, image, attitude, idea, *identifying* your ways with his" (55, emphasis in original). Burke sees identification as able to account for human interaction, in that it pertains to cooperation among groups, the formation of social cohesion, and the ways in which individuals in particular groups can be distinct from one another yet also be identified with one another. That is, for Burke, identification is not possible without division; this, he feels, is the irony of identification. Here, he notes that identification does not mean "the same as"; rather, it refers to the way in which "A" may be "identified with" "B." It does not mean "joined with," per se. He notes, for example, that a child is both related to and distinct from its parentage. Thus, identification does not deny distinctiveness, for a person may be identified with another person in a particular group while still being an "individual locus of motives" (Burke 1969, 20–21). As Barbara Biesecker (1997) also notes, "Through either explicit attempts at persuasion or more subtle forms of identification, 'A' becomes identified with 'B': the supersession of the individual and the consolidation of the social are accomplished by rhetorical exchange" (42). Of interest in this chapter is how such rhetorical exchanges can result in the idea of sex offenders becoming associated with collective perceptions about recidivism rates, amenability to treatment, or threats to public safety, for example.

Burke's ideas about identification then provide the basis for his understanding of consubstantiality. Whereas Burke's identification forms the basis for persuasion, or represents a lens through which we may conceptualize how persuasion can occur, his notion of consubstantiality then functions to establish a common ground or establish a consolidated social hierarchy through which that persuasive act may be sustained and perpetuated. As Ratcliffe (2005) describes it, "Consubstantiality signifies a place of bridged differences and common ground, a place from which to act for a common cause" (55). In our case, we understand this common ground to be related to a specific, deterministic view of sex offenders that portrays them as a singular Other. For example, even though Opheim had concluded his required treatment program, and even though his provisional discharge would be very closely supervised, with an immediate return to confinement if he violated those conditions, his case was nonetheless viewed through the sort of deterministic lens that sees recidivism as the likely outcome for released offenders. The media may then further perpetuate these kinds of identifications. One victim advocate, for example, described the political factors that influence the cycle of identification and the shaping of a public "common ground":

> So I think that the public is really unaware, and the media doesn't help inform them well, and then policy makers, I think, bend … I think that the safest position for anybody to take in this issue right [now] is to be tough on sex offenders, rather than to take the time to help the public understand. So I think that it's a marvelous combination of those three things. I mean I think that they all kind of feed one another.
>
> (C-4)

Given the potential for identification to flatten out or bridge differences in the name of creating social common ground, Ratcliffe (2005) suggests, and we agree, that it is within the space of these bridged differences that the potential limitations of Burke's theory become apparent:

> On the question of coexisting commonalities and differences, however, Burke's identification ... does not easily escape charges that it mystifies unfair ideological power plays (in its erasure of differences) ... Because it posits conjoined substance ... it demands commonalities.
>
> (58)

So then, Ratcliffe (2005) asks,

> which differences must be bridged and which differences must be deemed excess and relegated outside the consubstantial place of identification? In most cases, the answer is: the "I" with the power. For the "I" without power, Burke's metaphoric common ground may feel more like "not me" than "me." ... Given these considerations, the politics of identification emerge as incredibly complex.
>
> (59)

She then voices the following critique of identification: "In valorizing commonalities, though, it [Burke's identification] does not provide a sufficient recognition of differences as a place for rhetorical exchanges and subsequent actions. In Burke's theory, differences do not 'accede to power,' they learn to submit" (60).

Rhetorical Listening

This lack of space for rhetorical exchange reveals a need, says Ratcliffe (2005) for "concepts of identification and disidentification that engage differences" (60). Put differently, she wants to know how to best theorize identification as a place for what she calls "rhetorical listening." For Ratcliffe (2005), rhetorical listening is "a trope for interpretive invention," which "signifies a stance of openness that a person may choose to assume in relation to any person, text, or culture" (1). She says that "[a]s a place for rhetorical listening ... Burke's concept of identification is limited. It does not adequately address ... how to identify and negotiate troubled identifications; moreover, it does not address how to identify and negotiate conscious identifications functioning as ethical and political choices" (48). We find it critical to illuminate the political and social implications of identifications that function as political choices, and the ways in which those choices may lead to the Othering of sex offenders in public discourse and in policymaking.

For our purposes, as we have described here, identification is useful primarily in helping to account for some of the ways in which sex offenders become further alienated within society. That is, we look at the discourses perpetuated and sustained through the media and by policymakers, for example, as fostering those polarizing or alienating identifications. In considering the types of identities cast upon sex offenders in MSOP, we encounter the Othering of a feared group that justifies whatever means the public might think should be taken to feel protected from that group. In addition, we encounter the work of elected officials to distinguish themselves from those who might be perceived as "soft on crime"; that is, not to be viewed as "hard on crime" is to possibly lose one's professional status and credibility and therefore decision-making power.

Finally, we see a rhetorical situation in which those who wish to maintain their decision-making capacity seek commonality with the public and media by stressing the common dangers from sex offenders by creating a single social category of all sex offenders, or Opheim is just the same as Rodriquez, Shiue is just the same as Linehan, for example. At the same time, as we will show, much evidence exists that those offenders come to MSOP with distinct backgrounds and treatment needs. Thus, to consider how identification functions relative to public discourses about sex offenders allows us to better understand how identification works between power groups through alienation from the offenders, but it does not adequately extend the rhetorical and cultural implications of these identifications, or the ways in which these discourses serve to essentialize and Other a complex and controversial population. Thus, to better understand the complex identities of sex offenders and the social power of this Othered group requires that we examine additional ideas about identity theory and the discourses of stranger danger.

The Discourse of Stranger Danger

Ahmed (2000) accounts for some of the discursive processes by which communities understand and perpetuate ideas about strangers, when she describes the discourse of "stranger danger":

> [T]he discourse of stranger danger produces the stranger as a figure—a shape that appears to have linguistic and bodily integrity—which then comes to embody that which must be expelled from the purified space of the community, the purified life of the good citizen, the purified body of "the child."
>
> (22)

In accounting for some of the thought processes and emotions that then lead communities to points of political action, she invokes the category of sex offender: "[T]he paedophile comes to embody the most dangerous stranger as he poses the greatest risk to the vulnerable and pure body of the child" (35). Here, Ahmed (2000) writes:

> The child's innocence and purity becomes a matter of social and national responsibility: through figuring the stranger as too close to the child, the stranger becomes recognisable as an attack on the moral purity of nation space itself. It is over the bodies of children that the moral campaign against strangers is waged.
>
> (35)

It is particularly significant, then, that Opheim's selected victims were children, a fact that understandably added to the outrage about this provisional discharge from MSOP. The first words of the story in Minnesota's largest newspaper announcing Opheim's discharge, for example, read as follows:

> A man who had admitted to molesting 29 [other accounts raise this number to 100] children is about to become the first in over a decade to be freed from the state's St. Peter facility. His release will test the ability of behavioral science.
>
> (Wolfe 2012, February 19, n.p.)

These headlines are not unusual in stressing the perceived dangers to children whenever an offender reenters society. In Toronto, Canada, for example, the public was alerted when James Cooper reentered the community: "'Pure Evil' Pedophile Released from Prison After 21 Years," and then told that the Toronto police had issued a "rare public safety alert" because such offenders "cannot be fixed" (Clairmont, 2015, n.p.). Moreover, such stories seem to affirm that such offenders not only can never be fixed but also can never be trusted to self-manage, and so the possibility of controlling recidivism may be beyond the abilities of public officials. A pedophile released from prison in Florida, for example, who reoffended 18 months after he was released from prison, was given a "second chance" after state experts admitted to "straddling the fence" about his release (Zennie 2015, n.p.).

Thus, when communities understand sex offenders as a singular social group whose presence will yield a singular outcome, they react accordingly: "The recognition of dangerous strangers allows the enforcement of the boundaries of such communities: a definition of the purity of the 'we' against the monstrous 'it'" (Ahmed 2000, 34–35). Similarly, as Linda Alcoff (2000) describes, a "realistic identity politics ... recognizes that social categories of identity often helpfully name specific social locations from which individuals engage in, among other things, political judgment" (341). It is from this vantage point that we complicate what we contend are sometimes overly determined and insufficiently critiqued categorizations of sex offenders, which may then guide policymaking.

One outcome of Othering, as we will demonstrate, is that by alienating a group, such as, in this case, sex offenders, through discourses that invoke fear of that group, policymakers may inadvertently assign or give over power to that group, because by reinforcing the public's fears through practices of Othering, politicians lessen the potential for the sort of balanced, constructive dialogue that can lead to positive system change. Julia Kristeva (1982) explains how this fear may be traumatic and sickening, particularly when it falls into the category of the abject or the perversity that "turns aside" prohibitions, rules, and laws, and therefore points out the fragility of these borders and laws (15). When we engage in Othering, however, James Cherney (2011) notes, "We can think of the Other as a two-dimensional being, driven by indiscernible, illogical, and unrealistic ideas, but resist thinking about ourselves in this way" (n.p.). We follow Cherney's (2011) call for reform, to seek a common ground between us and who we consider "Others," which then "not only allows us a measure of empathy and understanding, it expands our awareness of our own unexamined biases" (n.p.). Sara McKinnon (2012) likewise calls for new frameworks

> that illuminate how audiences use their own identities and histories as sieves to categorize, interpret, and acknowledge those who stand and speak in their presence. Recognition necessitates that we do this work of decentering the singular subject in our thinking about subjectivity, insisting that we see the recognition of subjects always, already multiple and intersecting.
>
> (193)

McKinnon (2012) also attempts to account for how Othering happens when she says: "[W]hen we stand before another subject we do not merely see an Other, but recognize an Other in relation to ourselves and the relationship between the two selves" (193). While her focus here is more so on race, she makes an interesting and relevant point that "rather than engaging with the differences, some white people employ essentialist discourses of the Other to deny the validity and legitimacy of the subject" (195). Thus the positions of Cherney and McKinnon seem to share similarity with Ratcliffe's call for rhetorical listening, or greater openness when thinking critically about social groupings, texts, and cultures. That openness was offered, in part, by Leo Anderson, a Golden Valley resident, who when he heard that Opheim would move into his neighborhood, trusted the safeguards of Opheim's halfway house and referred to Opheim by the positive term of "gentleman," but still endorsed the strict division between Opheim and the rest of the community:

> All his [Opheim's] windows are locked. He can't even step outside the house to get a can of soda because he has the ankle bracelet. I'm not against the halfway house or the gentleman living there. As long as he stays in his provided area.
>
> (CBS News, 2012, n.p.)

The Role of the Media and Public Discourse in Othering

Working in the negative, however, the cycle of fear and Othering continues, as Ahmed (2000) cautions: "The community comes together through the recognition of such dangerous strangers" (35). As one victim advocate put it, when referring to the kidnapping and murder of Sjodin by Rodriguez, for example:

> We really fuel the fear pretty well. I get that if you don't know more about sexual violence and the dynamics and the data and so forth, you would be fearful to think, "This could have as easily happened to me." When, in fact, the Rodriguez case is very rare. It's awful. It doesn't make it less awful. But so you get the sort of heartstrings and the fear and the "We want these people to be Other."
>
> (C-4)

The words of this victim advocate illustrate not only the fear that perpetuates the Othering of sex offenders but also the lack of education about sex offenders that perpetuates the public's fear in the first place.

The Media, Policymakers, and Public Fear

The public's fear is reinforced by media portrayals of sex offenders, which has the effect of shaping the common ground or consubstantiality that contributes to the production of Othering. As one mental health professional concluded, for example:

> I think that the media does think that it needs to put an exclamation point behind [every statement]. And if they put every one of those stories in perspective, maybe they could help be part of a more thoughtful conversation.
>
> (T-3)

That is, the media tend to identify with their audiences in ways that reflect and perpetuate fears and concerns about the release of sex offenders from treatment programs. As Roger Lancaster (2011) notes in his study of sex panics, "These news stories provide an infinitely malleable template for the production of recurring narratives about victimization and innocence, the invention of new identities about these terms, and the manufacture of an inexhaustible need for ever more discerning modes of surveillance, supervision, and protection" (4).

Policymakers too, as one victim advocate described, may "bend" to the will of the public, thus further reinforcing the common ground that shapes public and political discourses about sex offenders (C-4). The words of a community corrections officer help to illustrate and complicate this point:

> The public perception and the perception of the political leaders is these individuals cannot be on the streets, and in some cases, they are right ... [P]ublic response and public demands from political response ... always present the [likelihood] of an overreaction, and that comes out of legitimate fear and anger, regarding the crime and other crimes that have occurred.
>
> (A-5)

This corrections officer acknowledged that in some cases, the public's perception that these individuals should not be "on the streets" is accurate; however, public and political pressures often prevent more nuanced discussions about when these views are accurate and when they might require further discussion. This "legitimate fear and anger," nonetheless, produces a singular view of sex offender identity.

Ahmed (2000) acknowledges a similar point about the public's perception of sex offenders when she conveys the views of the social organization *Parents Against Child Abuse*:

> The construction of sex offenders against children as child monsters who do not belong in a community is clear in the following statement from John O'Sullivan, from the pressure group, *Parents Against Child Abuse*: "If there is a wild lion loose in the street, the police would tell us. A paedophile in the neighbourhood is the same. They might not rip the flesh, but they are just as damaging to the mind of a child. We need to know who they are."
>
> (35)

Additionally, one judge also described how the public's essentialization of sex offenders produces a fear that prevents any "real discussion":

> [I]f you hear the word sex offender, everybody thinks you should run and lock your doors because it's somebody who is lurking in the bushes ... I don't think you ever get a real discussion of sex offenders. It's such a loaded word and frightens people so much.
>
> (J-1)

A Victim's Testimony

In an example that further illustrates this judge's point about the public's fear of sex offenders and the "loaded" nature of the debate, we turn to the recent federal court case about MSOP's constitutionality, *Karsjens et al. v. Jesson et al.* (2015). Again, in this civil suit a group of sex offenders alleged that their indefinite confinement and lack of periodic risk assessment reviews, and higher standards for discharge than for commitment, among other perceived problems, had violated their constitutional right to due process. At the time of the federal trial, judges, policymakers, concerned citizens, and the media heard several weeks of testimony from stakeholders familiar with MSOP, as well as from one victim of sexual assault, and even from offenders themselves.

On March 12, 2015, the Court heard what the local media referred to as "emotional" and "chilling" testimony from victim Tom McCartney, who, along with his wife Janet, was assaulted and raped by sex offender John Rydberg in 1975 (Serres 2015, March 12, n.p.). At the time of the assault, the McCartneys were at home with their young son, when Rydberg broke into their house. McCartney said he suspected the toys on the front lawn had drawn Rydberg to their home because he believed a young mother might be alone and vulnerable in the house. Rydberg wore a mask and carried a sawed-off shotgun. He ordered the couple "to bind each other's hands and feet; he then pulled pillow cases over their heads and raped them while their 3-year-old son slept upstairs" (Serres 2015, March 12, n.p.).

During the testimony, which was designed to represent victims of sexual assault, McCartney asked Judge Donovan Frank "to consider the plight of rape survivors before reaching a verdict in a trial that could decide the constitutionality of the Minnesota Sex Offender Program (MSOP)" (Serres 2015, March 12, n.p.). Here, then, McCartney's testimony not only recounted his and his family's trauma, or the trauma he had already encountered, but it was also meant to represent more broadly the potential trauma which has not yet been encountered—that which is preventable by, according to McCartney, permanent confinement of sex offenders such as Rydberg. As Ahmed (2000) has put it:

> The figure of the stranger is far from simply being strange; it is a figure that is painfully familiar in that very strange(r)ness. The stranger has already come too close; the stranger is "in my face." The stranger then is not simply the one whom we have not yet encountered, but the one whom we have already encountered, or already faced.
>
> (21)

Moreover, in a powerful statement that was quoted in the local media, McCartney turned to Judge Frank and said: "If you're really convinced that you want to let these people out, then why don't you take them home with you? Why should we be the guinea pigs?" (Serres 2015, March 12, n.p.). Part of what makes this statement so powerful is the image of the sex offender crossing the boundary from outside to inside—and into the home of a public figure such as a judge, no less. In his statement, McCartney is acknowledging the boundary of the home and the need to protect that boundary from the unwelcome stranger. As Ahmed (2000) notes: "It is the enforcement of the boundaries between those who are already recognised as out of place (even other fellow residents) that allows those boundaries to be established" (26). When he was asked to describe the impact of the assault on him and his family, McCartney said, "We don't have enough time for that" (Serres 2015, March 12, n.p.). McCartney did, however, note that he had taught his daughter, when she was just 13, how to shoot a gun, at a time when, as he put it, she "should be worrying about her first kiss" (Serres 2015, March 12, n.p.). He also described other ongoing, long-term trauma and effects of the assault, such as the onset of his wife's diabetes, and "argued that violent sex offenders such as Rydberg should never be released, but should be locked away for life or executed" (Serres 2015, March 12, n.p.). While the McCartneys' experience was clearly extreme and horrific, and the tenor of his comments and arguments is absolutely understandable, such narratives may also be seen as sustaining the fear of a population in which very extreme cases of violence become representative of the singular category of sex offender. In doing so, such discourses may inadvertently perpetuate deterministic views about recidivism and amenability to treatment.

The Other and the Community

One noted outcome of the public's fear of sex offenders is the hindrance of public education and awareness and the subsequent Othering of this population. A victim advocate, for example, again described a perceived lack of public awareness that leads to Othering:

> I am always stunned at how little the public knows ... There is a study that just came out about a year and a half ago from the Frameworks Institute where they compared what the public understands about sexual violence versus what experts understand, and for the public it kind of goes back to, "They are just really, really bad people. They are really like genetically, you know, poorly engineered people."
>
> (C-4)

Dr. Michael Farnsworth, a psychiatrist who helped design MSOP, asked, "How do you release somebody after building them up as monsters?" (Oakes 2011, n.p.). Farnsworth's comment is compatible with the views of scholars who understand fear of the Other as a determiner of Othering. Kristeva (1982), for example, reminds us that fear of the Other may be traumatic and may illicit extreme fear responses, especially if it threatens society's prohibitions, rules, and laws. Othering occurs, then, not only when the distinct backgrounds and needs of those offenders are not acknowledged by decision-makers or the public but also when that group is seen as separate from the rest of society.

The Sex Offender as Outsider

To view this Othered group as not part of the larger social sphere inscribes a social identity on the body through practices of domination that have both discursive and physical effects. Or, as Ahmed (2000) notes:

> [W]hen we face others, we seek to recognise who they are, by reading the signs on their body, or by reading their body as a sign … [S]uch acts of reading constitute 'the subject' in relation to "the stranger," who is recognised as "out of place" in a given place.
>
> (8)

One policymaker, for example, described the challenge of trying to assist sex offenders in finding a physical place to live, upon release into the community, when that community indeed perceives them as out of place: "Communities don't want these folks in their areas, and they are doing more and more things every year to avoid having them" (A-3).

Ahmed's (2000) ideas about the discourses of "stranger danger" help account for the resistance of communities to accept sex offenders into the community; she says:

> On the one hand, the fear of crime embedded in the discourse of stranger danger allows the protection of domestic, social and national space from the outsider inside, the stranger neighbour, by projecting danger onto the outsider. On the other hand, the stranger only appears as a figure of danger by coming too close to home: the boundary line is always crossed, both 'justifying' the fear and legitimating the enforcement.
>
> (37)

Similarly, Nancy Sabin, Director of the Jacob Wetterling Foundation, named after the St. Joseph, MN, boy who was abducted in 1989 and whose body was found in 2016, described a need to move past the view that perceives sex offenders as originating from outside of society: "Where are these guys coming from? They're coming from our own homes. … We have to own the problem so we learn how to get past the hysteria in order to find better solutions" (Oakes 2011, n.p.). As Ahmed (2000) likewise argues:

> The projection of danger onto the figure of the stranger allows violence to be figured as exceptional and extraordinary—as coming from outside the protective walls of the home, family, community or nation. As a result, the discourse of stranger danger involves *a refusal to recognise how violence is structured by, and legitimated through, the formation of home and community as such.*
>
> (36, emphasis in original)

In failing to acknowledge the closer-to-home sources of many sex offenses, the varied backgrounds of sex offenders and the range of crimes that they commit, and the essentialization that often occurs as a result of the smoothing over of these differences, then, we encounter the limits of Burke's (1969) theory of identification. That is, Burke's identification functions via consubstantiality and the bridging of differences; however, as Ratcliffe (2005) reminds us, his theory "does not easily escape charges that it mystifies unfair ideological power plays (in its erasure of differences)" (58). This singular categorization of the sex offender, as some policymakers note, "makes it hard to craft policies that recognize differences among offenders" (Oakes 2011, n.p.). As a probation officer concluded, for example:

> If we are starting to talk about first-time sex offenders, like a first-degree, I have a big problem with that, because it's lumping everyone in together. It's not looking at their amenability to treatment; it's not evidence-based practice. I mean it's not assessment-driven; it's offense-level-driven, and I kind of have a problem with that.
>
> (L-2)

Given these examples, we can now begin to see how public discourses about sex offenders function to produce a singular social category that does not acknowledge differences among this complex population. Such essentialized discourses emerged during the time of Ming Sen Shiue's parole hearing, when Mary Stauffer, in expressing her opinion that Shiue will reoffend if released, concluded that the assaults would "just end up happening again" and that no institution could guarantee public safety (Martinez 2010, n.p.). In citing concern that there is no community or institution that can satisfactorily house Shiue, the offender, as stranger, as monster, has effectively been deemed out of place, or expelled from the community. Or, as Edward Ingebretsen (2001) notes: "By locating monsters *off* the social map, we located the human—and, thus, we hope, ourselves—*on* it" (5, emphasis in original). Indeed, to think more critically about this Othered group, we must continue to examine the practices of domination that produce the already inscribed and determined category of sex offender, and the deterministic views that come with it.

The Problem of Public Shaming

In a recent article about the need for public education about the civil commitment process, Margretta Dwyer, a Minnesota psychologist who has worked with sex offenders, described the negative implications of shaming for the possible rehabilitation of sex offenders:

> We need to know who is dangerous and who is not ... We've got it all mixed up so that everybody's dangerous. That belief leads to panic, and shaming, which doesn't work ... Lack of empathy plays a major role in people perpetuating these sexual behaviors ... Once we shame them, they're likely to re-offend.
>
> (Rosenblum 2012, n.p.)

Thus, public shaming may then have consequences for the reintegration of sex offenders within the community.

In a recent media article, two offenders, for example, said that "they felt more comfortable living in the relative anonymity of the North Side [of Minneapolis], rather than face the public shaming that other sex offenders did when they tried to move to wealthier neighborhoods" (Stahl and Rao 2013, n.p.). Ahmed (2000) describes a similar phenomenon when she discusses the discursive implications of programs like Neighborhood Watch: "Neighbourhood Watch schemes are more common in the middle-class areas, where residents are more likely to want to co-operate with the police, and where there is more 'property' with value to protect" (27). These "middle-class spaces" then become viewed as valuable by way of their being watched; that is, as Ahmed (2000) notes, "the subject who watches out for crime, is also *maintaining the value of her or his* neighbourhood" (27, emphasis in original). In this way, the connection between valuable spaces, protectable property, and social privilege helps justify the need to defend communities against "unwelcome intrusions and intruders," and in the process creates "certain categories of strangers—those who don't belong in the leafy suburbs—that are socially legitimated and enforced" (Ahmed 2000, 27).

A mental health professional similarly noted the impact of public shaming and Othering on sex offenders, through the ways in which offenders reject the "monster" image for themselves but participate in imposing it on others:

> You know, I sometimes wonder what it's like coming to our program as a client for the first time and just standing in front of that door

> and thinking "What am I doing? I am going in here, and I am going to join a group of sex offenders." Of course, no one views themselves as one of them. The offenders themselves have the same biases and the same disgust for sex offenders as anyone else. And, that's in large part because of the community, the way it's been handled.
>
> (T-2)

The words of this mental health professional not only work against Othering by viewing the offender as an individual but also by implicitly acknowledging that the categories created through public discourse can have consequences on sex offenders' amenability to treatment and likelihood of recidivism.

Public shaming and Othering may also influence the ways in which sex offenders view their own offenses; as one policy specialist noted, from an offender's perspective, it might be more acceptable to think "'I am an offender. I did something wrong; therefore, I need to be in jail or prison,' as opposed to, 'I am mentally ill and dangerous'" (A-4). One judge similarly acknowledged that many sex offenders understand that they are a feared and loathed group and so might actually be more compliant: "Because they were, a lot of them were really afraid of going to prison. They thought ... that sex offenders were murdered in prison ... And, they could control their impulses enough to behave themselves" (J-1). And, as mentioned in Chapter 1, when Clarence Opheim's integration back into the community appeared initially successful, the mayor of the suburb where Opheim first resided praised the "system," including monitoring and social services, for working, demonstrating perhaps that it is possible to view such cases on an individual basis (*StarTribune* 2012, November 30, n.p.). So then, as the words of these policy specialists, mental health professionals, and law enforcement officials help demonstrate, it is possible to work against the Othering and essentializing of this feared group when we begin to consider the offender as an individual and consider the broader contexts of their offenses.

Working Against

To work against the Othering borne out of practices of essentialization and determinism thus requires viewing the challenge of sex offenders in a broader social and political context—a perspective not easily adopted by many concerned parties. A major challenge for mental health professionals who work with these offenders and believe in the possibility of their rehabilitation, then, is to prepare them for reintegration into a society that likely does not share this belief or feel that offenders deserve a second chance.

Viewing Sex Offenders in a Broader Context

"I tell the people in this program that I want them to learn to live honorably in a system that will not treat them with honor," says Warren Maas, Executive Director of Project Pathfinder, the organization that first housed Clarence Opheim (Wolfe 2012, February 19, n.p.). Such organizations as Project Pathfinder understand the sex offender as an individual rather than as a social group whose characteristics are predetermined. As Maas further described of sex offenders who are preparing to eventually reenter the community:

> 'We want the offenders to understand and take responsibility for the offense, and for how they got to this point in their lives ... Then they need to figure out how to move on ... Despite some heinous crimes in their past, these guys should be far better prepared to reenter the community safely' than many other felons.
>
> (Wolfe 2012, February 19, n.p.)

Throughout our study, we found that those who acknowledged the essentialization of sex offenders, and actively worked to avoid it, tended to demonstrate an understanding of the offender as an individual rather than as a member of a group whose characteristics were already determined. One attorney, for example, provided an example to describe the ways in which previous traumas may influence the crimes committed by sex offenders:

> I had a client who was a guy in his twenties who would run up to women in bus stops and throw them down on the ground and tear their clothes off. And, obviously people would immediately think, well, what a horrible guy. Well, it turned out when he was a very, very young child, his mother decided to raise him locked in the closet. So he spent his growing up years for, I don't know, about 8 or 10 years, locked in the closet.
>
> (C-3)

This attorney engaged in a sort of interpretive activity, akin to rhetorical listening, which works against the flattening out of difference by understanding the offender as an individual and looking at the situation from a different vantage point, understandably a difficult thing to do, given the crimes of this offender. The words of this attorney may be seen as putting into practice Cherney's (2011) call to find "similarities between our thoughts and those we ascribe to Others," in order to allow for "a measure of empathy and understanding" (n.p.).

Those who work against the essentialization of sex offenders also tend to acknowledge the range of offenses committed by perpetrators and the sentencing guidelines imposed for those offenses. They may avoid essentialization by considering whether the sentence was warranted given the perpetrator's specific offense. As one law enforcement official described in this hypothetical example, if a

> 17-year-old boy has sex with their 14-year-old girlfriend, that's a sex crime in Minnesota. We charge these individuals with third degree rape. So should we take 17-year-old-boys, hang them, castrate them, kill them, for having sex with an underage girl? It is rather amazing. (L-2)

Such critical reflections also point to the political effects of these broad social groupings, such as beliefs about public safety, likelihood of recidivism, and success of treatment. As one victim advocate described, for example: "[P]eople just don't believe that treatment works, people think if you are sex offender, you are always going to be a sex offender" (C-1). The societal effects of Othering through public discourse thus become clearer, not only for offenders but also for the public, when we consider how such discourses of alienation might lead to sex offenders becoming homeless or reoffending.

Considering Safety and Recidivism

"I'm a widow and I'm older, and I was scared," said Sonja Thygeson, who lived four houses down from Alfonso Rodriquez after his release from prison, "so I had my son-in-law come over and install a motion light after he [Rodriquez] moved in" (ABC News: Good Morning America 2003, n.p.). The sex offender is perceived to have the power to violate substantial physical boundaries and to fool expert surveillance. After all, Rodriquez was not civilly committed despite his Level 3 status, and Opheim had a long history of getting away with child sexual assault. Thygeson's statement represents the essentialized category of the sex offender, casting that offender into the role of the most aggressive and violent criminal and revealing a deterministic view of recidivism. One interview participant working on sexual abuse prevention within MSOP explained this reaction: "Generally speaking, clients in the Minnesota Sex Offender Program are the ones that stick in people's minds the most because they are the scariest cases of sexual violence" (T-1).

Next, we further account for some of the processes that call for or create obstacles in working against Othering the sex offender in public discourse: through perceptions of an increased need for public safety; through misperceptions of the risks of recidivism in light of statistical studies of who actually offends and reoffends; through the public's uneasiness with any successful treatment approaches for sex offenders; and through the idea of the sex offender as the stranger rapist, all of which prevent the public, the media, and policymakers from fully embracing intervention, education, and prevention.

Quoting Sartre (1956), Alcoff (2000) provides a way of discerning the power that the sex offender holds over the public's concern with safety:

> The Other looks at me and as such he holds the secret of my being, he knows what I am. Thus the profound meaning of my being is outside me, imprisoned in an absence. The Other has the advantage over me.
>
> (331)

In other words, the public may fear, "If the Other looks at me and knows who I am, and knows the fears I hold, how can I prevent risk to me and my family?" To Other the sex offender, rather than appease fear and address intervention, education, and prevention, again increases a sense of vulnerability within the public. The public relies on policymakers and law enforcement for protection, but these agents also know that they frequently offer only a false sense of protection. As one police officer stated, members of the public demand notification of the location of Level 3 offenders, because "'I wouldn't have let my kid go down the block if I knew that a sex offender was there'" (L-2).

As discussed in Chapter 1, those who manage sex offenders, whether civilly confined or released after they fulfill their prison sentences, assess the probability of recidivism or risk of re-offense either by the clinical method or by the actuarial method. The Risk Assessment/Community Notification Unit of the Minnesota Department of Corrections, for example, measures probability of recidivism for each offender who has completed his or her prison sentence. Based on that information, a county attorney may file a petition for civil commitment to the county Mental Health Court, which then makes a final decision. Statistical studies, however, proffer that the majority of sexual violence is most likely not committed by the released offender; as mentioned earlier, only one in seven sex offenders have a prior conviction for a sex offense. Those who are re-confined most likely "go back into the institution" for other crimes, according to one police officer, "because they are drinking, they assault their girlfriend, they beat people up, and they go back to prison for committing new crimes, but not new sex crimes" (L-2).

Despite these statistical reassurances about the low rate of recidivism, the cultural perception about sex offenders persists that we are all in danger from violent strangers and deserve a sure way to assess risk (see, for example, Becker et al. 2003; U.S. Department of Justice 2005; Wilcox, Jordan, and Pritchard 2006). Risk is created by cultural perception, particularly when extensive media coverage plays a role in unsettling the public and leads to overdependence on risk assessment tools. Lancaster (2011), furthermore, proposes that even placing sex offenders into the Level 1, 2, and 3 categories for risk "lends scientific credibility" to practices that are less based on scientific and predictive studies than aligned "with much older ideas about danger, taboo, and ritual pollution" (81–82; see also Beck 2007; Tullock 1999). A scan of media coverage on the national level confirms this inability to absolutely assess risk. Lawyer Jeff Green, for example, who was interviewed about sex offenders in federal prisons, summarized the risks as follows: "These are hideous crimes," he said, "but they demonstrate that the experts, in terms of identifying which individuals are dangerous, are no better than astrologers" (Totenberg 2010, n.p.).

Considering Treatment and Prevention

In order to leave Moose Lake or St. Peter, to lessen the perceived risk to the public, the sex offender must successfully complete treatment—be "cured" of or at least able to be managed regarding any propensity to reoffend. Among our interviewees, however, even the most optimistic about treatment were cautious and, at times, seemed to struggle to distinguish the sexually dangerous offender from other offenders and the curable from the incurable within the sex offender group, thus continuing to essentialize the image of the sexual predator that provokes such fear. As one legislator asserted, for example, it was much easier to predict the behavior of other offenders: "Well, it's almost to the point where people want a 100% certainty about what the future is like for these people, and that's a threshold, of course, that's not possible," particularly for sexual assault, which is "not like robbery, or you know vandalism, or even murder" (S-3). A probation officer further distinguished between sex offenders, who might "successfully complete treatment, never reoffend, have stabilized, you know, have families, support homes, sit next to you in church" and pedophiles, who "will never be treatable" and who, along with the stranger rapist, represent the worst of the worst among sex offenders (L-3). Moreover, a representative from a county attorney's office contrasted "people with mental health issues, chemical dependency issues," who "are not violating the law all the time," to sex offenders who "have had one or several attempts at treatment" and often go "back to committing the same types of offenses" (A-4). The problem, said a corrections officer, is that unlike an illness such as cancer, where the care givers would never say, "Okay, go now, you are done, you are fixed," similar social support after discharge from MSOP may not provide fully for the sex offender who has completed treatment (A-5; see also Rosenblum 2012, n.p.). Aspects of determinism represented in these perceptions about treatment reveal that sex offenders remain a distinct and Othered group, despite perceived differences between first offenders and repeat offenders, and between pedophiles and those with adult victims, because by their very being they are determined to have less chance of recovery and therefore receive less public support for their integration back into the community.

Policymakers and stakeholders also perceive treatment as frequently failing. After the Sjodin murder, for example, when Governor Pawlenty called for legislation that would enable sex offenders to be tracked for the rest of their lives; he concluded, "There are circumstances where sex offenders are not curable and they need to be incarcerated longer, be kept off the streets longer or worse" (ABC News: Good Morning America 2003, n.p.). A decade later, in opposing Governor Eliot Spitzer's proposal for civil commitment in New York, an editorial in *The New York Times* (2007) warned that the state would be the latest "to travel down a murky legal road, to a place where laws are made not in response to facts, but to wistfulness and fear" where sex offenders receive "psychological treatment that nearly always fails" (n.p.). Even the former executive director of MSOP, Dennis Benson, confided in legislators that the best way to minimize the risk to the public would be to strictly manage supervision of those provisionally discharged from MSOP because "[w]e don't believe we can cure these people" (McEnroe 2011, n.p.). Therapists and others involved in the treatment of sex offenders note that making progress in treatment depends on "your willingness to talk about all the terrible things," which might cause a listener to think, "Well, he has got all these things in his mental life that are terrible and horrible, and therefore maybe he is even a bigger risk than we thought" (A-2; S-3). As a Minnesota state senator concluded,

> I can point to drug treatment facilities that work. I can point to gambling addiction. I can point to all kinds of things that are social pathologies that people get themselves involved in, and there are people who successfully find ways to overcome them and live perfectly useful productive lives. I have not heard anything like that with sex offenders.
>
> (S-3)

Sex offenders, then, are potentially Othered by the "I with the power," to borrow from Ratcliffe's (2005) terms, or policymakers and stakeholders who may validate fear and anger with high demands for risk assessment or lack of faith in treatment. Finally, the image of the sex offender as the stranger rapist further essentializes the offender and thus limits effective policymaking, by neglecting to recognize the range of crimes that many sex offenders commit, such as acquaintance or date rape, engage in inappropriate sexual acts with children within their social or family circles, or force sex during attacks on intimate partners. Additionally, some who are civilly committed have served prison sentences for engaging in sex with partners who have not reached the age of consent.

Distinguishing Among Victims and Offenders

Not all stakeholders in the MSOP discussions essentialized the sex offender as the stranger rapist. According to a probation officer who supervises adult sex offenders, for example,

> When we are talking about an actual stranger rape ... grabbing a kid off of a playground, you know, we are talking about maybe 5 percent of all sex offenders ... It might be like 93 percent know their victim: it's your uncle, it's your babysitter, it's your dad, your teacher, your coach. That's the majority of sex offenders.
>
> (L-3; see also Janus 2006; Meloy 2006)

Other interview participants still struggled with perceived victim complicity in making such distinctions. One interview participant, for example, referred to the sexual assault victim and perpetrator as follows:

> A vast majority of our stranger rapes would be examples of women who are chemically dependent, they are addicted to drugs or alcohol, they will go to a drug house, they will be participating in a party and using drugs, and a stranger there will take them, lure them to like a basement, beat them up and rape them.
>
> (IP; see the Appendix for an explanation of this designation)

These interview participants went on to distinguish these events from much more unusual ones, such as "ladies who are coming home from church, getting jumped on by a complete stranger and raped in their yards or cars or homes," even though those second kind of assaults "are the ones that make the newspaper" (IP). In some cases, then, essentializing the sex offender as the stranger rapist seems to accompany essentializing the victim of sexual assault.

In some courts and police precincts, in order to be a genuine victim of sexual assault, according to Jeffrey Spears (2005), a woman still has to be perceived to have a good moral character, not engage in risk-taking behavior, be raped by a stranger, resist her attacker, and report the crime immediately to the police (see also Konradi 1996; Schafron 1992; Wood 2005). The irony is that, on the one hand, the victim of stranger sexual assault might have a hard time substantiating her claim if she does not conform to this image of the "good" or "real" victim, but on the other hand, the offender is also cast into that group of Others who are depicted as stranger rapists and characterized as terrorists or as pedophiles who cannot be cured. Impressions may stem from what Ratcliffe (2005) again noted as an unfortunate lack of complicating such identification, by failing to provide sufficient recognition of differences or address troubled identifications.

Such identifications may carry over into perceptions about the domestic violence victim who is sexually assaulted, perhaps making her task of achieving credibility more difficult. Perhaps as a consequence, as Cheryl Hanna (1997–1998) points out, many stakeholders and policymakers believe: "One who abuses women needs help; one who abuses a stranger is dangerous" (1540; see also Schuster and Propen 2011). Elizabeth Schneider (2000) relates how this distinction curtails efforts to question the Othering of the sex offender and to support educational and intervention efforts:

> Because it is acknowledged that all women can be targets of stranger rape, it is easier for the public to see how the fear of rape shapes women's actions than to see how the generally unacknowledged assertion of power and control or violence within an intimate relationship shapes the fabric of women's lives.
>
> (190)

A mental health professional who works with adult sex offenders further noted that because "people have a feeling of inevitability of sexual violence," policymakers focus on how to deal with the perpetrator "afterwards" rather than moving attention and resources "upstream" (C-4; see also Stahl and Rao 2013, n.p.). Such an "upstream" focus would parallel the public health model of early intervention and education to treat the troubled person before he or she becomes an offender. Intervention might have made a difference in the life of the offender who was kept locked in a closet for years and took out his anger toward his mother on other women.

The Othering of the sex offender, particularly as the stranger rapist, thus affects perceptions of public safety; distorts understandings of recidivism and therefore high risk among these offenders; presents a pessimistic view of treatment; and distracts from intervention, education, and prevention efforts. In the final section of this chapter, we will explain how elected officials may respond to this deterministic and essentialized portrayal of the sex offender by being "tough on crime." In this way, they are able to protect their positions and avoid the burden of releasing an offender who might reoffend, but they may also perpetuate the Othering of the sex offender and, in essence, the public's fear. We conclude by demonstrating how complicating these discourses that result in Othering the sex offender go beyond Burke's ideas about identification and, then how, through public discourse, stakeholders may unwittingly give over power.

Public Fear and the Redistribution of Power

Judges, legislators, county attorneys, sheriffs, and police chiefs all depend on satisfying their constituents with their stance on crime, among other things. If the public, based in part on media coverage, is fearful of sex offenders and believes that only confinement, rather than treatment and education, can prevent recidivism, then the elected official must be cautious about being labeled "soft on crime." As one interview participant conveyed:

> Because if you do have a petition for commitment, in [a small county], where you have got one judge and not a lot going on for the newspaper to cover probably, except what is going on in the court, that judge likes his or her job most likely and knows that one of the best ways to draw a challenge [in reelection] and maybe lose it is to give some sexual predator a break.
>
> (IP)

Policymakers may enter into a situation where, as a result of their concern or hesitancy, and in an effort to retain their credibility with the public, they may inadvertently lessen their power to deliberate openly about the challenge of how to handle sex offenders. In other words, we argue that responses that remain rooted in the public's fear may serve to exacerbate that fear. Thus, by remaining "tough on crime," the cycle of Othering rooted in public fear continues.

After the Rodriguez case, Governor Pawlenty tried to avoid opening up the possibility that decision makers could be "soft on crime," saying initially that the officials who had released Rodriguez "guessed wrong," although, as Robson (2004) notes, Pawlenty's spokesman later remarked that this was perhaps a "poor choice of words" (n.p.). Additionally, if a county attorney did not recommend civil commitment to a sex offender, the governor proposed giving the state attorney general the authority to overrule that county attorney (Robson 2004, n.p.). The Rodriguez case and Pawlenty's reaction contributed greatly to the Othering of sex offenders that continues today, according to one media report: "Many blame the tortured, emotional politics of the issue, which paralyzes lawmakers who are loath to appear soft on one of society's most heinous crimes" (McEnroe 2011, n.p.).

Here, again, we see one potential outcome of identification at work. That is, to borrow Ratcliffe's (2005) terms, the "socializing functions of discourse" initiate pressures to perform attitudes that mesh with those of the dominant discourse (29). Policymakers who push up against those dominant discourses may lose their credibility and political power. At the same time, a double bind ensues, whereby maintaining political credibility means perpetuating and sustaining public fear of sex offenders through policies that may be reactive rather than proactive. In a sense, then, through their efforts to maintain their power and credibility, policymakers may also give a sort of power to sex offenders through the public fear that they invoke. That is, sex offenders are not necessarily asking for power, per se, but rather, politicians are simultaneously disempowered by way of reactive discourses that might otherwise be more empowering or productive from a policymaking standpoint. As Ingebretsen (2001) interestingly notes: "Like Cerberus, they [monsters] guard bridges and gates, protecting human boundaries against those who think to test them by crossing out. Monsters warn by example: they are themselves terrible consequences" (xiv). That is, the sex offender, as monster, becomes an inadvertent or unwitting gatekeeper; to be feared within society is to hold the power to illicit a strong emotional and rhetorical public response that stymies or blocks productive policymaking. That public response is in many ways reflective of the consequences of that fear, creating a sort of cycle of Othering.

Along with responding to what elected officials perceive are the demands of their constituents, decision makers also understandably do not want to suffer guilt if they release a sex offender who reoffends, "because nobody wants to be responsible for a death," as one Minnesota state senator put it (S-2). And so, according to one attorney with expertise about sex offenders, if the county attorneys who consider these civil commitment cases "are going to make a mistake, they are going to make a mistake on the side of confining somebody who doesn't really need to be confined" (C-3). Othering the sex offender, then, appears the safest approach for those elected officials who want to keep their positions and avoid jeopardizing public safety. Finally, as seen in the Rodriguez case and the Opheim discharge, to impose blame for a decision that led to disaster becomes the norm. One police officer, for example, recalled in the Rodriguez case that "the local county sheriff's office wanted to blame the Department of Corrections; the Department of Corrections said, 'Hey, we notified your county attorney that this guy was being released, and you didn't do anything about it'" (L-2).

Task forces, legislative committees, the Minnesota Legislative Auditor in his evaluation report on *Civil Commitment of Sex Offenders* (2011), and MSOP and Department of Corrections leaders have recommended a number of ways to avoid such pressure on decision makers, particularly elected officials. Many of these involved bi-partisan involvement, and appointed, rather than elected, reviewers of civil commitment petitions. The Legislative Auditor, for example, recommended that one way to avoid inconsistency in the submission and the approval of civil commitment petitions was to establish "a centralized prosecution structure and a single commitment court for sex offenders" (Minnesota Legislative Auditor 2011, 48). One judge recommended an independent parole board with staggered terms to alleviate the pressure on judges who might release somebody on bail and "hope that this guy doesn't go home and kill his wife," while a legislator suggested asking retired judges to serve on review boards; additionally, a therapist recommended that half of the parole board be appointed by the state Supreme Court and the other half by the Commissioner of Corrections and the Commissioner of Human Services (J-1; S-1; T-3). To avoid reform of MSOP might leave the federal court little choice but to discharge many offenders presently confined in MSOP. The federal court, predicted former state Chief Justice Eric Magnuson, head of the task force appointed to respond to Chief U.S. Magistrate Boylan's demands, would "act as a sword, not a scalpel" (*StarTribune* 2013, March 30, n.p.).

After the Mitchell Hamline School of Law symposium, reporter D. J. Tice (2013, January 23), who served as a panelist, noted, "Minnesota leaders really have begun a calmer, more constructive discussion worth noting and encouraging" (n.p.). More than a year later, however, the local newspaper for which Tice works, was still calling for "calm reform" (*StarTribune* 2013, March 30, n.p.) Moreover, Minnesota State Representative Tina Liebling foresaw what could happen to stall the proposed bill on less-restrictive housing for civilly confined sex offenders, the first task force recommendation: "We have to have bipartisan support to do something," she said; "In the past it's gotten demagogued, and that kills the ability to solve the problems we have" (Schade 2013, n.p.). And then, in the meantime, Clarence Opheim continues to live quietly in supervised housing, but the public continues to live in fear of his and other sex offenders' presence in their neighborhoods. And, Ming Sen Shuie likewise will be civilly committed if he is ever released from prison.

Sex offenders, then, through social practices of Othering and policies aimed at fighting a danger within society, continue to inadvertently hold a sort of power through the fear they invoke. We may recall the ideas of Alcoff (2000), who describes the power of the Other to invoke fear, despite, or perhaps through, their marginalization within society. Sex offenders illicit a public response of fear and anger because the public may feel backed into a corner and may not have access to the sort of discussions that would prompt a different sort of conversation. The "I with the power," or policymakers who do not want to appear soft on crime, then respond by validating and perpetuating that fear response through subtle practices of determinism and essentializing. Ahmed's (2000) ideas about the discourses of "stranger danger" also help account for the public's resistance to accept sex offenders into the community. Moreover, in considering the theories of Kristeva (1982), we might speculate that the impulse to see sexual assault as a result of stranger rape could be the result of recognizing an uncomfortable understanding of the perpetrator of acquaintance rape or domestic violence.

Thus, based on the findings of our research and analysis, we contend there remains a need for the sort of constructive discussion that might better constitute "rhetorical listening" when it comes to the discourses surrounding the civil commitment of sex offenders in Minnesota. Relative to our study, Ratcliffe's (2005) work also helps to complicate and illuminate the limitations of Burke's theory in the following ways: 1) We must resurrect and examine the differences that get displaced in Burkean analysis. For example, as we have described through our analysis, not all sex offenders are the same—and not all public officials agree with the essentialization of sex offenders. There remain unresolved areas, such as questions about the usefulness of therapy and the mixed perceptions of recidivism, which cannot be dismissed. 2) Public discourses group all sex offenders into a single social category, which then serves to escalate fear and confinement. 3) The public may be unconsciously persuaded through the "socializing functions of discourse," which take shape largely through the media's decisions about how to narrate an incident and how to quote officials (Ratcliffe 2005, 29). In these ways, the myths surrounding the stranger rapist as opposed to the acquaintance rapist or perpetrator of domestic violence may become solidified. 4) Thus, the sex offender becomes objectified or assigned a static grouping; the public then aligns itself against that group through the belief that the offender cannot change and should thus be confined indefinitely. Given these considerations, as Ratcliffe (2005) suggests, "the politics of identification emerge as incredibly complex" (55).

Given these ideas and calls from scholars like Cherney (2011) for critical awareness around practices of Othering, we have endeavored in this chapter to add a new layer in questions about the practices of Othering—a layer that considers the discursive implications of inadvertently giving power to a group through discourses that serve to perpetuate fear of that group. That is, to perpetuate and sustain discourses of fear related to sex offenders is to inadvertently assign power to that group; and that very power, then, has the effect of not only further Othering this marginalized group but also disempowering policymakers. We believe that this new approach to conceptualizing the discursive implications of Othering a feared or loathed group within society may help shape new ideas about approaches to policymaking and their relevance to rhetorical and professional communication studies.

4 Moving Between Text and Context

The Challenges of Systemic and Cultural Change Regarding Gender and Violence

Two years after killing Teri Lee and Timothy Hawkinson, Sr., Steven Van Keuren appealed his first-degree premeditated murder conviction before the Supreme Court of Minnesota. There Van Keuren and his attorneys argued that the district court erred when it failed to instruct the jury that first-degree "heat-of-passion" manslaughter was a lesser-included offense of first-degree premeditated murder. A lesser-included offense is "necessarily committed during the perpetration of a greater crime because the lesser crime contains some of the same elements of the greater crime" and allows a lesser sentence (Legal Information Institute 2015a, n.p.). With a heat-of-passion argument, the defendant's emotional state at the time of the killing is of primary importance. Van Keuren claimed that unexpectedly finding his former girlfriend in bed with another man justified his extreme emotional response. The Court, however, denied his appeal, recalling Van Keuren's own trial testimony that upon discovering Hawkinson with Lee, he "simply moved forward with his plan to shoot himself in Lee's presence" and killed Hawkinson by accident. Specifically, the Court acknowledged that the Lee and Hawkinson murders showed "a pervading characteristic of anger," but legal precedent determined that anger alone was not sufficient to establish the element under first-degree manslaughter; the offender's reason had to be clouded and his willpower weakened, and Van Keuren's actions showed instead "vengeful planning, and preparation" (*State of Minnesota v. Steven Van Keuren* 2008, n.p.).

Although domestic homicides are often ripe with anger and jealousy as in the Van Keuren case, these expressions of power and control extend beyond the effects on the individual victim to reveal broad concerns about public safety and firm roots in cultural gender roles. From these perspectives, some features of the Van Keuren case are common in instigation and result. One study, for example, found that in 2011, there were an estimated 1,382 murder-suicides in the US; 90 percent of the offenders were male and involved intimate partners, 89.5 percent of incidents involved a firearm, and 84 percent of the incidents occurred in the home (Violence Policy Center 2012, 2–3, 5–6). Justice Alan Page, in concurring with the decision in the Van Keuren appeal, noted other commonalities: Van Keuren knew that Lee was dating another man, and a no-contact order was in place at the time of the murders. Moreover, Justice Page pointed out the threats to public safety posed by Van Keuren because he had "created the situation that provoked his aggression," having broken into Lee's house "with a loaded gun and extra ammunition and prepared to shoot himself in the presence of the victim" (*State of Minnesota v. Steven Van Keuren* 2008, n.p.). Tom Lininger (2009) summarizes the complications of domestic violence both legally and socially, as we see echoed in the Van Keuren case: "A defendant who repeatedly batters his intimate partner does not do so by mistake. The repetition of violence belies any defense that the violence is attributable to abrupt provocation or 'the heat of the moment'" (901). In many cases, says Lininger (2009), the offender intends to isolate the victim in that he has observed "the effects of terrorizing his intimate partner including her acquiescence, her unwillingness to break from the relationship, and her refusal to bring charges against him—and the persistence of his violence indicates that he intends to perpetuate these effects" (901). Public safety issues thus require the sanctioned intervention of the law to establish a penalty for disobeying the pertaining legal statutes, to protect the victim, to manage the offender in the future, and ultimately to prevent such violence.

In this chapter, we return to the Lethality Assessment Protocol (LAP) to explore the relationship between this protocol and the cultural and systemic attitudes toward gender and violence. To do so, we often shift between rhetorical analysis of texts and feminist investigations of cultural contexts to show the challenges of curtailing domestic violence and sexual assault as well as confirm the necessity of such broad interdisciplinary analyses in professional communication research. Our explorations, include deconstructing dichotomies, a problematic strategy often used to sustain an argument; for example, we examine the dichotomies of lethality versus non-lethality as proposed in LAP, agency versus victimization as articulated in caring for the domestic violence victim, and victim-centered programs versus offender-management and offender-rehabilitation programs as supported within the legal arena. Our analysis also includes looking specifically at legal and metaphorical language to reveal cultural attitudes toward gender and violence. Finally, we believe that in exploring both text and context regarding domestic violence, we extend rhetorical and professional communication perspectives on the relationship between discourse and cultural norms that sustain or counter the "Othering" or marginalization we examined in Chapter 3.

Cultural gender roles certainly play into how assault victims and offenders are viewed as a group and the extent to which prevention is possible. As Liz Kelly (1988) succinctly puts these influences, "Male violence arises out of men's power and women's resistance to it" (23). Shonna Trinch (2010), among many other feminist scholars, extends the notion that domestic violence and sexual assault are consequences of patriarchy, defined as "a broader system of power and gender inequality that privileges masculinity at an ideological as well as a structural level, thus affording men violent access to women without serious sanctions" (395). In terms of the law, Jennifer Andrus (2015) reminds us, "[G]ender is a factor in, a product of, and affected by legal language ideologies located in the intertextual discourses of the law from the trial to the precedent" (29). Therefore, although the Van Keuren case invites us to examine the actions of individual offenders, effective intervention and prevention require challenging long-held systemic and cultural perspectives, which are most likely reflected within cultural discourse as well as legal language and ideologies. That is, according to Janus (2006), "[S]exual violence is not a pathologically isolated cancer but a systemic dysfunction, spread broadly throughout the normal relationships of society" (79).

Thus, effective systemic changes regarding gender violence must counter these patriarchal and hierarchical norms. Systemic changes happen over time, with the anticipated results that the "experiences of practitioners and service providers over decades have helped refine, expand, and adapt interventions to serve survivors more effectively" (Arnold and Akie 2013, 562). Such reform, however, is quite complex. On the one hand, Nancy Berns (2001), for example, notes the pitfall of looking at power but not at gender. She cautions that "degendering the problem" of domestic violence and sexual assault, by substituting "human violence" for gender violence, "undermines the role of gender and power in abusive relationships" and resists "any attempts to situate social problems within a patriarchal framework" (265–266). On the other hand, "gendering the blame," says Berns, can dwell on such things as the "culpability of women" by "holding female victims responsible for their role in their own victimization" (269). Moreover, scholars such as Natalie Sokoloff (2004) question gender inequality as the main or only factor contributing to domestic violence and therefore call for the examination and reform of other systems of power and inequality such as sexual identity, race, ethnicity, class, and immigration and disability status.

In Chapter 2, we examined LAP as a disrupting and potentially enlightening and advancing genre, created by the Maryland Network Against Domestic Violence and adopted in Minnesota in the *kairos* following the Van Keuren murders. Representatives from various Minnesota county agencies identified the goals of LAP as allocating limited resources, ensuring cooperation of first responders on the domestic violence scene, influencing judges and prosecutors to pursue high-risk cases more vigorously, and persuading victims to seek advocacy sources and, in most cases, to leave their abusers. Examining these goals revealed a tension between changing systemic responses to domestic violence and managing resources more efficiently within existing legal and judicial systems. Those victims who refused to cooperate in LAP expressed distrust of the legal system, feared retaliation from their abusers, worried about transitioning to a life without the financial and emotional support of their partners, and desired to continue working on their emotional relationships with those partners. To overcome such resistance, law enforcement and others often employed fear-based arguments with LAP, in essence asking victims to exchange *fear of retaliation* for *fear of death.*

We begin this chapter by identifying these transformational challenges from feminist, rhetorical, and legal perspectives and ground these perspectives by recalling the Van Keuren case and by examining a domestic homicide-suicide case in Colorado. We also return to our interviews with those administering LAP in Minnesota counties to test and extend these theoretical perspectives. We then focus on how LAP has served as a companion genre or a catalyst for two new protocols to help the domestic violence victim and to manage the offender, in particular, providing victims with additional advocacy help and safety planning and urging offenders to engage in pre-trial counseling. With a focus in this chapter on the tendency at times to essentialize or even manipulate the domestic violence victim, we rely heavily on our discussions from Chapter 3 on Othering. We end this chapter by returning to the cultural construction of gender and gender violence to suggest ways to address systemic obstacles to curtailing domestic violence.

We do engage in these analyses with some optimism despite how our examination of text and context reveals entrenched notions of gender and violence. We recall that certainly LAP and accompanying efforts have disrupted existing individual beliefs, even though to be most effective they also have to challenge the patriarchal and hierarchical system that misunderstands, endures, and even tolerates gender violence. Our interviews with Minnesota stakeholders, for instance, reveal some successes already in meeting those challenges. A first responder, for example, determined that his previous custom of asking the victim "Why don't you just leave him?" was a kind of "knuckle dragging thought," given how administering LAP enlightened him about the complications of domestic violence (P-17; again see the Appendix for our interview citation style). Another first responder said that after administering LAP to domestic violence victims, he so realized the danger of separation assault that he "changed the way I have approached domestic violence, because I am pretty sure that I have told people in my 15 years, when I recognized that this is pretty serious … 'You have to leave him.'" Now this officer gives victims another kind of message: "Because that's the most dangerous time for them … I will tell them, 'If you choose to leave him, it needs to be planned. And you can't just tell him'" (W-1).

Success, however, also lies in balancing the management of the offender with the needs of the victim. To fail to achieve this balance will continue to marginalize and silence the victim on the local level and inadvertently maintain the patriarchal and hierarchical tolerance of domestic violence on the cultural level. However, we believe that if LAP and subsequent systemic changes meet expectations, not only will domestic homicide be reduced but also scholars and activists can better recognize the mechanisms by which such major systemic and cultural changes are introduced and ultimately considered successful.

Theoretical Approaches to Domestic Violence

To ground the theoretical approaches to gender, violence, and the law, and to examine systemic challenges on the broadest level, we rely on one more case review, that of *Town of Castle Rock, Colorado v. Gonzales* (2005). Safeguards such as no-contact orders and orders for protection, as we saw in the Van Keuren case, often fail the victim. Again, because Minnesota police would not cross into Wisconsin to arrest Van Keuren on a no-contact violation, he remained free to harass and eventually kill Teri Lee. Legislatures have attempted to address such failures. The Minnesota legislature, for example, recently determined that the sentences for violations of orders for protection should be enhanced. Specifically, the first violation of an order for protection is a misdemeanor, the second within ten years of a previous violation a gross misdemeanor, and the third within ten years a felony carrying a possible imprisonment of up to five years (Minnesota Statutes 2014, 518B.01). Despite such efforts, this method of protecting the victim has often floundered.

Particularly revealing in this regard is the *Gonzales* case, a case that went through a federal district court, the U.S. Court of Appeals, Tenth Circuit, and the U.S. Supreme Court. In May 1999, Jessica Gonzales obtained an order for protection (called a temporary restraining order in Colorado) against her estranged husband, Simon, in connection with their divorce proceedings. Under the order, Mr. Gonzales was excluded from the family home and prohibited from "molesting and disturbing" Ms. Gonzales and their three daughters, ages ten, nine, and seven. The order allowed Mr. Gonzales parenting time with the girls on alternating weekends and for two weeks during the summer, but he needed permission to visit the girls at other times. On June 22, 1999, sometime between 5:00 pm and 5:30 pm, Mr. Gonzales abducted his daughters, Rebecca, Katheryn, and Leslie, while they were playing outside their home. Ms. Gonzales suspected immediately that Mr. Gonzales, who had a history of erratic behavior and suicidal threats, had taken the children, and she called the Castle Rock police for help. When the police arrived, Ms. Gonzales requested that her restraining order be enforced and the children returned to her, but the officers stated that there was nothing that they could do and suggested that Ms. Gonzales call again if the girls were not back home by later that evening. At 8:30 pm, Ms. Gonzales reached Simon, who told her that he and the children were at an amusement park in Denver. She again called the Castle Rock police to request that they arrest Mr. Gonzales and return the children. She was told to wait another two hours to see if Mr. Gonzales would return the children on his own, and so she called the police again at 10:00 pm and then at midnight to report that he had not done so. The police took an incident report at midnight but did not attempt to enforce the restraining order or locate the children; instead, the responding officer went to dinner. Shortly after 3:00 am, Mr. Gonzales arrived at the Castle Rock police station and opened fire with a semiautomatic handgun. The police returned his fire and killed him. Inside Mr. Gonzales' truck, the police found the bodies of all three girls, whom he had murdered earlier in the evening. Ms. Gonzales sued the town of Castle Rock for violating her substantive and procedural Fourteenth Amendment due process rights when failing to enforce the restraining order against Simon Gonzales.

The *Gonzales* case raises again the general question of what legal strategies are most effective in protecting the victim of domestic violence. Kathryn Moracco et al. (2010), for example, caution about domestic violence coming to the attention of the legal system by way of orders for protection and no-contact orders. The problem is that such an order usually "reflects chronic behavior, not an isolated or initial assault," say Moracco et al., and the court's and law enforcement's awareness of this likelihood is particularly important given "the field's current lack of precision in predicting recidivism and our limited ability to assess abusers' lethality" (1217–1218). Moreover, some protective orders can be harmful, according to Andrea Nichols (2013); when protective orders are "predicted to fail," as they certainly would in the Gonzales case given the emotional instability of Mr. Gonzales, the focus should be instead on "extensive safety planning to mitigate batterer-based revictimization" (1417). LAP is designed to address these problems, and yet victims often rely on such protective orders to serve as the primary and sometimes only barrier between them and their abusers. The *Gonzales* case offers the opportunity to examine from gender, rhetorical, and discursive perspectives the cultural context in which this failure to protect the victim and her family may occur.

Gender Perspectives on Proprietariness and Privacy

Feminist scholars and activists have looked closely at cultural gender roles in relationship to such violence. Early on, Karen Offen (1988) defined feminism "as a concept that can encompass both an ideology and a movement for sociopolitical change based on a critical analysis of male privilege and women's subordination within any given society" (151). According to Offen, feminism "opposes women's subordination to men in the family and society, along with men's claims to define what is best for women without consulting them; it thereby offers a frontal challenge to patriarchal thought, social organization, and control mechanisms" (151). Kathryn Bell and Amy Naugle (2008) break down this definition into specific causes of violent domestic relationships, such as "sexism and female inequality within patriarchal societies," gender roles that are "defined by society and taught to individuals during childhood that are thought to place men in positions of power over women," and "various tactics including physical violence" used by men "to control and exert their dominance over women and their families" (1097).

These gendered expressions of power and control are often expressions of male proprietariness, a hypermasculine response that may emerge during estrangement, as in the *Gonzales* case, and leads to "escalated coercion, such that possessive men may be more motivated to kill when they perceive their female partners intend to leave them" (Serran and Firestone 2004, 4). In exercising hypermasculinity, again as Vokey, Tefft, and Tysiaczny (2013) define the phenomenon, abusers perceive violence as part of normal masculinity. In Anderson and Umberson's (2001) exploration of hypermasculinity, for example, male batterers excused their behavior, rationalized their actions, justified their responses, and minimized their violence against their female partners by depicting their violence "as rational, effective, and explosive whereas women's violence was represented as hysterical, trivial, and ineffectual" (363). Moreover, some scholars assert that male proprietariness results from behaviors and attitudes toward female sexual infidelity that have evolved over decades, if not centuries: "For example, men who dropped by unexpectedly to see what their partner was doing or who told their partner that they would 'die' if she ever left him were most likely to use serious violence against their partners" (Goetz et al. 2008, 485). These men seem to embrace the belief that "violence and the threat of violence can prevent a partner from leaving a mateship, or encourage a woman who has temporarily left to return to that relationship" (Buss and Duntley 2011, 416). Although it is impossible to capture with absolute confidence Simon Gonzales' proprietary motivation in kidnapping and murdering his three children, his actions do seem designed to punish Ms. Gonzales for separating from him, just as his suicide threats seem initiated to persuade her to return to him. As we see next, in the *Gonzales* opinion, at times the courts mirror proprietary notions stemming from gender roles by debating constitutional entitlement to personal safety and by denying the negative effect of their decisions on overall attempts to curtail domestic violence. Moreover, the dissenting justices in the opinion pointed out that the reaction from law enforcement sustained the view that domestic violence is a "private" affair, not a public concern.

The U.S. District Court, District of Colorado, dismissed Ms. Gonzales' initial complaint on the basis that no principle of substantive or procedural due process allowed her to sue a local government for failing to enforce a restraining order. The case then went through the U.S. Court of Appeals twice, the first time before a panel for the Tenth Circuit, which found that Ms. Gonzales could indeed present a legitimate procedural due process claim. The panel, however, noted that in an earlier case (*DeShaney* 1989), the U.S. Supreme Court had found that "nothing in the language of the Due Process Clause itself requires the State to protect the life, liberty, and property of its citizens against invasion by private actors" (195). State laws could address such concerns, but the Constitution did not require it. Moreover, the Appellate panel found that failure to enforce the restraining order in the *Gonzales* case, "while it did not reduce the danger posed by Simon Gonzales' abduction of the girls, did not create or enhance that danger," and therefore this "lack of affirmative conduct" was "fatal" to Ms. Gonzales' substantial due process claim (*Gonzales v. Castle Rock* 2002, n.p.). The panel concluded, however, that the defendant police officers used no means, "reasonable or otherwise," to enforce the restraining orders, in reference to the requirements of the Colorado state statutes, and therefore, the panel remanded the case for further proceedings based on these distinctions and limitations (*Gonzales v. Castle Rock* 2002, n.p.; Colorado Revised Statutes 2002, n.p.). In other words, Ms. Gonzales had at least some limited grounds to proceed with her suit.

A rehearing by the full Appellate Court indeed found that Ms. Gonzales had a "protected *property* interest [a certain benefit to which the individual is entitled under due process] in the enforcement of the terms of her restraining order," an interest that the Castle Rock police violated (*Gonzales v. Castle Rock* 2004, n.p., emphasis added). The full Court affirmed this interest because "Ms. Gonzales and her daughters relied on the enforcement of the restraining order to go about their daily lives," and that reliance was "arbitrarily undermined" by the officers' failure to enforce the order, "resulting in an unspeakably tragic outcome" (n.p.). At this point, it seemed that Ms. Gonzales would prevail.

But then in another reversal, by a 7–2 decision, the U.S. Supreme Court found instead that Ms. Gonzales did not have a constitutionally protected property right to the mandatory enforcement of the restraining order and therefore could not claim that the Castle Rock police had violated her due process rights. To have such a property interest in such an abstract benefit as a restraining order, the Supreme Court said that Ms. Gonzales would have to prove a "legitimate claim of entitlement" to the benefit. Moreover, Justice Antonin Scalia, in writing the majority opinion, found that the Colorado statutes allowed the police to arrest the subject who violated a restraining order *at their discretion*. Justice Scalia also declared that one statement from the Appellate Court was "sheer hyperbole," the statement that any other result than the required enforcement of an order for protection "would render domestic abuse restraining orders utterly valueless." Instead, Scalia determined that the very creation of the statutory grounds on which Mr. Gonzales could *possibly* "be arrested, criminally prosecuted, and held in contempt" were "hardly 'valueless'"—"even if the prospect of those sanctions ultimately failed to prevent him from committing three murders and a suicide" (*Town of Castle Rock, Colorado v. Gonzales* 2005, n.p.).

The dissent in the *Gonzales* opinion, written by Justice Stevens with Justice Ginsberg joining, opined that the majority had placed "undue weight" on state statutes that "seemingly mandate police enforcement but are generally understood to preserve police discretion" and that the Court failed to take seriously that the restraining order was "specifically intended to provide protection" to a "narrow class of persons who are beneficiaries of domestic restraining orders (*Town of Castle Rock, Colorado v. Gonzales* 2005, n.p.). Also, the dissenting justices argued that Ms. Gonzales property interest was "just as concrete and worthy of protection" as "any other important services" provided by the government (*Town of Castle Rock, Colorado v. Gonzales* 2005, n.p.). But most important to our analysis is the dissenting justices' focus on a comparable reform in law enforcement: mandatory arrest laws, the reform we covered in our Introduction. The dissenting justices note that the Colorado General Assembly in adopting mandatory arrest laws joined a nationwide movement that "took aim at the crisis of police underenforcement" (*Town of Castle Rock, Colorado v. Gonzales* 2005, n.p.). Moreover, one cause of such underenforcement, according to the dissenting justices, was "the perception by police departments and police officers that domestic violence was a private, 'family' matter and that arrest was to be used as a last resort" (*Town of Castle Rock, Colorado v. Gonzales* 2005, n.p.). Rhetorical and legal scholars such as Andrus (2015) have argued that this ideology extends throughout the legal system: "Crimes involving non-intimate individuals, often men, are assumed to have public consequences, whereas domestic incidents, only recently criminal, are assumed to always be merely private affairs" (99).

Both the National Coalition Against Domestic Violence and the National Center for Victims of Crime had warned that a defeat for Ms. Gonzales would "represent a step backward in the struggle against family abuse" (Lane 2005, A02). Thus, the dissenting justices as well as advocacy groups found the *Gonzales* decision a disappointment in affirming that Colorado police officers could decide whether to enforce protective orders on a case-by-case basis. The *Gonzales* case left domestic violence victims in Colorado uncertain as to whether their orders for protection would be enforced and, if violated, lead to an arrest of the offender.

Taking a more proactive role after their experiences with LAP, however, many of those implementing and administering LAP in Minnesota seem to reject such attitudes as those that emerged regarding the *Gonzales* case. A city attorney, for example, commented that when he encountered a case screened in on the LAP questionnaire as high risk, he would

> take this case more seriously because … the last thing I want to do is open the paper tomorrow and find that somebody that got assaulted in White Bear got killed because we foolishly let the guy go back there.
>
> (W-21; White Bear Township spans Washington and Ramsey Counties, MN)

A community corrections officer added that because administering LAP and identifying a high-risk victim might lead to a no-contact order and other responses, first responders now feel

> like they are more a part of the process … that in fact they know what's going on with the case … [and] there is a mutual response about this kind of work, and this implementation of this tool has really helped that.
>
> (W-3)

Finally, a member of a county attorney's office contrasted the office's involvement before LAP when "we went to scenes, we made arrests, we had victims in contact with the Alexandra House [victim advocacy organization and shelter]" to their current involvement when they can "look at the history that led to events" (K-9).

These comments certainly confirm that LAP might serve as a catalyst to gain that broader history in a domestic violence incident, which in turn not only better protects the victim and manages the offender but also has the potential to counter cultural assumptions about gender and violence. Next, looking at such issues through the lens of rhetorical analysis, particularly going back to our discussion of Othering in Chapter 3, we illuminate further the challenge and successes of curtailing domestic violence.

Rhetorical Perspectives on Othering and Dichotomization

Recognizing the *kairos* or exigency involved in a systemic focus on domestic violence, Gretchen Arnold and Jami Ake (2013) assert that the goal of ending violence against women "has always been rhetorically present" in the battered women or feminist movement, "but the degree to which it has been given priority as a tangible objective has varied" (572). Moreover, changing "cultural and structural underpinning of the violence," say Arnold and Ake, must "prevent violence against women by bringing about real structural change instead of criminal justice and social service approaches that mitigate the effects of violence on individuals after it has occurred" (572). Again, the National Coalition Against Domestic Violence and the National Center for Victims of Crime warned in the *Gonzales* case that the court's decisions could undermine structural efforts to protect domestic violence victims by way of orders for protection or no-contact orders. Rhetorical analysis, particularly of Othering and dichotomization, reveals not only these criminal justice and social service changes for which LAP and other efforts serve as a catalyst but also some of the challenges to such changes.

In Chapter 2, we looked specifically at the persuasive elements of the LAP questionnaire. Certainly, those first responders who had experience in administering the questionnaire acknowledged those persuasive elements. One first responder, for example, concluded that not only do certain questions, particularly those using words such as "kill" or "weapon," get the attention of victims who "don't consciously think about their daily activities," but also "when those questions are asked, that gets them to start understanding and realizing how they have gotten themselves into kind of a dangerous situation" (R-16). Another first responder noted that administering this questionnaire on the scene is particularly kairotic because some victims, for whom violence is "just a part of life," do not at the moment when LAP is administered "have the intuition to try to hide or minimize what is actually going on" (W-2). The victim's answers to the LAP questionnaire have somewhat the qualities and reception of the excited utterance, an exception to the rules of evidence that usually exclude hearsay testimony in court. Andrus (2015) explores why "spontaneous utterances are more trustworthy than rhetorical or subjective ones," such as when a first responder testifies as to what a victim might have shouted out when law enforcement arrived on the scene of a domestic assault (152). The victim is ill-prepared to strategically frame her statements to protect her abuser, for example, and therefore her answers to the LAP questionnaire might be considered noteworthy even if later recanted. The assumption may be then that the domestic violence victim is inclined to lie unless so caught up in the moment that she cannot censure her outbursts—here she might be completely trustworthy.

And again, another rhetorical strategy of LAP is to persuade the victim that remaining with her abuser is not "normal." As a first responder noted, the goal is to help the victim realize as the police officer or deputy sheriff administers the LAP questionnaire, that this violence "isn't necessarily normal or, you know, how a relationship should be" (R-13). Moreover, a victim advocate concluded that because her organization would "spend more time on going over her [the victim's LAP] questions that she answered 'yes' to, it kind of brings more of an awareness to her that 'OK, this [violent] behavior is not normal'" (G-12). In essence, the very act of administering the LAP questionnaire and sharing the scoring with the victim is designed to persuade her that living with domestic violence is abnormal or places her in a marginalized social group.

As we discussed extensively in Chapter 3, this rhetorical act of Othering distinguishes those who are perceived to be different from that mainstream and imposes this subject position within society upon them. Again, Cherney (2011) finds that the act of Othering includes considering certain two-dimensional beings to be illogical and unrealistic, holding notions that so-considered normal persons are expected not only to dismiss but also to employ in distinguishing themselves from those Others (n.p.). In essence, the act of Othering conveys to a domestic violence victim that she can move from abnormal victimization to normal agency only when she is awakened to her danger and takes steps to leave her abuser. And so, those in power might mark either the abusive or abused as Other, until a person or group resists that so-considered abnormal position and negotiates a different one. Moreover, as Judith Butler (1990) asserts, in reaction to the work of Mary Douglas, "all social systems are vulnerable at their margins, and ... all margins are accordingly considered dangerous" (132). Until a kairotic moment, perhaps during administration of the LAP questionnaire, the domestic violence victim remains suspect because she is part of a dangerous dynamic that disturbs public safety.

Therefore, to repeat the perspective of Dunn and Powell-Williams (2007), the mainstream and the agencies charged with protecting domestic violence victims can so Other them to create a "new kind of deviance in the form of pathetic victims" (983). Laurie Kohn (2008), for example, suggests that both the judicial and the law enforcement systems "can convey the message that victims cannot make rational, informed decisions about themselves, their families, and their futures" (240). And so, the "easiest way to deal with fragile, uncooperative, mentally ill, or indecisive individuals," says Kohn, "is to remove them [victims] from the decision-making role," in essence making the victims' voices irrelevant and creating in them "a profound sense of disempowerment" (241). And, of course, their abusers have already Othered domestic violence victims, by what Dobash and Dobash (2011) call "dehumanization and impersonalization," actions that can then lead abusers into "divesting victims of human qualities, thus blunting self-sanctions when individuals are no longer seen as worthy of respect" (115–116). Therefore, Othering marks the victim as deviant, irrational, uninformed, fragile, uncooperative, indecisive, unworthy, inhuman, and even dangerous, features that those in the mainstream use to distinguish themselves from the victim and to justify speaking for that victim.

In the act of such Othering, victimization and agency can be falsely dichotomized. Rhetorical analysis reveals such dichotomies or dilemmas as false when an argument presents two options as mutually exclusive and disregards other alternatives. These choices appear to be mutually exclusive, just as the mainstream may designate the normal and the abnormal as two separate categories or groups. In such a dichotomy, movement from one category to another is possible but only by leaving the first assigned category completely behind. A false dichotomy is therefore called black-and-white thinking, the fallacy of false choice, or the fallacy of the excluded middle, among other labels. False dichotomies can be posed by accidental omission, or they can be created as a deliberate strategy to force a choice, determine an outcome, or impose politicized thinking upon a marginalized person or group. And so, rhetoric scholars, such as John Searle (1995), have long argued that if distinctions between people and groups do not allow for marginalized and divergent cases, their arguments and deliberations are indeed suspect.

Along these lines, Neil Websdale (2000), in his critique of lethality assessment tools, has warned that the "absolute distinction between lethal and non-lethal cases" could be such a false dichotomy (1). The primary problem with such predictive tools, said Websdale, is that "they employ a scientific language that seeks to foretell the future" and they so rely on "clean data" by the checked boxes of a questionnaire that "women's lives are stripped of their idiosyncrasies, their complexities, and subsumed into a final score or final solution that obscures the richness of their personal experience" (5). The solution, according to Websdale, is to allow first responders to also follow their instincts in identifying cases as high or low risk, an option that LAP includes. But, we certainly see dichotomization in the *Gonzales* case when Ms. Gonzales attempted to assert her voice before law enforcement and her rights before the courts. Were her rights as a victim curtailed because the violence was a private matter or were they confirmed to ensure public safety? Was she a victim needing protection or an agent demanding remedy? The law presumes that some individuals are sovereign agents and others are not, but as Andrus (2015) argues, "Agency is slippery, difficult to define, and contentious" (147). Likewise, Caroline Picart (2003) adds that the rhetorical move of dichotomizing the victimization and agency "reifies the same picture of the monolithic woman as pure victim, one who must be protected from 'evil' and predatorial forces because she is incapable of any acts of agency to defend herself" and ignores "the complexities that victims live, with their divided loyalties and the chiaroscuro of agency and powerlessness they straddle from day to day" (97). Schneider (1993) likewise notes in that within violent relationships abused women still may exercise agency to protect themselves and their children (387–388). Thus, a dichotomy of victimization versus agency, or sovereign agency versus constrained agency, miscasts the roles and positions in domestic violence.

Dunn and Powell-Williams (2007), however, warn that "the idea of agency is so entrenched in the sea of American culture that it cannot be submerged no matter the rhetorical circumstances but keeps bobbing to the surface" (980). In their interviews with 32 domestic violence victim advocates, these researchers found that regardless of experiences of the battered women the advocates encountered, they "continue to construct them as victims even in the face of their apparent agency" (985); therefore, "victimization is a vocabulary or rhetoric to be drawn on" by these advocates, and "central to this vocabulary is the removal of agency" (982). Finally, in their examination of the consequences of allowing individuals to define their own sexual or domestic violence experiences, Charlene Muehlenhard and Leigh Ann Kimes (1999) found that legislatures, police, and prosecutors often rejected the notion of allowing victims themselves to identify incidents as domestic violence, a rejection that "implies that it is clear a priori who is a victim and hence who is entitled to label the incident" (237). Through rhetorical criticism, then, we see that the victim can be cast as either agent or victim and be so Othered to ignore the steps she has already taken to preserve her own safety and that of her family. Next we look at how specific language can mark the domestic violence victim as Other, alerting rhetorical and professional communication scholars once again to the cultural context of specific word choices.

Discursive Perspectives on Verbal Violence

Othering is accomplished through language or discourse. Lucinda Finley (1989), for example, summarily identified this potential in the very origin of legal language: "Rather, legal language is a male language because it is principally informed by men's experience and because it derives from the powerful social situation of men, relative to women" (893). Finley goes on to qualify her statement in that the law has, on the one hand, recognized women to be subjects or contemplated targets of many laws, including those laws designed to protect them. On the other hand, Finley still finds that "men's understanding of women, women's nature, women's capacities, and women's experiences" has informed those laws (894). Moreover, Muehlenhard and Kimes (1999) caution that in the law, there are no objective definitions, and therefore words not only "reflect the interests of the people who create and promote them" but these words also "mean whatever people with power agree what they mean" (243; see also Rosenberg 1982).

In the *Gonzales* case, for example, the Appellate Court noted that the restraining order Ms. Gonzales obtained contained the following words, which served as a warning to Simon Gonzales: The issuing court "finds that physical or emotional harm would result if you are not excluded from the family home," and "[i]f you violate this order thinking that the other party or a child named in this order has given you permission, you are wrong, and can be arrested and prosecuted" (*Gonzales v. Castle Rock* 2004, n.p.). Regardless of these stern directives to

Mr. Gonzales, the Appellate Court panel, the full Appellate Court, and the U.S. Supreme Court focused more on the language of the Colorado statute regarding the enforcement of restraining orders, specifically the phrasing determining the duties of police officers: These officers "shall use every reasonable means to enforce a restraining order" (Colorado Revised Statutes 2002, n.p.). The Supreme Court interpreted the words "shall" and "reasonable" to indicate choice rather than absolute duty:

> We do not believe that these provisions of the Colorado law truly made enforcement of restraining order *mandatory* ... It is hard to imagine that a Colorado peace officer would not have some discretion to determine that ... the circumstances of the violation or the competing duties of that officer or his agency counsel decisively against enforcement in a particular instance.
>
> (*Town of Castle Rock, Colorado v. Gonzales* 2005, n.p., emphasis in original)

In response, Ms. Gonzales complained that the city of Castle Rock maintained a "custom and policy of failing to respond properly to complaints of domestic restraining order violations" (*Gonzales v. Castle Rock* 2004, n.p.). Of course, it is the obligation of the U.S. Supreme Court to interpret legal language to determine the constitutionality of state statutes; however, this decision seemed to leave domestic violence victims who rely on orders of protection less safe than they imagined they might be because of the interpretation of the words within the state statutes and the support of the customs and policies of local law enforcement.

If the *Gonzales* case rested on the definition of the words "shall" and "reasonable" as set within the context of a problematic custom and policy, the metaphorical language used by our Minnesota interviewees in regard to LAP perhaps at times indicates unconscious Othering of the domestic violence victim. In metaphorical language, a word or phrase is applied to an object or action as symbolic or representative of something else, particularly something unfamiliar or abstract. According to Rudolf Arnheim (1969),

> Experience indicates that it is easier to describe items in comparison with others than by themselves. This is so because the confrontation underscores the dimensions by which the items can be compared and thereby sharpens the perception of these particular qualities.
>
> (63)

Metaphorical language highlights particular qualities and suppresses others in the audience's mind, in what Arnheim calls visual thinking. Metaphor, according to Gunther Kress and Theo van Leeuwen (2001), can thus support a material rhetoric in that "our experience of moving our bodies in space and of interacting with the material world forms the basis of our ability to develop abstract concepts from metaphor" (75). Examining such metaphors, say Kress and van Leeuwen, illuminates the dominant values of culture; for example, "softness is highly valued for women, but not highly valued in the culture as a whole, with the result that *women* are not highly valued" (75, emphasis in original). And, as Andrus (2015) concluded, these metaphorical constructions "make the link between the linguistic and the social appear to be natural and normal" (45).

Again, one of the goals of LAP is to encourage high-risk domestic violence victims to realize the danger in staying with their abusers, again to exchange fear of retaliation for fear of death. The metaphors used by our interview participants to describe the means of achieving that goal were often visual and material. More than once, for example, an interview participant used the metaphor "sugar coat" to describe how the victim might disregard the danger from domestic violence prior to the implementation of LAP:

> When there was an arrest made, and he goes to jail, she has every opportunity to minimize the abuse and sugar coat it, because there is no one at the scene at the moment asking her questions, and there are no follow-up questions being made.
>
> (IP; again, see the Appendix for an explanation of this designation)

After the implementation of LAP, another interview participant said that first responders were no longer

> dancing around the topic, like, "Gee, have you thought that this could happen again?" Kind of sugar coat. It's really plain, "Has he or she ever threatened to kill you?" And I think that, for a lot of victims, is a point where they think, "Wow, this is serious."
>
> (IP)

The metaphor of "sugar coating" represents how domestic violence might be perceived as so common in the life of the victim that she has accepted it, just as law enforcement in the past might not have directly confronted her about the abuse. To get the victim to change her impression, however, some interviewees used other metaphorical language of necessary abrupt or even violent awakening to danger. One first responder, for example, commented that LAP "gets victims thinking about a pattern of behavior that they have gotten used to" and therefore "opens a lot of these women's eyes" (G-16). Another interview participant compared the process to a "huge eye opener" and related how the domestic violence victim's reactions are like

> the frog in the water on the stove. It just keeps getting warmer and warmer and warmer and warmer. And so, there is no guy on

> the planet that on the first date that punches you in the face. You wouldn't go out with him again. And, so it slowly, gradually builds up, and you build up your tolerance, and you just don't realize how violent and dangerous the situation is because that's what you are living with.
>
> (IP)

The story symbolizes how the frog, the victim in this story, eventually dies without realizing the dire situation, boiling to death without feeling the increasing heat and danger. What this victim needs, according to another interview participant, is "a real slap in the face," a symbolic assault on the victim, because when a victim has lived in a "crappy relationship for a long time," she doesn't "come to appreciate" the danger she is in (IP). To convince victims of their high-risk for lethality, again victims will hear from first responders, "Women in your situation have been killed by their partners." According to a community corrections staff member, that statement is "very impactful" because victims "have never heard someone say that directly to their face" (W-8). These metaphors indicate that the victim needs to have her physical senses awakened, senses that have been muted and a situation so minimized that direct confrontation, a symbolic "eye opener" or "slap in the face," is required.

In contrast, the metaphorical language used by those praising LAP stresses increased collaboration and cooperation among agencies. A police chief described the effect of LAP on judicial process as

> painting a picture from a blank slate, and you have to paint that picture so that everybody can understand what it is. It's not like that picture that if you look at it one way, it's an old woman, and if you look at it the other way, it's the young girl. You are really painting the picture so everyone sees the same thing, the same event.
>
> (R-15)

In describing how LAP enhanced the enforcement of no-contact orders, a community corrections officer said that because community corrections staff were "trained with advocates, with first responders, with a few from the County Attorney's Office ... one of the best things was, now the right hand knows what the left hand is doing" (W-8). The fear-based persuasive strategies of LAP, however, still indicate how domestic violence victims might be Othered or manipulated despite the good intentions of those agencies involved, all now cooperating to keep these victims safe. A community corrections officer summed up these strategies as follows: A victim might think,

> Oh, man, now what's going to happen. He's going to get out [of jail], and he is going to be madder ... Now he is the one who is providing

> for my kids. With him being in jail that's going to be problematic for our family.

Therefore, it's important that the first responder tell the victim, "Based on what you shared with me, there is a high probability that other women in your situation, or victims in your situation, have been killed" (W-3). These strategies must overcome what Lininger (2009) calls the "control motive," a proprietary response in which "batterers threaten reprisals if their victims testify or otherwise cooperate with law enforcement. Reprisals might include renewed violence, abduction of children, or economic retaliation" (868). Through metaphorical choices, a kind of metadiscourse, victims are placed within the social situation of Other, as law enforcement and other agencies represent mainstream cooperation in convincing those victims to move from social margins, from the abnormal to the normal. And, such movement might best be accomplished by sudden and even violent verbal messages.

With these gender, rhetorical, and discursive perspectives in mind, we next examine two LAP-related Minnesota programs, looking in particular not only for problematic dichotomies and Othering but also for attempts to revise systemic responses to domestic violence. In focusing on these two programs, we again identify additional persuasive strategies used to modify the behavior as well as to alter the minds and values of both victims and abusers.

Systemic and Structural Changes: Protecting the Victim and Managing the Offender

Several domestic violence programs and protocols were expanded or created around the time of the Van Keuren murders and the introduction of LAP into Minnesota counties. In this section, we focus on two such programs: additional safety planning offered by victim advocates and an intensive domestic abuse pre-trial program managed by community corrections staff. Although these programs are not unique to Minnesota (see, for example, the Idaho Domestic Violence Court Website 2015; the Florida Misdemeanor Pretrial Diversion Program 2015), they indicate again how LAP as a new genre may serve as a catalyst for systemic or structural change and perhaps provide inroads into resisting the entrenched cultural attitudes toward gender and violence we have just reviewed.

Honoring Victim Agency through Additional Safety Planning

Victim advocacy organizations have long struggled to protect their clients both from further violence by their abusers and from pressure by state agencies to aid in prosecution. Kohn (2008) points out the extremes of this second source of pressure: "By bulldozing victims, ignoring their needs and preferences, and substituting the state's interests for the victim's, the state coerces victims into compliance in the same way as the typical batterer might" (243). Moreover, the victim advocate as well as the victim can be challenged by the victim/agent dichotomy, at this point with a problematic definition of agency. As Schneider (1993) says, "Traditional views of agency are based on notions of individual choice and responsibility, individual will and action: perceptions of a world composed of atomized individuals, acting alone, unconstrained by social forces, unmediated by social structures and systemic hardship" (395–396). Certainly the domestic violence victim, regardless of her decision and in light of these pressures, illuminates these problematic perceptions of agency.

When victim advocates work with domestic abuse victims, the issues of victimization and agency may fall instead along a continuum, a more effective approach than pressuring the victim to reach a fanciful status of agency. Dunn and Powell-Williams (2007) did find that for some advocates, "It is the women, not their abusers, whom they seem to expect to 'turn around,' 'make the changes,' and 'make a better life,'" and the "only choice the advocates see as appropriate, the only acceptable agency, is leaving the violence relationship" (993). Nichols (2013) also confirmed that although victim advocates provide information about orders for protection, assist victims in obtaining such an order, and help victims develop safety plans, quite often these actions are designed primarily to support the victim who has left or is preparing to leave her abuser. However, Nichols (2013) also discovered that often

> such choices were collaboratively made with the advocates ... consistent with the empowerment model of feminist advocacy that assumes women's agency, rationality, and puts control of the decision making in the hands of victims to best provide for safety.
>
> (1418)

Rejecting the victim/agent dichotomy for a victim-centered approach, as one Minnesota county attorney concluded, not only helps the victim accept advocacy services but also increases "the likelihood that a victim will stay with us, end up trusting the police and the prosecutor and the advocate more than the person that did the battery" (P-6). The challenge, according to this prosecutor, is to keep the victim safe, help her achieve a sense of choice, and still satisfy the need for the state to manage the abuser through prosecution and rehabilitation. Moreover, cooperation across state agencies and advocacy groups can ensure that the victim has this sense of choice, decided this prosecutor.

With the introduction of LAP, now victim advocacy services begin safety planning immediately, particularly when a victim is screened in at high risk. Previously, an advocacy group relied on information from the police report and would contact the victim a day or two after first responders had left the scene. After LAP, safety planning begins with the phone call made by the first responder on the scene of the incident and continues when a victim arrives at the shelter and/or takes advantage of advocacy services. For those victims who decide to remain in the domestic relationship, one Minnesota community advocacy service offers such advice as, during an argument, "Avoid rooms with no exits like the bathroom or rooms with weapons like the kitchen" and "Establish a 'code word or sign' so that family, friends, teachers, or co-workers know when to call for help." For those who choose to leave these relationships, advocates advise, "Vary your routine," and "Save and document all contacts, message, injuries, or other incidents involving the abusive partner" (Tubman Family Crisis and Support Services n.d, 24–25). Such advice is standard across such advocacy groups and across the nation (see, for example, Alexandra House n.d., n.p.; Texas Council on Family Violence n.d., n.p.).

Even though agency and return to normalcy are still linked by many advocates to separation, and despite the somewhat coercive language we highlighted earlier in the LAP questionnaire, victim advocates do note that analyzing a victim's answers to the LAP screening questionnaire allows them to take a more individualized approach to the victim. According to one advocate, LAP "really does open, for our advocates with victims, good conversations"; for example,

> it's easier for us to do a safety plan because we know where her needs are going to be ... and it's easier for us to have her start thinking about is this the kind of relationship she wants to be in.
>
> (G-12)

LAP, however, also serves as a check against "sugar coating" by the victim. As another advocate said,

> When we are safety planning ... and if the victim is kind of minimizing or saying, "Well, you know, nothing like this has really happened before," we can come back and say, "OK, remember what you said on this [LAP questionnaire]."
>
> (W-4)

According to this advocate, "having the actual [LAP] form, it's a nice visual to say, 'You know you do screen in high risk' instead of just saying, 'We are worried about you'" (W-4). Finally, a judge confirmed the credibility of safety planning based on the LAP results by saying that she would vacate a no-contact order only after the victim had engaged in enhanced safety planning through victim advocacy: "Someone with a little coaching can make a different choice in terms of how bad things get before they seek some safety or get out of the situation quicker" (W-25). Safety planning, thus, can be individualized through the specific details an advocacy group gains from the LAP questionnaire.

Keeping in mind again that the LAP questionnaire is meant to be a persuasive document, we offer the results of one recently published quantitative study that measures the relationship between victims' protective actions and women's risk of domestic homicide as measured by the Danger Assessment (DA), the predecessor to LAP. After interviewing 432 women who had experienced domestic violence and subsequent police involvement in Oklahoma, Messing et al. (2014) found that women who were screened in at a high risk for being killed by their abusers were significantly more likely than low-risk victims to take protective actions. These actions included hiding money, keys, and other belongings; establishing a code with family and friends; removing or hiding weapons; packing a bag and locating important documents; and applying for an order for protection. Surprisingly, given these results, the study also found that high-risk victims were not more likely to seek *formal* advocacy services: only 5.09 percent reported that they received shelter services, and only 12.73 percent reported that they received safety planning, legal advocacy, and/or counseling, a "troubling" finding, "particularly given that these services have been demonstrated to be helpful in most cases" (Messing et al. 2014, 558). In light of these results, Messing and her colleagues, who included DA-creator Jacquelyn Campbell, urged researchers and practitioners to "develop unique ways to reach out" to victims who take protective actions but are not seeking those formal services because "it is important to build upon their strengths and provide empowering interventions while respecting women's autonomy and self-determination" (559–560). The entire protocol that we identify as LAP seems a positive step forward in this regard.

Finally, much as in Oklahoma, additional safety planning appears to be the most victim-focused program in the Minnesota counties in which LAP was introduced. The question remains as to whether the program in Minnesota is as effective as anticipated and whether any ineffectiveness is caused by victims' reluctance to relinquish their own sense of choice, their resentment of the Othering that places them outside the social norm, or the failure of LAP to change their minds about the source of danger. Safety planning might enhance a victim's sense of control in some ways, but the question remains as to whether she can do so on her terms, given possible conflicts among an advocacy group's mission to honor the victim's voice, a county attorney's wish to prosecute the abuser, and the fear-based arguments contained within LAP. The next LAP-related program we discuss further illuminates the challenges of changing behavioral patterns, this time of abusers' patterns supported by the cultural norms of male proprietariness or hypermasculinity.

Changing Abuser Behavior through Intensive Domestic Assault Pre-Trial Programs

The intensive domestic assault pretrial program (IDAPP) in Anoka County, MN, relies on identifying domestic abusers in high-risk cases through the LAP questionnaire and then directing them toward community corrections before any major decisions are made about a penalty for their offense. The plan is to supervise the abuser on a pre-trial basis "from arrest to sentencing using treatment programming, home electronic monitoring devices, drug/alcohol testing and case management" (Anoka County Community Corrections n.d., n.p.). Through IDAPP, offenders are offered three options: stay in jail, post bail, or participate in IDAPP. If defendants choose to participate in IDAPP, they receive intensive supervision, including bi-weekly personal contacts and random home/work visits. Much as does LAP, IDAPP depends on persuasive strategies, in this case, to convince the offender he has been identified as being at risk of continuing his abusive behavior and therefore suffering additional legal restrictions or consequences. In essence, he has been marked as Other as we saw in Chapter 3: dangerous, needing management, and unlikely to succeed in rehabilitation, but he might reduce his upcoming sentence greatly by engaging in counseling now rather than subsequently as a condition of probation or supervised release from prison.

Across the US, such pre-trial release programs were created originally to ease jail-crowding by placing offenders of various crimes back into the community on house arrest or electronic monitoring while they awaited their trial (see, for example, Prince William County Government in Virginia 2015, n.p.). Now some jurisdictions have dedicated domestic violence courts, such as in Ann Arbor, MI, where a "mini danger assessment" is completed before pretrial release is considered, and defendants must report to a pretrial review group to receive a consistent message: In such a pretrial review group, notes Jane Sadusky (2006), "we talk about how violations have serious consequences and ... that there are no 'accidental' violations," particularly of no-contact orders (15, 19). Again, these pretrial programs focus on the perpetrator, a focus that such scholars as Lisa Goodman and Deborah Epstein (2005) caution lacks enough flexibility to meet the needs of individual victims:

> For example, if a victim seeks to drop charges so that the father of her children can continue to work and provide financial support, a prosecutor is likely to refuse on the grounds that this would not serve the interests of the state in punishing violations of the social contract.
>
> (481)

Along with this potential disregard for victim needs and interests, again the benefits of participating in IDAPP are strongly conveyed to the abuser on the basis of self-interest. Offenders know that courts are informed of such efforts; in fact, one judge endorsed telling any high-risk defendant that, by following the conditions of such IDAPP supervision, "You could influence this [outcome] by how you act between now and then [sentencing]" (W-25; see also Clair 2011). Moreover, one Minnesota prosecutor tells all the defense attorneys he works with, "If your clients take advantage of that [voluntarily participating in IDAPP], I will take that into consideration" (G-24). Finally, a county attorney staff member reflected:

> A lot of the offenders ... don't want to get into domestic abuse counseling, and they are a whole lot less likely to do it if they haven't had to do it for 9 or 10 months since the last attack,

but IDAPP "gives them some incentive and motivation to do it" (K-27). The question is, however, whether the offender who completes IDAPP has conformed to required behavior in the short term or whether he has changed his beliefs about and impulses toward proprietariness, hypermasculinty, and subsequent violence. As the county attorney staff member quoted above said, "Our job here can't be to just punish" (K-27). Therefore, a corrections officer added that if LAP "really draws the victim into the solution," IDAPP could "draw the perpetrator to a better and quicker treatment remedy" which in turn "may reduce some level of victimization or harm" (K-20). The ultimate goal of IDAPP would be to "create a long-term better reality" by changing "the mind-set that creates" domestic violence (Sakry 2012, June 29, n.p.).

Both the expanded safety planning offered to domestic violence victims by advocates and the intensive pre-trial domestic violence therapeutic and monitoring program offered to abusers by community corrections employ persuasive strategies to attract and retain participants. In terms of safety planning, these strategies expand upon the fear-based persuasive of LAP; in terms of pre-trial behavior modification, these strategies stress how abusers themselves might benefit when going before the court. Moreover, the programs focus on behavior management and changes: leave your abuser or at least have a safety plan; stop abusing and participate in therapy. The ultimate goal again is to change not only behavior but also beliefs and values; however, affecting cultural change regarding gender, violence, and the law is difficult and requires different strategies, as we explore in the final section of this chapter.

The Ultimate Challenges of Cultural Change in Behavior and Belief About Gender and Violence

Those implementing and administering LAP hope that one distinct benefit of the protocol is that "it all comes back to the victim" (W-8); in turn, "victims feel like their voices are being heard" (W-4) as the protocol "really draws the victim into the solution" (K-20). Certainly these statements attest to the presence and the value of the victim's sense of agency and choice during the process. Along with attempting to bring those Othered victims back from the margins of the mainstream, at its best LAP offers "a bigger picture" (W-5; K-9), builds "a history" (W-8), or captures the "historical context" (W-2) of the violence within a relationship. This history helps various agencies and advocacy groups engage as fully as possible with the victim to find a solution to the violence within her relationship and to "draw the perpetrator to a better and quicker treatment remedy" (K-20). Given these endorsements of LAP, even with the limitations we identified earlier in this chapter and in Chapter 2, again it does not seem overly optimistic to anticipate that cultural perspectives on gender and violence could be affected and even altered as LAP and LAP-related programs, such as the two we reviewed above, are implemented.

As Andrus (2015) points out, however, "Gender identity is not singular and an internal and cohesive element of the individual, but rather it is situational and rhetorical, developed and deployed in different ways depending on what the interaction calls for" (27). Likewise, Merry (2009) reminds us that violence is a complex cultural construct, which "impacts the everyday lives of people yet remains invisible and normalized. It includes poverty, racism, pollution, displacement, and hunger"; moreover, gender violence "is deeply rooted in the cultural understandings of gender and power, whether it takes place within a marriage or among strangers" (16). Indeed, as one Minnesota retired police chief mentioned, her dream was to "live long enough to hang the 'For Sale' sign on the front door of the local women's shelter ... not because we needed a bigger shelter, but because we no longer needed shelters" (R-5). However, even though the local law enforcement with which she had worked had assumed "proactive perspective" under LAP, she found "we still continue to see the increase in domestic homicides" (R-5). The domestic homicides and suicides that took place in the Van Keuren and Gonzales cases reflect the cultural challenges and complexity of gender and violence as we explore below.

Both Steven Van Keuren and Simon Gonzales threatened suicide during the estrangement from their partners, and both committed homicide, Van Keuren murdering Teri Lee and Timothy Hawkinson, Sr., and Gonzales murdering his three daughters. According to Andrew Starzonski and David Nussbaum (2000), there appears to be some evidence that some men who engage in domestic homicide-suicide might suffer from depression, jealousy, despair, anxiety, paranoia, and borderline personality traits, but most cases involve men who "become untethered from anchors of meaning in their life, typically the emotional structure of their marital and familial relationships and/or career," often with "immediate loss of attention, intimacy, and nurturing" as well as potential disapproval and shame (473). Moreover, the men whom Starzonski and

Nussbaum (2000) studied found a way to "make hostile external attributions for their intimate problems," including blaming their partners rather than themselves (473). And again, Serran and Firestone (2004) attribute the vast number of domestic homicides to male proprietariness, in particular, exacerbated by the female partner's infidelity or decision to leave the relationship and by feelings of jealousy and by viewing the woman "as property to be taken in death" (12). Dobash and Dobash (2011) in studying 104 case files of men convicted of murdering their partners found that in most cases the men considered the violence acceptable because the women were "defined as 'out of line' with the man's notions of the appropriate behavior for a wife, mother, or housekeeper" (114). Most likely, Simon Gonzales attempted first to intimidate his estranged wife into not divorcing him, but he became motivated to kill when she carried through with her plans to leave him. Moreover, scholars such as Carrie Brown (2008) found that these traits of power imbalance, social isolation, and internalized discrimination based on gender roles may carry over into violence and murder-suicide in same-sex intimate relationships among men and women. More specifically, Dena Hassouneh and Nancy Glass (2008) discovered that among the 52 women they studied who self-reported domestic violence in a same-sex relationship, the "dominant Western gender-role stereotyping" affects women's ability to identify domestic violence in their same-sex relationships and in turn to work with advocacy services (323).

The cultural assumptions about the roles of men and women in regard to violence seem quite entrenched. As Judith Butler (1990) proposed, "Gender proves to be performative—that is, constituting the identity it is purported to be. In this sense, gender is always doing" (25). James Ptacek (1999) extended this theory to domestic violence: "From a performative perspective, doing violence is a way of doing gender" (11). Based on interviews with 33 heterosexual men who have committed acts of domestic violence, Anderson and Umberson (2001) found that young men

> often learn to view themselves as capable perpetrators of violence through rough play and contact sports, to exhibit fearlessness in the face of physical confrontation, and to accept the harm and injury associated with violence as "natural."
>
> (363; see also Hollander 2001; Wilkinson and Hamerschlag 2005)

Moreover, when men who hold traditional beliefs about the male gender role feel a loss of power and control over their female partners, they experience what Gallagher and Parrott (2011) define as "masculine gender role stress" and use violence to subordinate women (570; see also Basile, Hall, and Walters 2013). And, women in such situations often recognize and report these "patriarchal notions of family and gender" as "internalized and reinforced" during domestic violence (Gillis et al. 2006, 1156).

The challenge on the cultural level is to disrupt, through invention and education, these gender performances as linked to violence. The wife of a police officer, for example, reported that when her husband's colleagues got together at her house, they might start talking about a domestic violence case:

> "Well, you know, she is letting him back in, and if she is really afraid of him, why is she doing that?" And, it's hard for me to bite my tongue. I have to step in at that point and say: "Well, you know, there are probably a lot of other reasons, like he is not giving her support, she doesn't have any other place to go."
>
> (W-5)

This interviewee reminds these first responders that women who experience domestic violence "make these decisions on a completely different level" in that they "might give up their safety for some of those real practical considerations," decisions that it takes a "deep understanding" to appreciate (W-5) and an understanding that must be "lived out within a wider cultural context of gender relationships" (121), as Dobash and Dobash (2011) say.

Another challenge to disrupting cultural assumptions about gender and violence rests in embracing the intersectionality of the issues. As well as the effect of assumed gender roles in same sex relationships, we now know more about how other aspects of identity affect violence. Patricia Hill Collins (1998) cautions, "American understanding of violence, for example, only makes sense in the particular historical context of hierarchical power relations of race, gender, class, nationality and heterosexism in the United States" (920; see also Bograd 1999; Weldon 2006). Two research studies exemplify these challenges and complexities of intersectionality. On the one hand, in interviews with 14 Black couples and one Indian heterosexual couple done in South Africa, Floretta Boonzaier (2008) found that feminine and masculine subjectivities were "far from being fixed, stable and unambiguous" (202); therefore, violence was not a natural expression of masculinity among these couples but instead "an effort to reconstruct a contested and unstable masculinity," a finding that, according to Boonzaier, counters essentialist readings of men's violence against women in U.S. popular culture (375). On the other hand, Joseph Vandello and Dov Cohen (2003) looked at honor codes among men within and outside the US and found that men's lost honor, particularly in the face of female infidelity "can be at least partially redeemed" through the use of violence, and female loyalty in the face of such violence "is not seen as weakness but as a sign of warmth and goodness" (2008). Although the class, race, and ethnicity of the interview participants and the populations of the Minnesota counties in which they live and work do not allow such in-depth intersectional studies, we acknowledge the ways in which diversity complicates cultural change.

Finally, systemic changes, let alone cultural disruption, that include these intersectional approaches are possible but often hard fought. The Violence Against Women Act (VAWA), for example, was established as a federal law in 1994 and provided $1.6 billion toward the investigation and prosecution of violence crimes against women, imposed mandatory restitution for these victims, and allowed civil redress for those cases not prosecuted. As a result, the Office on Violence Against Women within the Department of Justice awards special grants to those initiating effective systemic changes on the local level, one of which was awarded to Anoka County, MN. When the VAWA came up for reauthorization in 2013, however, hard fought were the new protections for Native American women, which would extend tribal jurisdiction over non-native offenders who committed domestic violence and sexual assault against a Native spouse or partner (Chekuru 2013, n.p.). As Sarah Deer, Professor of Law at Mitchell Hamline School of Law and member of the Muscogee Creek Nation described, violence against native women is rooted in a "history of racism and oppression" and reflects a deep-seated belief that women are vulnerable and "not protected by the system" (qtd. in Chekuru 2013, n.p.). Working against this issue, Deer says, involves both changing the conversation about the "cultural values about women" and creating tribal justice systems so that "tribes aren't depending on the state government or the federal government to take action, but can take action on their own terms" (qtd. in Chekuru 2013, n.p.). Thus, as Deer implies, to change the political system involves a shift in cultural values, which in many ways is reflected in and perpetuated by public and political discourse on the issue of violence against Native women.

Certainly the LAP questionnaire, as we examined in Chapter 2, and the two LAP-associated programs, as we explored them in this chapter, were designed to initiate broad systemic and cultural changes regarding gender, violence, and the law. The minimum requirements for such programs and protocols nationwide seem to be system-wide cooperation and implementation as well as immediate contact between the victim and advocacy services, such as Anne DePrince et al. (2012) confirmed in their study of a domestic violence triage intervention service in Denver, CO. Such reform programs, as they are called by Merry (2009), "endeavor to change batterers and their victims, to reshape the way both men and women understand and enact their gendered identities" (48). Moreover, these initiatives should recognize that a domestic violence victim may take quite a long time to reach what Dianne Follingstad, Ann Neckman, and Julia Vormbrock (1988) consider the fifth stage of ending an abusive relationship, the stage that includes the restructuring of the self in which "women must change their self image of being a battered woman and to view themselves as survivors rather than victims" (386). Finally, these reform programs are successful only if they embrace not only intervention but also education. As a county attorney staff member put it,

> What's our goal here? If our goal is to get better, let's honestly strip down some of the myths and really start looking at it [domestic violence] ... we need to say what's best here for family units and children and sometimes that's not a popular position, but at the end of the day, long term, I think that we'll be proven to show that it was the better position.
>
> (K-27)

For all these reasons, in our next chapter, we endorse a public health approach to domestic violence.

We mention again that those agencies and advocacy groups that see LAP as the catalyst for systemic change and an inroad into cultural change express a guarded but optimistic perspective. A county attorney staff member concluded that "domestic violence is going to continue to happen, and whatever we can do to see if we can help make victims safer ... to provide better services whether it's law enforcement or advocacy services or prosecution services ... is great" (W-5). A community corrections officer involved in IDAPP agreed with this perspective:

> Domestic violence is an ongoing dilemma that we will probably never cure, but we will certain try to utilize the services that we have available to enhance the delivery to some level of additional public safety. That's our goal—a safer community.
>
> (K-20)

Thus, a first responder learned that domestic violence victims "are not going to leave until they are ready to leave," but eventually may begin "to believe that they don't need this person"; this responder supplements the administration of the LAP questionnaire with such comments as "'Let's think about this. Does this sound like a good environment for you and your kids?'" (W-7). The goal is to avoid Othering the victim and to resist focusing exclusively on punishing or managing the offender and instead turn to better addressing and changing cultural values.

Certainly, throughout this book, the Van Keuren case, and within this chapter, the Gonzales case, illustrate the complicated roles of gender identity and performance in domestic violence. Jealousy, anger, insecurity, and proprietariness all contribute to this complexity as do the false dichotomy of agency and victimization and the place of cultural norms seen within Othering. Particularly hopeful in overcoming these challenges are the Lethality Assessment Protocol, additional LAP-related advocacy programs, and pre-trial counseling. Whether victim-centered or abuser-centered, the two LAP-related programs depend on persuasive strategies ranging from fear of death as supported, at times, by verbally violent language to self-benefit as affirmed by judges and prosecutors. The challenge remains as to whether LAP and the associated programs can achieve behavior modification and management as well as change cultural mind-sets and values. Finally, feminist, rhetorical, and discursive perspectives illuminate these challenges. Texts set within organizations and systems such as probation offices, judicial chambers and public courtrooms, and victim advocacy groups have long been the focus of professional communication researchers. Rhetorical scholars have likewise examined new genres, such as the LAP questionnaire, and deconstruction of dichotomies and metaphorical language illuminate the values that inform discourse. Othering, marginalizing, and predictive stereotyping of offenders, as we demonstrated in Chapter 3 and as a focus of rhetorical as well as feminist scholars, can inadvertently reduce the power of stakeholders to resolve conflict and mismanagement. Such Othering of domestic violence victims seems based on the assumption that the unguided victim will recant and return to her abuser. In the next, our concluding chapter, we not only review the theoretical and applied significance of our study but we also update the reader on the current status of MSOP and LAP, as well as the public and political response to the *Karsjens* opinion.

5 Final Perspectives

The Rhetoric of the Civil Commitment Debate and the Lethality Assessment Protocol

Throughout this book, rhetorical analysis and professional communication perspectives, in conjunction with feminist and cultural analysis, have revealed the complexities regarding legal, legislative, and public discourse about two types of violent crimes against women: domestic violence and sexual assault. We have focused on two specific studies to illuminate the different directions that policymaking and protocols have taken regarding that violence against women: the debate over civil commitment of sex offenders, as exemplified by the Minnesota Sex Offender Program (MSOP), and attempts to identify high-risk domestic violence victims, as in the Lethality Assessment Protocol (LAP). In this concluding chapter, we refer back to MSOP as a study that demonstrates how policy solutions can be derailed by media coverage, public fear, and partisanship sustained in public discourse. We also remind our readers that when fear is out of balance with actual risk and with offender treatment needs, then attempts at reform, education, and intervention tend not to succeed. We then review LAP as a catalyst for change in judicial and legal systems, throughout the country and more specifically in the Minnesota counties of Anoka and Washington, by reflecting again on the experiences of those now administering and responding to LAP and the additional protocols and genres that have come from LAP.

In the remainder of the chapter and in keeping with our pattern of grounding theoretical perspectives in examples and anecdotes, we bring our readers up to date on the situations in Minnesota involving MSOP and LAP as of this writing. We first describe a community meeting intended to educate the public about the integration of a sex offender into the rural community of Le Center, MN, and the ways in which that meeting reflects many of the ideas about moral panic and Othering that we discussed in Chapters 1 and 3. We then describe in more detail the judge's decision in the 2015 federal trial, *Karsjens et al. v. Jesson et al.*, which found the state statutes governing MSOP to be unconstitutional as written and as applied, the reaction to which shows some signs of continuing and yet some signs of easing the kairotic cycle of political pressure described in Chapter 1. That is, by February 2016, six sex offenders had been conditionally discharged from MSOP. These actions were speculated to be caused by "a possible easing of attitudes toward offenders," according to "experts" interviewed for media coverage (Serres 2016, February 10, n.p.). We end our discussions of MSOP by comparing Minnesota's program with the civil commitment policies of Wisconsin, much as did experts testifying in the *Karsjens* case, to demonstrate how such discursive acts as community education can support such potentially controversial programs.

Finally, we move back to LAP to consider an expedited case program in Anoka County and a new stalking initiative in Washington and Hennepin Counties. These LAP-related programs further demonstrate how the protocol has served as a catalyst for continued communication and collaboration, as described in Chapters 2 and 4. We then consider the idea of taking a public health perspective for domestic violence, and in particular sharing how, in public health, nurses are involved in furthering LAP systemic change to curtail violence against women. And, we end this chapter and this book with a reminder of how such studies of domestic violence and sexual assault can contribute to rhetoric and professional communication perspectives for both scholars and activists.

A Brief Review of the MSOP and LAP Chapters

In Chapter 1, we demonstrated how sex offenders elicit a public response of fear and anger, for example, a kind of moral panic seen in what we called kairotic cycles, because the public may feel backed into a corner and may not have access to the sort of discussions that would prompt a different sort of discourse and lead to effective systemic change. As we have also shown in Chapter 3, when sex offenders are Othered, policymakers and stakeholders actually lose a type of power and agency—the power to create solutions that address the overcrowding in civil commitment facilities, the high cost of civilly confining offenders after they have completed their prison sentences, the disregard for the constitutional rights of offenders, and the failure to reintegrate offenders back into the community in a timely but safe manner. Additionally, using the theoretical framework we introduced in Chapters 1 and 3, we have shown that there remains a need for constructive discussion that might better constitute a sort of "rhetorical listening" when it comes to the discourses surrounding the civil commitment of sex offenders. From Ratcliffe (2005), that is, we recall that rhetorical listening is an interpretive mode that "signifies a stance of openness that a person may choose to assume in relation to any person, text, or culture" (55). Moreover, we have endeavored to add a new layer to questions about the practices of Othering—a layer that considers the discursive implications of assigning power to a group through discourses that serve to perpetuate fear of that group. We hope that this new approach to conceptualizing the discursive implications of Othering a feared or loathed group within society may help shape new ideas about approaches to policymaking and their relevance to rhetorical and professional communication studies, as well as illuminate ways to make progress in civil commitment programs and policy that can also help address the issue of violence against women.

In Chapters 2 and 4, in our analysis of the rhetorical work of LAP, we explored the intersections of genre theory and gender studies in order to better understand how the LAP has shaped and sustained ongoing collaboration and systemic changes to policies regarding domestic violence intervention. In Chapter 2, we demonstrated how the LAP questionnaire, as a new genre within an expansive protocol, aims to work against the discursive and cultural assumptions associated with the domestic violence victim and subsequently must stand up to the high expectations placed upon it. As we described, LAP is meant to change the perception and subsequent behavior of the victim of domestic violence so that she might choose to take certain actions, such as separate from her abuser—a difficult and, at times, unsafe decision for the victim. Our analysis of LAP thus pushes the boundaries of genre theory by considering not only the extent to which LAP changes current domestic violence policies, but also how a genre may be used to alter not only actions but also beliefs—again, a result that those in the legal and judicial systems greatly encourage, but one that the victim might fear and resist for good reason. Chapter 4 continued the focus on how LAP has served as a catalyst for major systemic changes in the Minnesota counties of Anoka and Washington through a discussion of additional LAP-related advocacy programs, although we also revealed the problematic dichotomy of agency versus victimization as well as victim-focused versus offender-focused domestic violence programs. Thus, we considered whether, given cultural gender roles, LAP may inadvertently Other the domestic violence victim, if a victim does not change her mind about the level of danger she might be in or the source of that danger. While domestic violence remains an ongoing dilemma, agencies and advocacy groups view LAP with quiet optimism, as it continues to shape new protocols intended to assist the domestic violence victim as she attempts to locate resources and potentially leave her abuser.

Overall, then, we hope that throughout this book we have identified not only how such perspectives can illuminate the challenges of curtailing sexual assault and domestic violence but also how scholars and activists may recognize the strategies by which major organizational and social changes are introduced and ultimately either considered successful or remain unrealized.

The Current Status of the Minnesota Sex Offender Program

The MSOP debate continues to develop and, in some cases, potentially stall in response to changing discourses and policies based on sometimes shifting but sometimes stagnant ideas about public safety and the treatment of offenders in sexual assault cases. A public meeting about the integration of Level 3 sex offender Robert Jeno into the community of Le Center, MN, for example, illustrates the ways in which fear and moral panic continue to function in the civil commitment debate.

Moral Panic and the Othering of a Sex Offender in Le Center, MN

On December 16, 2014, one of us attended and observed a community meeting, open to the public, in which residents of Le Center, MN, gathered at the Tri-City United Le Center gymnasium to learn about and discuss the upcoming provisional discharge of sex offender Robert Jeno from MSOP into the community. Jeno, a Level 3 sex offender who sexually assaulted two adult women in 1982 and 1983, served almost 11 years in prison and was moved to MSOP in 1992 (Associated Press 2014, n.p.). Jeno did not commit his prior offenses in Le Center, a small rural community of approximately 2,500 people. The town was chosen as the community for his reintegration partially because he had family living in the area (Associated Press 2014, n.p.). Additionally, Shiloh's Hope, an all-male adult care facility in Le Center, was prepared to accept him. Like Ming Sen Shiue, whom if ever paroled from federal prison or finished with his criminal sentence, would be immediately transferred to MSOP, Jeno was civilly committed because he was found to be likely to reoffend; however, Jeno was provisionally discharged because he was considered "no longer dangerous" (Minnesota Statutes 2014, 253D.29; 253D.02 subd 15; 253D.02 subd 16).

The Le Center community meeting included an introduction and endorsement of the discharge given by the Le Center Police Department and a presentation by a representative from the Department of Corrections (DOC). Several news organizations attended, along with about 70 people from the community, as well as Representative Tony Cornish, who had sponsored the failed House bill to extend prison sentences for sex offenders rather than indefinitely civilly committing them; the MSOP reintegration director; a representative from the Rice County Attorney's Office (the county where Jeno committed his offences and which originally petitioned to have him civilly committed); and two representatives from Shiloh's Hope. The DOC representative began by stressing the educational goal of the meeting—discussing recidivism statistics, introducing aspects of the law, and giving tips to parents on how to avoid acquaintance and familial rape. The educational goals of the meeting included deflecting the audience's attention from possible fear of Jeno and instead teaching the audience about the myths of sexual assault by strangers, the responsible ways in which Jeno would be managed in Le Center, and the legal requirements of how Jeno must be managed. After all, at this time Jeno was only the third sex offender provisionally discharged from MSOP in two decades, and certainly Le Center had no experience with the process.

The DOC representative conveyed to the residents of Le Center that Jeno was not any more of a threat, and even less of a threat, than those sex offenders already in the area but largely unknown to the community. She noted, for example, that offenders are civilly committed according to the definitions in the statutes. She described that community notification must take place for all Level 3 sex offenders when they move into a community—and for all provisionally discharged from MSOP regardless of their level (Minnesota Statutes 2014, 244.052; 253D.29). She went on to distinguish for the audience the differences between the registration of sex offenders and the supervision of sex offenders and then noted that as of January 1, 2014, there were 17,500 "active" predatory offenders registered in MN, and eleven already living in Le Center, a statistic that certainly would surprise most members of the audience.

The DOC representative then explained how risk levels are actuarially arrived at and stressed the statistics that demonstrated how little the community had to fear from Jeno himself. For example, only 10 percent of sex offenders had a prior conviction; 90 percent would not reoffend and could live safely in close proximity to community members; and 86 to 90 percent were known by the victim, not strangers such as Jeno but instead family members and acquaintances. Moreover, she pointed out that during a three-year study in Minnesota, between 1990–2002, there was a 2.5 percent reduction of reconviction of sex offenders, and in a more recent four-year MN study, the recidivism rate was just slightly higher, at 3.3 percent, thus demonstrating that community members had very little to fear from Robert Jeno in contrast to other types of offenders. The DOC representative also outlined Jeno's prior and continuing treatment for mental health and chemical dependency issues and his registration as a sex offender for life. Thus, she stressed that the DOC and MSOP knew everything about Jeno and were prepared to help the community stay safe from him.

The DOC representative also showed a slide on risk management as particular to Jeno, describing court-imposed conditions ranging from GPS monitoring to polygraphs to random drug tests. Jeno would also be subject to other protective factors such as supervised housing and expectations of employment, although at most, given his developmental disabilities, Jeno might be able to handle part-time work. She stressed that MSOP reintegration specialists would be involved with the case, and that Jeno would have daily face-to-face meetings for the first 30 days of his provisional discharge. Jeno would also have 24-hour supervision and treatment and no direct or indirect contact with minors. Finally, she emphasized again that people should really direct their attention to the eleven other already registered sex offenders in Le Center and ended her presentation with tips for parents on how to protect children, monitor teenagers, recognize behavioral signs of abuse, and be alert to any red flags when adults were around children.

Following the presentation, audience members had the opportunity to ask questions, most of which were fielded by the MSOP reintegration director. Despite the specific details and thorough information provided during this meeting, the emphasis on public safety and on low recidivism did not seem to reassure members of the audience, many of whom were outspoken with their questions and concerns. The DOC representative's emphasis on the fact that sex offenders already resided in the community—and the greater danger of acquaintance or familial abuse—did not seem to allay overall fear and panic. As we discussed in Chapter 1, moral panic might constitute an expected response to Jeno's provisional discharge from MSOP, for, as Cohen (1980) might put it, Jeno's provisional discharge can be seen as constituting "a threat to societal values and interests" (9). As Garland (2008) further interpreted Cohen's ideas, Jeno's discharge could incite a moral panic, or a "sudden and excessive feeling of alarm and fear ... leading to extravagant or injudicious efforts to secure safety" (10). Consistent with these ideas, we captured some representative questions and comments from the audience at the Le Center public meeting, which revealed a sort of moral panic to be taking place, despite the presenters' thorough discussion and attempts to allay such fears.

One audience member, for example, asked what sort of recent bad behavior Jeno had exhibited, to which the MSOP reintegration director responded that he had been very compliant throughout his civil commitment and had been working for the last three years on his provisional discharge plan and community reintegration preparation. Consistent with Ahmed's (2000) ideas about the discourses of "stranger danger," many of these citizens seem concerned with "[t]he enforcement of boundaries," which thus requires, or assumes, as Ahmed puts it, "that some-body ... has already crossed the line, has already come too close" (21–22). One audience member asked, for example, why Jeno would be integrated into a 2500-person community where everyone knows everyone else; this person noted, we are "good heartwarming people," but doubted that this would be the best situation for him. Were there no other options? The MSOP reintegration director reasserted the care with which the MSOP community reintegration staff study the totality of what each offender needs. Similarly, another audience member noted that Shiloh's Hope was located in a very active part of the community—that members of the community sit out in their backyards. The response here was again that this location was desirable for Jeno's support system—that he must be housed in a typical neighborhood for successful reintegration. When one audience member likewise asked why Jeno must live in Le Center, another woman shouted: "People like Jeno never change!" Another community member also asked the DOC representative with a challenging tone, "Do you have any offenders in your backyard?" Here, her response was: "Absolutely, there are sex offenders in every community." Again, consistent with some of Ahmed's ideas, the audience members seemed to describe Le Center as a community that had produced a sort of pure, homogeneous space by way of living together closely; as Ahmed (2000) says:

> The model of the neighbourhood as an organic community—where a sense of community arises from the simple fact of shared residence—defines social health in terms of the production of purified spaces and the expulsion of difference through ways of living together.
>
> (25)

Citing concerns about public safety and recidivism, audience members also asked, if once in Le Center, Jeno might just be waiting for an opening to reoffend; that is, whether, on a solo outing, he would go directly to where he was supposed to be going, such as a convenience store, and what steps Shiloh's Hope itself would take to keep the community safe. Here, the MSOP reintegration director and others noted that Shiloh's Hope had male overnight staff, that there would be increased staffing there and additional staff training, as well as alarms on Jeno's windows and the back door. When asked what would happen if Jeno escaped, it was noted that he would be wearing a GPS monitor and that authorities would learn very quickly of the situation. The audience's continued questions reflected their persisting fears. Another audience member asked again how quickly the GPS would work, and another asked if Jeno would ever appear out in the yard at Shiloh house, near a play area for children, even though the DOC representative had emphasized more than once that Jeno's criminal history did not include victimizing children (Moniz 2014, n.p.). Again, as Ahmed (2000) describes, the discourse of "stranger danger" also invokes "the vulnerable body, the one who is most at risk. Here, 'the child' becomes the figure of vulnerability, the purified body that is most endangered by the contaminating desires of strangers" (34). It is possible to see, then, that the Le Center public meeting about Robert Jeno illustrates the continuing challenge of reintegrating provisionally discharged sex offenders into the community after they have completed treatment during civil commitment. The idea of provisionally discharging convicted sex offenders into the community continues to invoke public fear and moral panic, which then perpetuates the Othering of sex offenders.

Possible Political and Public Impasse after Karsjens et al. v. Jesson et al.

The judge's decision in *Karsjens et al. v. Jesson et al.* (2015) served as the catalyst for another possible kairotic moment in the cycle of political impasse to reform civil commitment in Minnesota. After almost six weeks of testimony in the *Karsjens* case, on June 17, 2015, United States District Judge Donovan W. Frank found in the class action suit brought by 14 named plaintiffs, all current MSOP clients, that the Minnesota statutes governing civil commitment and treatment of sex offenders were unconstitutional as written and as applied. Immediately, Minnesota Governor Dayton indicated that he would appeal the decision, and Department of Human Services (DHS) Commissioner Lucinda Jesson, who oversees MSOP and was one of the named defendants in the trial, publicly disagreed with Frank's decision. However, in July 2015, Judge Frank denied the state's motion for appeal and appointed a special master to oversee the litigation challenging the program (Serres 2015, July 24, n.p.). And currently, the MSOP and others are awaiting a decision from the Eighth Circuit Court of Appeals.

In his decision, Judge Frank asserted that the *Karsjens* case challenged "the boundaries that we the people set on the notions of individual liberty and freedom, the bedrock principles embedded in the United States Constitution"; the preservation of such liberties demanded scrutiny to ensure that any process that deprives a person's liberty must be "narrowly tailored" so that detention was "absolutely limited to a period of time necessary to achieve these narrow governmental objectives" (*Karsjens* 2015, 2). Moreover, Frank challenged the Othering that potentially occurs under such detention: "One reason why we must be so careful about civil commitment is that it can be used by the state to segregate undesirables from society by labeling them with a mental abnormality or personality disorder" (*Karsjens* 2015, 3). In his own scrutiny of MSOP, Frank determined that the plaintiffs' testimony had been convincing in terms of the disadvantaged status of MSOP clients. Certainly there are some sex offenders confined through MSOP, wrote the judge, "who are truly dangerous and who should not be released" but there were others "who should have been released, provisionally or otherwise, some time ago" (*Karsjens* 2015, 5). However, Judge Frank also reassured all stakeholders that Moose Lake and St. Peter, the high-security MSOP settings, would not be closed instantly and all offenders released, but that there were other changes "that could be made immediately" to remedy the problems discerned in MSOP. Two primary changes might be to perform annual risk assessments on all MSOP clients to see if they still met the criteria for confinement and to reconcile the criteria for discharge with the criteria for confinement, the latter of which was more stringent than the former.

Certainly any hint of closing MSOP facilities and releasing a number of civilly committed sex offenders would cause moral panic, again, as we saw in Chapter 1 and as defined by Cohen (1980), Filler (2003), and others. Demonized for threatening social values, those events upsetting to the so-called "normal" within society cause extreme emotional and often irrational response. Instead, Judge Frank, as did the plaintiffs in the case, cast MSOP clients in the role of victims involved in an unfair game of chance. The civil commitment statute, as applied by MSOP, "is a three-phased treatment system," said the judge, "with 'chutes-and-ladders'-type mechanisms for impeding progress, without periodic review of progress, which has the effect of confinement to the MSOP facilities for life" (*Karsjens* 2015, 65). In a similar strategy, this time addressed to politicians as well as their constituents, Judge Frank anticipated those features of moral panic identified by Garland (2008) that can lead to "extravagant and injudicious efforts to secure safety" (10), particularly by policymakers in response to public outcry. However, the judge warned, "The Court must emphasize that politics and political pressures cannot trump the fundamental rights of Class Members who, pursuant to state law, have been civilly committed to receive treatment. The Constitution protects individual rights even when they are unpopular" (*Karsjens* 2015, 68). And, in what seemed an attempt to avoid destructive divisions, the judge reminded his readers that he "is sensitive to the interests of all individuals affected by this matter, as well as the fears and concerns of the public at large, including, of course, victims of these heinous and tragic crimes" (*Karsjens* 2015, 68–69). To meet the Court's "obligation to all citizens to not only honor their constitutional rights, but to do so without compromising public safety and the interests of justice," the judge pledged to meet that goal: "The balance is a delicate and important one, but it can and will be done" (*Karsjens* 2015, 69).

Judge Frank, then, in these "Findings of Fact, Conclusions of Law, and Order," appeared to try to stem what we have identified in Chapter 1 as a kairotic cycle of moments condemned to repeat without resolution, when *kairos* is so heavily influenced by moral panic and inaccurate perceptions of risk that the right choice cannot be persuasive or obtainable. As we did in Chapter 1, we looked at recent media coverage to help predict whether the MSOP debate might sink back into unresolvable kairotic cycles again or might achieve the delicate balance that Judge Frank envisioned. Again, according to Hall (1978), Zatz (1978), and more recently Welch, Price, and Yankey (2002), the media often contribute to public feelings about risk—in this case, the risk that high-risk sex offenders will be discharged from a reformed MSOP. Certainly, Judge Frank's ruling caught the attention of the local news media, which, within hours of the decision, characterized it as "scathing," a ruling that "sets the stage for what could be a long and bruising battle between the courts and state officials" (Serres 2015, June 17, n.p.). The attorney for the plaintiffs in the case predicted the debate would continue, regardless of the judge's August 2015 remedy proposal pre-hearing: "'[N]o one is going to go out on a limb and agree to reforms until everyone is in agreement,'" to do otherwise would be "'politically unwise'" (Serres 2015, June 17, n.p.).

Those long involved in MSOP began to express their support of Judge Frank's thinking. Don Betzold (2015), for example, a former state senator who helped rewrite the 1939 civil commitment law on civil commitment of psychopathic personalities, wrote in the local *StarTribune* that he had long ago stressed that civil commitment was for treatment rather than incarceration and that a number of MSOP clients are "not now dangerous at all"—in fact, some "are old men in wheelchairs and on walkers" (n.p.). Betzold (2015) also credited Judge Frank for the reasonableness in giving "Minnesota officials one last chance to work with him to change the law and the program, so that we can keep the really dangerous offenders in a realistic treatment program" (n.p.). Moreover, Jeffrey Brown (2015), one of the first psychologists hired to do risk assessment for sex offenders scheduled for release from Minnesota prisons, confirmed that civil commitment had become too politicized since the Dru Sjodin kidnapping and murder. Finally, the Editorial Board (2015) of the *StarTribune* urged policymakers to cooperate with Judge Frank on MSOP reforms. Quoting Governor Dayton's resolve to "defend Minnesota's law," MSOP, and the civil commitment statutes, the Board warned, "Daring the court to act again by displaying unwillingness to cooperate is imprudent" (n.p.). The Board found Judge Frank's approach "careful, deliberate and sensitive to understandable public fears," but noted that it "doesn't let Minnesota's political leaders duck their responsibility to fix this troubled program" (n.p.). State political leaders have long known, the Board claimed, that MSOP was "very likely unconstitutional," but did nothing, "self-servingly fearing that political opponents would accuse them of being 'soft on crime'" (n.p.). Not only was there a turn in local media coverage from the earlier Clarence Opheim provisional discharge, a turn to now calming the public, praising the judge, and pointing the finger at entrenched policymakers, but also the national media weighed in similarly on the judge's ruling. Again, *The New York Times* offered that the decision was being watched by the 19 other states in which civil commitment of some sort was the practice.

At the time we write this conclusion to our book, the broader implications of the *Karsjens* ruling remain unclear. But again, in early August 2015, Benjamin Gissendanner, "who raped a woman in an alley in New York City in 1970 and then 11 years later twice raped a St. Paul college student after breaking into her apartment," was granted provisional discharge after a Supreme Court Appeals Panel decided that he had made sufficient treatment progress to justify being moved from MSOP to a less restricive placement and into the community (Serres 2015, August 11, n.p.). Then, in late August, the decision to provisionally discharge Chris Coker ignited controversy, largely because of the severity of his crimes and the disagreement by some state officials and mental health professionals about his progress in treatment and cooperation while in MSOP. On the one hand, a three-judge panel ruled that he had demonstrated "great progress away from sexual dangerousness" (Serres 2015, August 26, n.p.). On the other hand, one judge on the panel that approved Coker's petition for discharge "wrote a rare dissenting opinion, arguing that his 'lack of cooperation with his treatment team' and opposition to terms of his discharge plan made him unfit for living in the community" (Serres 2015, August 26, n.p.). Finally, one of the most well-known local media outlets in the Twin Cities, the *StarTribune*, interviewed Richard Williams, a 61-year-old sex offender ready for conditional discharge from MSOP. Along with describing the treatment that Williams had and the monitoring that he would experience once back in the community, the newspaper offered Williams' view of his situation: "Even now, after years of therapy, Williams rejects the ideas that he can be 'cured,' like someone with a disease. In his view, sex crimes result from underlying feelings of rejection and resentment that can be 'managed,' but never cured" (Serres 2016, February 20, n.p.). Moreover, Williams admitted during the interview: "You can never be sure you're not going to reoffend ... I agree with that because once you've done something, it's easier the next time" (Serres 2016, February 20, n.p.). In turn, one reader responded to Williams' frank assessment by saying:

> For many of us, rape would be a near-death experience that would leave its mark for the rest of our lives. I believe that the risks are too high, and unless the offender is physically unable to do further lifelong harm, he should not be released to any venue where there is a chance he could slip away.
>
> (Johnson, Carol, 2016, n.p.)

These decisions to conditionally discharge more sex offenders from MSOP may reflect, as noted months earlier, "the intense pressure the state is facing to reform the MSOP" (Serres 2015, August 26, n.p.). The state clearly is facing strong pressures to reform MSOP, and it remains to be seen, to a degree of optimism as yet realized in these civil commitment debates, whether the *Karsjens* decision and the political response that follows will quiet public fears and political maneuvering and thus lead to reform—that "delicate" balance that Judge Frank envisioned.

The Discourse of Public Education in Wisconsin

For those imagining how to achieve that balance, the participants in the 2012 Mitchell Hamline symposium, the experts who testified at the *Karsjens* case, and even Judge Frank in his ruling mentioned other states where broader systemic management of sex offenders rely on continuing public education. In considering other systemic approaches to managing sex offenders, Judge Frank and four court-appointed expert witnesses or "Rule 706 experts" (Legal Information Institute 2015b, n.p.) invoked the civil commitment policies and programs in Wisconsin as another persuasive strategy to support the reform of MSOP.

Before August 2015, no sex offender had ever been unconditionally discharged from MSOP, and only three had been provisionally discharged, two successfully and one unsuccessfully. Wisconsin, on the other hand, during this same period had "fully discharged 118 offenders and placed about 135 on supervised release since 1994" (Serres 2015, June 17, n.p.). These statistics point out an uncomfortable contrast between the failure of MSOP to discharge its clients and the so-called success of another system. As mentioned above, Judge Frank felt that two primary and necessary changes to MSOP might be to perform annual risk assessments on all MSOP clients to see if they still met the criteria for confinement and to reconcile the criteria for discharge with the criteria for confinement. In the *Karsjens* trial, for example, the plaintiffs revealed that forensic risk assessments were conducted only at the time a client himself took the initiative to petition for discharge or for a transfer in custody. Annual risk assessments, the plaintiffs felt, were needed to measure progress in treatment and could correct not only for the great increases in civil commitments after the Rodriguez case but also the lack of any full discharges and the extremely low number of provisional discharges. According to one Rule 706 expert testifying in *Karsjens*, these more accurate assessment tools might reveal that a number of clients confined to MSOP might not indeed "meet the statutory requirements for confinement" (Miner 2015, n.p.). Moreover, a senior staff psychologist from the secure juvenile treatment facility in Wisconsin testified, "a fresh set of eyes" was very important to "rule out a lot of people who should have never been committed" (Caldwell 2015, n.p.). In testimony, the sex offenders civilly committed to MSOP were not Othered as a dangerous group but instead cast as victims of a system because of unfair limitations of constitutionally protected freedoms.

In the Wisconsin program at Sand Ridge Secure Treatment Center (SRSTC), for example, as Freeman et al. (2014) describe in the Rule 706 Experts' *Report and Recommendations*, submitted pre-trial, planning for release begins upon admission and continues throughout treatment. Additionally, a client may be released from SRSTC at any time during their placement, thus initiating a systemic approach of ensuring that "patients and staff are continuously planning for release" and "targeting community reintegration issues" from the start (Freeman et al. 2014, 92). And so, with regard to supervised release (SR), Wisconsin has conveyed a commitment to prepare and inform the community in tandem with preparing the client, in order to alleviate fear and encourage compassion.

As Freeman et al. (2014) describe, SR includes tailored community notification by local law enforcement, and also what is called a "Core Team" approach, "which includes a multi-disciplinary team of stakeholders that assists law enforcement in determining the level of community notification" (95–96). This is a highly collaborative, systemic process that involves parole officers, case managers, victim advocates, and other professionals. The Core Team, for example, meets to determine the level of notification needed; levels may range from notifying schools and neighbors via flyers to notification via media release and/or a public community notification meeting. In Wisconsin, at community meetings,

> order is maintained by law enforcement and, if necessary, unruly citizens are asked to leave. To reduce spontaneous outcries by audience members, attendees are not permitted to ask questions from the floor, but rather are provided with notecards upon which to write their questions, which are addressed by presenters during the meeting. (97)

Such a practice may be understood as encouraging listening over speaking, which could potentially prevent the sort of Othering that was perpetuated by some remarks at the Le Center, MN, community meeting, as well as possibly promote a calmer atmosphere that may result in more productive conversation and education. In a sense, then, the practice of submitting written questions in advance may be read as a form of "rhetorical listening," borrowing again from Ratcliffe (2005), in which audience members' questions become texts that are then read, heard, and interpreted within the context of the community meeting. Along similar lines, Wisconsin's program also sees public education as part of its goal, and "has taken the position that it is responsible for providing education and information whenever the opportunity arises in order to dispel myths and provide accurate information about safety measures that can be employed to reduce vulnerability to sexual assault" (Freeman et al. 2014, 98).

While Robert Jeno committed his offences in Rice County, he was provisionally discharged to Le Center, which is in Le Sueur County. In Wisconsin, on the other hand, as Freeman et al. (2014) note, sex offenders released from civil commitment are returned to their communities of residence, "an important factor" that is conveyed not only to the communities and stakeholders but to the media: "[I]t is critical to citizens and stakeholders of any given county to hear that the court's order is to return sexual offenders they consider 'their own' and not others from other counties" (98). On the one hand, this can help work against Othering by creating a sense of fairness; on the other hand, however, as Freeman et al. (2014) note, "[I]t is not the panacea of accepting the return of persons who sexually offend in communities and the program continues to be challenged with developing and implementing SR plans to return civilly committed sexual offenders to the community" (98). For in many ways, as Ahmed (2000) says, "The neighbour who is also a stranger—who only passes as a neighbour—is hence the danger that may always threaten the community from within" (26). Nonetheless, while Wisconsin's program is not without its challenges, the Rule 706 experts generally contrasted it to MSOP, stressing a systemic approach to the management of sex offenders along with a careful management of community reaction. In the *Karsjens* trial this contrast fulfilled the rhetorical function of refuting the defendants' claims that MSOP functioned successfully.

The Current Status of the Lethality Assessment Protocol

Similar systemic and collaborative approaches to domestic violence characterize the LAP-initiated or LAP–related programs within Anoka and Washington Counties, MN, as of August 2015. The first of these is the expedited domestic violence case program in Anoka County. Although a nuanced view of this program shows the continuing tension between attending to the needs of the victim and yet serving the requirements of the legal system, in this case prosecution of offenders, the program has achieved its goals.

Managing Recantation in an Expedited Domestic Violence Case Program

As Kohn (2008) and others have found, domestic violence victims are viewed as "unreliable partners" by law enforcement, prosecution, and even advocates, an image enforced by cultural gender roles. Kohn even finds that the widely endorsed Duluth Power and Control Wheel "reinforces the image of domestic violence victims as unable to act in their best interests" (208; see also, Domestic Abuse Intervention Project n.d). One aspect of that so-called unreliability occurs when a victim recants her complaint against an abuser and withdraws her cooperation with prosecution before the case is settled or goes to trial. As one judge commented,

> I think that a lot of our victims go for 10 days or 4 weeks or 5 weeks, and, you know, of course the breadwinner is not home and is spending money somewhere else to live, or there is a huge economic impact of the no-contact order, and the child care issues, for instance, are immediately influenced.
>
> (W-25; again, see our Appendix for our interview citation style)

In reaction to this propensity for the victim to recant and in connection with LAP, Anoka County began an expedited domestic violence case program, a program that according to the County Attorney's Office "can benefit victim safety and recovery, and provide for more offender accountability" (Anoka County Attorney's Office n.d., n.p.). Specifically, the expedited program calls for a trial date to be set within three months of a felony defendant's first appearance in court, rather than within six to nine months or more as seen in the past. For misdemeanors and gross misdemeanors, the goal is two months from first appearance to conclusion. The program, which began in September 2011, saw 75 serious domestic violence cases expedited by March 2012, cases that had been determined to be high risk by the LAP screening questionnaire (Chanen 2012, March 29, n.p.). Moreover, the program was exceeding its goal by August 2013 when the average time in the system for a case was 78 days (K-26). Finally, the program directors saw fewer victims recant and make requests to drop no-contact orders.

Certainly, the expedited domestic violence program was designed to help the victim reach resolution and stability as quickly as possible, as well as aid her in getting the services to be safe and perhaps separate from her offender. However, others working within the LAP-related expedited program may still dwell on the perceived characteristics of victimization and struggle with the tension between helping the victim versus more efficiently using legal and judicial resources, a tension that we revealed in Chapter 2. One characteristic that can be assigned to the recanting victim, for example, is lack of honesty about the incident. As a first responder noted about victims who recant despite their answers on the LAP questionnaire, "It boils down to honesty and integrity, and, you know, 'Are you going to change your answers?'" (R-15). A community corrections staff member uses LAP as a tool to avoid recantation:

> And, I think that advocates use this, I have used it, "But wait a minute when you completed this [LAP questionnaire] on the night of the offense, you said that he has choked you in the past" ... when victims talk about going back to their partners or if they are going to recant their statements.
>
> (W-8)

Finally, a city attorney understood how "disruptive to the family environment" no-contact orders were and how victims are more likely to recant the longer the legal process takes, as "time heals all wounds"; a shorter time in the process, however, also "allows them to be on board and assist us in doing the right thing" (K-24). Time seems to help the victim "sugar coat" the incident and avoid cooperating with prosecution in doing the "right thing," metaphorical features of victimization such as those we explored in Chapter 4.

Therefore, a first responder described the challenge faced in expedited case programs to balance system efficiency with helping the victim: If a case takes 6 to 9 months,

> the couple could be working things out, which is good ... but then nobody is getting any help if they need it; the victim is not getting the services, and the defendant is not being held responsible for his actions.
>
> (K-9)

Knowing that recanting might occur despite case expedition, law enforcement in Anoka County, according to this officer, is now tape recording statements on the scene to capture "the exact words and the exact feelings at the time" as well as administering LAP, a strategy to hold victims accountable should they recant (K-9). A member of the County Attorney's staff expressed this same tension in that, given the new timetable, collecting sufficient evidence and locating witnesses to prosecute an offender were challenges, but "lingering cases are almost never good for anybody, including the victims" (K-27). The public may comment that the office was "not doing enough" in high-profile domestic violence cases, but this County Attorney's staff decided to ask: "'Do we want to get a mediocre result in nine or 10 months? Or do we try to get a better and more just result in three months?" (K-27). This decision was made in part to refute public accusation, to support prosecution, and to encourage the victim to take advantage immediately of the services within LAP.

Anoka County's expedited case program reflects the potential for Othering the victim even within efforts to understand her financial and psychological dilemma. Again, if that victim recants, prosecution is hindered in managing and punishing the offender. But to expedite cases, some compromises might be necessary in collecting evidence, accepting plea agreements, and arguing for more severe sentences.

Intervening Early in a Threat Assessment Advisory Group

The second LAP-related program we examine is in the initial stages of development but has great potential to curtail domestic violence systemically and before escalation of violence. According to the National Center for Victims of Crime (2015), 7.5 million people per year are stalked in the US, and 15 percent of women and 6 percent of men have experienced stalking in which they feared being harmed or killed. Moreover, as with Teri Lee and her children before she was killed by Steven Van Keuren, 76 percent of female domestic violence victims have been stalked by their intimate partners, and 54 percent of these victims reported to police that they were being stalked before they were ultimately killed by their stalkers. In response to these statistics, states such as Wisconsin have made stalking a felony offense and defined stalking accordingly:

> The actor knows or should know that at least one of the acts that constitute the course of conduct will cause the specific person to suffer serious emotional distress or place the person in reasonable fear of bodily injury or the death of himself or herself or a member of his or her family or household.
>
> (Wisconsin State Legislature 2015, n.p.)

Regardless of these responses and increasing knowledge about the alarming link between stalking and domestic homicide, stalking cases are still difficult to charge and prosecute. Nancy Halverson (2014) from Minnesota's Hennepin County Department of Community Corrections and Rehabilitation, for example, summarizes that challenge: "It is about perseverance rather than perfection. The reality of it is so few cases are actually charged and convicted of stalking, most of the time it is other stuff," such as property damage and trespassing (1). And yet again, intervening into a stalking situation may prevent the escalation to domestic abuse or sexual assault and eventual homicide.

Inspired by LAP and by the similar efforts in Oregon to better control and manage stalking cases, Hennepin and Washington Counties cooperated to create the Threat Assessment Advisory Group (TAG), one active participant of which initiated LAP into Washington County. The Oregon Threat Advisory Team, like TAG, does not manage or investigate cases but instead shares information and knowledge with law enforcement agencies, in particular, on how to handle such cases (Marin County n.d.). The Oregon team consists of representatives from law enforcement as well as from the courts, county attorneys, school districts, and health departments throughout the state. In Minnesota, TAG works in a similar fashion by helping agencies with "early identification of warning behaviors, the communication of risk, a coordinated and evidence-based response/management plan, and the sharing of vital information" (Threat Assessment Twin Cities n.d., n.p.). TAG states that by recognizing both stabilizing and destabilizing factors and certain triggers in specific cases, "violence may very well be averted" (n.p.). In this case, education of policymakers and law enforcement about stalking helps to preserve public safety.

A new genre, a questionnaire similar to that associated with LAP, is being piloted by TAG in Minnesota, but the data come not from victims but from law enforcement investigating stalking cases. Lorraine Sheridan and Karl Rogers (2011) created the questionnaire to enhance their study done in Wales and England because "it is well known that stalking victims often feel that no one takes them seriously, and the current evidence strongly suggests that we should listen carefully to these victims and act swiftly and accordingly" (269). The purpose of the stalking questionnaire is to help law enforcement "identify stalking, obsessional behaviors, and then accurately assess them for risk of violence" and then triage police, advocacy, and other resources (E-1). The stalking questionnaire was designed to focus on dynamic behaviors, behaviors going on at the moment, rather that the static behaviors that the LAP questionnaire might capture or the "has he or she ever" form of questions. Moreover, according to the first responder leading the implementation of the stalking questionnaire, unlike LAP, which as an actuarial tool looks at how the individual fits into a specific low- or high-risk group, the stalking form tries to capture individual risk factors or "get specific with the victims" and better manage the offenders (E-1). Finally, TAG identifies three or four officers in each department to follow up with stalking victims.

Minnesota's TAG and Oregon's Threat Advisory Team attempt to avoid the high- and low-risk dichotomies of LAP and instead focus on advising agencies on how to help the victim as well as manage not only the offender but also limited resources. With an individual approach to each case and yet systemic collaboration, false dichotomies might be avoided. Ideally agencies will come away from TAG with a new perspective; for example, probation might cooperate with law enforcement or prosecution by making such calls as the following: "Heh, Joe Blow, he is on our papers right now; he is on probation ... I just heard about this [stalking] case with him. We need to do A, B, and C with him" (E-1). The expedited domestic violence case program, as well as Hennepin and Washington Counties' TAG program, represent the future of systemic approaches to curtail domestic violence through intervention and education—policy and protocols supporting by discourse.

Widening the System through Public Health Involvement

To maintain or improve systemic approaches to both domestic violence and sexual assault, such as administering risk assessment protocols, offering intervention and treatment, and maintaining public safety, some stakeholders suggest public health involvement, an approach we highly endorse. This involvement can be based on adopting the philosophy or perspectives of a public health approach as well as the inclusion of public health practitioners in the processes. Janus (2006), for example, has suggested a public health approach to sexual assault, or as he defines it, "a systemic application of scientific learning aimed at understanding and addressing root causes," much like that used to control infectious diseases (116). And, more than one interview participant discussing MSOP suggested that the best way to address sexual offenses was not to legislate regulations but to approach the problem as a public health problem: "If we were talking about, you know, we might get 200 guys a year with tuberculosis, people would be planning; they wouldn't be like creating kind of a leper colony [such as MSOP]" (C-3). This public health discourse serves to alter conceptions of Others who must be isolated, to people who deserve treatment and acceptance.

A public health approach, according to Janus, involves primary prevention efforts, secondary identification of high-risk cases, and tertiary efforts to reduce future outbreaks. In regard to domestic violence and within these three categories, the LAP questionnaire itself would be a secondary intervention approach, and the entire protocol, including the LAP-related programs that we covered above and in Chapter 4, would constitute an attempt to reduce future violence on the tertiary level.

This approach leads to thinking about violence "from the perspective of the population as a whole" (Janus 2006, 117), or as Louise Dixon and Nicola Graham-Kevan (2011) put it, when the principles of public health are used to understand the causes and consequences of violence, the goal is "to provide maximum benefit for the largest number of people possible" (1151). The first approach, which involves prevention efforts, might focus, as Serran and Firestone (2004) suggest, on early intervention into the home, particularly when children witness domestic violence, not only to provide family violence programs but also to challenge "our view about the private nature of family life" (10), countering cultural gender roles that may limit discourse about and progress toward curtailing domestic violence.

The public health approach matches the approaches to gender violence taken by the World Health Organization (WHO), which range from recognizing the effects of growing up with violence to promoting gender equity to prevent violence (WHO 2004; see also Abramsky et al. 2011). The perspective of WHO regarding domestic violence is as follows: "In addition to being a breach of human rights, intimate partner violence is associated with serious public-health consequences that should be addressed in national and global health policies and programmes" (Ellsberg et al. 2008, 1165). Taking a broad look at the effects of domestic violence on public health, a WHO study of such violence in 10 countries concluded that abused women suffer from a wide range of physical and psychological ailments, including gynecological disorders, chronic pain, depression, anxiety, post-traumatic stress disorder, and alcohol and drug abuse, irrespective of their cultural and racial backgrounds (Ellsberg et al. 2008, 1165, 1171; see also Campbell 2002; Garcia-Moreno 2005).

Nurses and other health care providers have adopted the perspective that domestic violence is not only an individual health issue but also a public health challenge. From Sweden, in the *Journal of Epidemiology & Community Health* (Krantz 2002), domestic violence is analogized to other diseases: "Worldwide it has been estimated that violence against women is as serious a cause of death and incapacity among women of reproductive age as cancer, and a greater cause of ill health than traffic accidents and malaria combined" (242). Similarly, the American Association of Colleges of Nursing (AACN) (2000) offered this stance: "Violence is a public health issue as perilous as any microbial disease" (64). Such analogies offer persuasive evidence that domestic violence deserves worldwide attention. Therefore, in the *International Journal of Gynecology and Obstetrics* (Ellsberg 2006), reproductive health programs, in particular, have been noted as providing "a unique window of opportunity to address the needs of abused women," and therefore routine inquiry and screening for violence is recommended for all women who attend health services regardless of the reason for the visit (328). Moreover, the AACN (2000) recommended that nurses be taught interventions "to reduce vulnerability and increase safety," the "legal and ethical issues" in treating and reporting domestic violence, and "assessment skills to identify and document abuse and its health effects" (63; see also Cann et al. 2001; Glass, Dearwater, and Campbell 2001). These perspectives constitute a "system-wide approach to domestic violence," including, according to Mary Ellsberg (2006), "training for providers, a domestic violence protocol, chart prompts, public health campaigns, provider feedback, quality improvements, and an on-site domestic violence coordinator" (328).

Those administering LAP in Minnesota Counties not only recognize the validity of a public health approach to domestic violence but also include public health departments in administering the protocol. For example, the Anoka County Attorney's Office directed their VAWA grant accordingly, because "we are looking at this as we would a public health issue, [and] public health can get into schools" (K-27). The Ramsey County Attorney's Office also decided, "One of the things we need to be doing is looking at domestic violence from a public health perspective ... and look at the data and try to understand who is most susceptible to being a batterer, to being a victim" (P-6). And so, when an advocacy group worked with high-risk victims as identified by LAP, the victim advocates asked permission to refer pregnant victims or those with children under the age of five years old to public health, a "really cool piece" of the protocol (K-18).

That "cool" piece of the protocol is carried out by public health nurses, who believe that trust is the foundation for their work with at-risk women and children. That trust is essential for victims to disclose their predicaments and wishes, and for public health nurses to connect these victims with services. Public health agencies do risk assessment screening, such as The Relationship Assessment Tool (2015), to measure women's experiences in violent relationships, or they rely on referrals from child protective services, medical clinics, schools, and such. These public health nurses look for stressors in a relationship such as children in the family under the age of five years old, stressors that increase the risk for violence. But that trust is established by the public health nurses by way of their evidence-based programs, their "reputable medical and social" expertise, and because of LAP, according to one interviewee, their additional "awareness and visibility" in communities (E-2). This interviewee confirmed that the nurses within her department rely on the "Power and Control Wheel" (Domestic Abuse Intervention Project, n.d.) to educate domestic violence victims who "can't see outside their situation," the most challenging task that these nurses might face because many such victims wish to "maintain that [abusive] relationship" (E-2). These public health nurses "help those victims to get help" (E-2).

And so, one goal in the Anoka County Community Health Improvement Plan for 2015–2019 includes continuing to "contribute to the work of the Anoka County Attorney's Office Domestic Violence Lethality Assessment Project" (Anoka County Community Health and Environmental Services 2015, 12). Finally indicating the possible success of a system-wide approach to domestic violence that includes public health perspectives, a study done in Duluth, MN, of public health nurses' experiences with a domestic violence assessment protocol in a maternal and child health visiting program revealed: "If one of the goals of public health nursing visits is prevention of health problems, these nurses clearly became knowledgeable, comfortable, and willing to work collaboratively with community resources regarding issues of domestic violence" (Shepard et al. 1999, 365).

If resolving the problems of MSOP, according to Judge Donovan Frank, requires a "delicate" balance of public safety concerns and the treatment needs and constitutional rights of civilly committed sex offenders, certainly extending what promises to be an effective lethality assessment protocol requires balancing the management of domestic abusers with the protection and agency of victims. The LAP-related programs as well as the public health perspectives we explored above arose in collaborative efforts and community support, with very little, if any, political opposition. For this reason, there is cause for optimism, if not celebration.

We end this book with our continued hope that within the detailed stories and legal cases related to MSOP and to LAP, we have demonstrated that rhetorical and professional communication studies of domestic violence and sexual assault can allow scholars and activists to more easily identify and analyze the challenges of curtailing, at the systemic level, what are essentially problems of violence against women. Although that systemic level might occur within organizations or agencies, such as a county attorney's office or a victim advocacy group, obviously to prove most effective some change must take place on the cultural level, such as in the gender roles and hierarchies that we have explored throughout this book. Moreover, such a theoretical framework may allow scholars and activists to recognize the strategies by which major organizational and social changes are introduced and ultimately considered successful or not. Whether that framework simply identifies the analogies and metaphors used to mark victims and offenders, extends our notions of how a genre disrupts the values and ideologies of a system, or contributes new perspectives on *kairos* and kairotic cycles, having the tools to identify the persuasive strategies in the discourse about sexual assault and domestic violence benefits us all.

Reflecting on the theoretical perspectives offered in Chapters 1 and 3, we believe that our approach to conceptualizing the discursive implications of Othering can help illuminate new, rhetorically informed ideas about how to approach policymaking and ultimately make progress in civil commitment programs and policy. Reflecting on Chapters 2 and 4, we believe that our discursive analysis of LAP pushes the boundaries of genre theory by revealing the ways in which LAP changes current domestic violence policies and by illustrating how a genre may attempt to alter the victim's actions and beliefs in ways that might be risky at first but safer in the long term.

As we have described in earlier work, efforts to institute positive, systemic change in many ways constitutes advocacy work, and "is all about knowledge making" (Schuster and Propen 2011, 160). Through this book, we have tried to reflect some of these ongoing systemic efforts and the persuasive practices that shape and inform them. We hope that we have represented our interview participants respectfully, for without them we would have had very little to say. Finally, we accept that the debate about civil commitment is not over, and the tragic and horrendous acts involved in sexual assault and domestic violence might never be totally eliminated from our cultural landscape. We believe, however, that future scholars and activists will continue the dialogue we have begun here.

Appendix

Research Design, Data Collection, and Analytical Perspectives

To understand the kairotic events, cycles, and contexts concerning the Minnesota Sex Offender Program (MSOP) and the implementation and administration of the Lethality Assessment Protocol (LAP) within Minnesota county agencies and advocacy groups, we conducted an interpretive, qualitative study by collecting, triangulating, and analyzing data in several ways. Thus, although we grounded our findings in some statistics gathered from other sources and about other locations, we found the specific comments from individuals involved in MSOP and LAP and passages from the documents relating to these two programs most revealing.

In both the case of MSOP and LAP, we certainly recognize that those in same sex relationships encounter violence as do non-intimate family members. Because of the events and documents that emerged within our study of MSOP and LAP, however, we chose to focus on female victims of domestic violence and domestic homicide. Moreover, females (76 percent) experience more domestic violence than do males (24 percent), males more frequently perpetrate domestic violence, and a greater percentage of domestic violence is committed by intimate partners than by immediate family members or other relatives (Bureau of Justice Statistics 2014, n.p.; Centers for Disease Control, 2010, n.p.). Moreover, of the more than 700 sex offenders confined to the MSOP at the time of this writing, only one is a female perpetrator. Therefore, throughout this book, we use "she" rather than "he/she" when referring to a domestic violence or sexual assault victim, and we use "he" when referring to an abuser or perpetrator.

Also, we use the term "domestic violence," rather than "intimate partner violence," because the former term is used more frequently by the participants in the MSOP and LAP debates and efforts. We recognize, however, that domestic violence is most often initiated by a husband, ex-husband, boyfriend, or ex-boyfriend; that such violence can take place anywhere; and that the partners need not be living together for that emotional, financial, identity, physical, and sexual abuse to take place. Finally, we believe that the term "domestic violence" frames a necessary contrast and correction to the misconceptions about the frequency of sexual assault and "stranger rape." According to a study done by the Center for Sex Offender Management (2000), for example, up to 76 percent of sexual assaults are committed by a current or former husband, partner, or acquaintance, rather than by a stranger.

For the MSOP portion for this study, we observed and analyzed several public events. These events included a day-long symposium on civil commitment at Mitchell Hamline School of Law in St. Paul, MN, as well as the Minnesota House Health and Human Services Reform committee hearing about the upcoming provisional discharge from MSOP of sex offender Clarence Opheim. We were able to double-check our personal impressions and notes against the videotapes of the two events. We also observed the Community Education and Notification Meeting in Le Center, MN, a few days before sex offender Robert Jeno was due to be provisionally discharged from MSOP in December 2014. Finally, we observed the trial, held in the U.S. District Court, District of Minnesota, in February and March 2015, for the class-action lawsuit *Karsjens et al. v. Jesson et al.* brought by MSOP clients in which they challenged the constitutionality of the program. These 136 hours of trial observation, as well as a study of the complaint, concluding argument, and decision, greatly sharpened our understanding of the challenges of treating and civilly confining sex offenders given the necessary balance of public safety and preservation of liberty. In referring to testimony in the trial, we identify the witness, the date, and the role of the witness, such as testifying for the plaintiffs or being cross-examined by the defense. We do note that Judge Donovan Frank in collaboration with both the plaintiffs and the defendants charged four Rule 706 experts under the Federal Rules of Evidence to evaluate MSOP, write a report about their findings (see Freeman et al. 2014), and testify in court. Rule 706 appears in the Federal Rules of Evidence, Article VII, "Opinions and Expert Testimony" and allows a court to appoint an expert whom both parties agree upon to explore an issue in depth for the parties (see Rule 706. Court-Appointed Expert Witnesses. 2015. Federal Rules of Evidence. Article VII. "Opinions and Expert Testimony." https://www.law.cornell.edu/rules/fre/rule_706).

We also analyzed several written texts emerging from the MSOP controversies. We looked for primary concerns and arguments reflected within the March 2011 Minnesota Legislative Auditor's Report on civil commitment and compared recommendations in this report with those from prior task forces and study groups on civil commitment. We also followed the introduction and two engrossments of Minnesota House File 6 (2011) during the 87th Minnesota Legislative session of 2011–2012, a bill designed to ease the number of those civilly committed by extending the prison sentences of sex offenders. In addition, we captured the media coverage of these events and documents.

To further contextualize the MSOP study, we conducted 21 face-to-face interviews with 23 parties involved in the MSOP debates. We created a standardized interview guide based on our knowledge of the local situation and on an extensive review of the literature on civil commitment of sex offenders. (See our interview questions at the end of this appendix.) We identified interview participants primarily by prior activity in creating pertinent documents, participating in the events we observed, or taking a public stand on civil commitment. Moreover, we used "snowballing sampling," what scholars such as Andrea Nichols (2013) call an "effective practice in qualitative research," by "providing credibility in recruiting research participants through trusted coworkers" (1407). After interviewing a legislator, for example, we might ask what other senators or representatives were involved in the MSOP debate. We coded the interview data independently for themes related to the research questions, using the coding and analysis techniques from an open-coding approach and grounded theory analysis following Barney Glaser and Anselm Strauss (2011). Not only did we specifically focus on finding common themes but we also identified alternative perspectives.

To maintain our promise of confidentiality, we assigned these parties to groups and cited each group as follows: S—state senators and representatives; A—administrators, such as county attorneys or employees of the Department of Corrections or MSOP; C—civic group representatives, including victim advocacy organizations or public attorneys who represent sex offenders; J—judges; L—law enforcement officials, such as sheriffs, probation officers, and police officers; and T—mental health providers, therapists, and others who work directly with sex offenders. We then assigned each member of a group a random number, which we use parenthetically in citations, such as (A-l) or (C-3). However, to protect the identity of those interview participants who might share particularly sensitive or controversial information, a few times we simply attribute the comment to an "interview participant," along with the more general parenthetical citation (IP). Again, we recognize that we have captured and interpreted our interview participants' perceptions of the situation and, at times, of the motivations and values of others. However, given the volatile nature of the civil commitment debate in Minnesota and the fact that several participants were elected officials, conscious of their constituents' potential reactions to their comments, we felt privileged to have so many parties agree to speak with us.

Finally, we set the conversations and controversies surrounding MSOP within a national context by exploring the release or discharge practices of civil commitment programs in other states, particularly New York and Wisconsin, and the foundational federal and state law cases that confirmed the constitutionality of such programs when they were first introduced.

For the LAP portion of this study, we collected and analyzed all the documents concerning the use of risk assessment tools supporting or resulting from the introduction of LAP. These documents included the

20-item Danger Assessment scoring instrument created by Dr. Jacquelyn Campbell at Johns Hopkins University in 1985 and revised in 1988, which is made widely available nationwide. Using genre analysis, we analyzed the format and purpose of the two versions of LAP used in Minnesota, for example, the 11-question version used in Washington County and the 12-question version used in Anoka County and in parts of Ramsey County. We recognize that some users defined LAP as a "Lethality Assessment Program," but we adopted the more frequent and, we believe, more appropriate term "Protocol" to represent both the administrative directions given to first responders as well as the systemic changes initiated by the assessment questionnaire itself. We also studied the nation-wide LAP training materials as well as the documents resulting from local LAP-related efforts, such as the Anoka County Sheriff Patrol Procedural Guidelines on when to initiate and how to conduct the lethality assessment and on how to react to the victim during the administration of LAP. Finally, we gathered our impressions of the goals of LAP and related efforts from not only local documents, such as the Anoka County grant applications submitted and funded by the Office on Violence Against Women and the U.S. Department of Justice, but also from materials generated in other states and from federal and national efforts to assess lethality in domestic violence situations.

To further contextualize these LAP-related documents, we conducted 24 face-to-face interviews with 27 parties who were directly involved in promoting LAP in their counties and who administer LAP to victims on the scene of domestic violence incidents. (See our interview questions at the end of this appendix.). We followed the same identification, interview, and coding techniques as with the MSOP portion of this study. We invited interview participants, for example, who were identified in the LAP documents or in local news coverage as being involved in the introduction, training, or use of LAP in their various Minnesota agencies. Our interview participants represented the following: first responders, including police officers and sheriff deputies; county attorneys and their staff; municipal or city attorneys; advocacy organizations and shelters; probation, parole, or community corrections administrators and staff; and judges. We went into four Minnesota counties for our interviews (Washington, Anoka, Ramsey, and Chisago), conducting the majority of interviews in the first two counties given their early piloting of LAP. We also spoke with representatives from St. Paul; although located in Ramsey County, the city has adapted its own risk assessment tool and resources, named Blue Print for Safety, which we do not explore in depth.

To maintain confidentiality, we group interview participants not by name but instead by location and responsibility. In quoting from these interviews, Washington County is referred to as W, Anoka as K, Ramsey as R, Chisago as G, and St Paul, which uses a completely different risk assessment tool, as P. We then assigned each participant from the county a random number, which we use parenthetically in citations, such as (W-l) or (G-3). Again, however, to protect the identity of those interview participants who might share particularly sensitive or controversial information, a few times we simply attribute the comment to an "interview participant" or (IP). We also conducted a follow-up interview with a law enforcement specialist instrumental in introducing LAP who went on to create a cross-county domestic violence stalking resource center. Because we did not ask the same interview questions, we did not code this source's responses and refer to this source or expert as E-1. We did another follow-up interview with a public health specialist involved in working with those domestic violence victims identified as high-risk in LAP. Again we created specific questions for this expert, whom we call E-2. Finally, we set the introduction and implementation of LAP within a national conversation about the gaps and challenges of risk assessment, as well as conversations conducted by advocacy groups, first responders, and others who must measure whether they have achieved the goals of such assessment tools.

For both the LAP and MSOP portion of this study, we focused at times on the most widely viewed and read media coverage of the issues within Minnesota, including the two largest state newspapers (*Minneapolis StarTribune* and *St. Paul Pioneer Press*), and the local television news affiliates, such as CBS Minnesota's WCCO. In this way, we avoided so-called niche media as well as social media that might represent a particular point of view in coverage or appeal to a more limited audience. In referring to media coverage of LAP, we are aware of the conclusions of Lane Gillespie et al. (2013) in that

> the media are, in fact, both the problem and the solution ... the fact remains that many femicides continue to be explained away, as commonplace or their magnitude is obscured by placing blame on the victim, failing to hold the perpetrator fully responsible, or by diverting attention to more easily championed issues ... and the media miss the opportunity to use their influence to portray femicide as an issue deserving public outrage and intensified policy development.
>
> (240)

Also, in referring to the media coverage of MSOP, we agree with the general conclusions of such scholars as Clare Williams, Jenny Kitzinger, and Lesley Henderson (2003), in that the media "do have a strong influence on what, and how, things come to be defined as public issues. The framing of stories, the selective presentations of particular themes, oppositions, associations, 'templates,' 'facts,' and claims rather than others is a critical part" of this media influence (795–796). To completely contextualize MSOP and LAP, however, we must refer to this news coverage. Finally, we recognize that there exist no direct measures of public response to the MSOP debates, but instead we must rely on the reporting and perceptions of that response. We assess that reporting and those perceptions with confidence, however, given the commonality in media description and analysis among our interview participants.

The Institutional Review Board (IRB) at the University of Minnesota, where the project originated and the research was conducted, reviewed and approved our interview questions, consent form, and other documents used to collect our research data. For both studies, the IRB determined the study to be exempt from review under federal guidelines 45 CFR Part 46.101 (b) category #2 Surveys/Interviews; Observation of Public Behavior. The IRB assigned the MSOP study number 1103E97176 and the LAP study number 1304E31064. The Office of Research, Human Subjects Committee at the University of California, Santa Barbara deemed research activities pertaining to this project, protocol number 2-16-0784, exempt from the Federal Regulations at 45 CFR 46.101(b) category #4.

Interview Questions for MSOP Study

1 Please describe your involvement in past or current discussions about the laws and processes involving civil commitment of sexually violent persons or the Minnesota Sex Offender Program (MSOP).
2 What is your understanding of the state of current civil commitment laws regarding sexually violent persons or MSOP? What is the purpose of MSOP? How successful is it?
3 To what extent do you think that discussions about civil commitment laws or programs are a response to public pressure? To media coverage of specific incidents and crimes such as the Dru Sjodin case? Does the public, the media, or the Legislature initiate such laws and programs?
4 Are there problems with the current civil commitment processes or with the Moose Lake or St. Peter facilities? If so, what are they?
5 Are you familiar with the Legislative Auditor's 2011 report on *Civil Commitment of Sex Offenders*? If so, do you have any areas of agreement or disagreement?
6 Please describe your position on possible changes in the state statute regarding civil commitment of sex offenders.
7 If you are in favor of changes, are there possible changes or revisions that you would favor more than others? Please describe your reasoning.
8 Recently proposed legislation (House File 6) focuses on the increase in the statutory maximum indeterminate sentence or doubling the current statutory maximum sentences. Do you support this emphasis?

9 Do you think that this public and legislative discussion of civil commitment laws enhances or distracts from our understanding of other crimes such as non-stranger sexual assault and domestic violence?

10 Is there anything else you would like to share with us about MSOP? About civil commitment? About release of sex offenders into the community? Or other related topics? Finally, is there anyone else we should talk to in order to gain understanding of MSOP or civil commitment?

Interview Questions for LAP Study

1 How long have you been in your current position? What experience and education have you had in dealing with domestic violence victims? Can you describe the capacity in which you work with first responders, advocacy groups, victims, offenders, and others involved in domestic violence cases or prevention efforts?

2 Did you take the Lethality Assessment Program (LAP) training? If so, when? How long have you been using the questionnaire or working with others who might administer the questionnaire? Or how long have you been responding to victims who have completed the questionnaire?

3 Based on your LAP training, what is your understanding of the goals of the LAP questionnaire? In training, did you get any specific ideas about how those goals are to be accomplished? If you did not take LAP training yourself, what goals do you understand the questionnaire is meant to achieve?

4 Now that you have been using the LAP questionnaire for a while, what features does the LAP questionnaire contain to achieve these goals? Could you point these out? (Interviewees were handed a copy of the questionnaire.) Or if you have not administered the questionnaire yourself, do you have a sense of what features are meant to achieve these goals? If you use a similar procedure or document, could you describe that or show that to me?

5 In your experience, is there any one feature on the questionnaire that influences the victim more than other features? Or does completing a list of questions in and of itself seem to affect victims? Again, if you use a similar procedure or document, could you describe that procedure or document or show those features to me?

6 How might your approach to domestic violence victims differ in using the LAP questionnaire from earlier approaches without using such a document? Or does it?

7 Does your interaction with the victim go beyond using the LAP questionnaire? If so, what might you say to a victim that goes beyond the information you gather by using the LAP questionnaire?

8 Have you had victims refuse to answer the questions within the LAP questionnaire? If so, how have you responded? Are there particular factors that you have observed that might prevent the victim from taking part in this process? Have you had victims refuse to take the phone and speak with the crisis center after completing the LAP questionnaire? If so, how have you responded? Are there particular factors that you have observed that might prevent the victim from taking the phone?
9 If you were to change, delete, or add any questions within the LAP questionnaire, what might those be? Why?
10 Are there questions that we should have asked you about the LAP process and similar tools that we haven't? Is there anything else you want to tell us about your experiences engaging with LAP or similar ways of working with victims of domestic violence? Or with working with domestic violence victims in particular? Finally, is there anyone else we should talk to in order to gain understanding of this approach to working with domestic violence victims?

References

Abbott, Andrew. 1988. *The System of Professions: An Essay on the Division of Expert Labor.* Chicago: University of Chicago Press.

ABC News: Good Morning America. 2003, December 2. "Sjodin Case: Why Was Sex Offender Free?" http://abcnews.go.com/GMA/story?id=128168&page=1, (accessed November 21, 2016).

Abracen, Jeffrey, and Jan Looman. 2006. "Evaluation of Civil Commitment Criteria in a High Risk Sample of Sex Offenders." *Journal of Sexual Offender Civil Commitment: Science and the Law* 1: 121–140.

Abramsky, Tanya, et al. 2011. "What Factors Are Associated with Recent Intimate Partner Violence? Findings from the WHO Multi-County Study on Women's Health and Domestic Violence." *BMC Public Health* 11: 1–17.

Ackerman, Jeffrey, and Tony P. Love. 2014. "Ethnic Group Differences in Police Notification about Intimate Partner Violence." *Violence Against Women* 20: 162–185.

Adame, Jaime. 2014, February 24. "Are Domestic Violence Homicides Preventable?" *The Crime Report: Your Complete Criminal Justice Resource.* Inside Criminal Justice Section. http://www.thecrimereport.org/news/inside-criminal-justice/2014-02-are-domestic-violence-homicides-preventable#, (accessed November 21, 2016).

Adelman, Madelaine, Hillary Haldane, and Jennifer Wies. 2012. "Mobilizing Culture as an Asset: A Transdisciplinary Effort to Rethink Gender Violence." *Violence Against Women* 18: 691–700.

Ahmed, Sara. 2000. *Strange Encounters: Embodied Others in Post-Coloniality.* London: Routledge.

Alcoff, Linda Martin. 2000. "Who's Afraid of Identity Politics?" In *Reclaiming Identity: Realist Theory and the Predicament of Postmodernism*, edited by Paula M. Moya and Michael Hames-Garcia, 312–345. Berkeley: University of California Press.

Alexandra House. n.d. "Safety Planning Sessions." http://www.alexandra-house.org/domestic-violence-resources/safety-planning/, (accessed November 21, 2016).

Alexandra House. 2014. "What To Do If You've Just Been Sexually Assaulted." http://www.alexandrahouse.org/resources/sexual-violence/, (accessed November 21, 2016).

Amanor-Boadu, Yvonne, Jill Messing, Sandra Stith, Jared Anderson, Chris O'Sullivan, and Jacquelyn Campbell. 2010. "Immigrant and Nonimmigrant Women: Factors That Predict Leaving an Abusive Relationship." *Violence against Women* 18: 611–633.

American Association of Colleges of Nursing (AACN). 2000. "Violence as a Public Health Problem." *Journal of Professional Nursing* 16: 63–69.

American Psychological Association. 2014. "Intimate Partner Violence: Facts & Resources." http://www.apa.org/topics/violence/partner.aspx, (accessed November 21, 2016).

Anderson, Kristin L., and Debra Umberson. 2001. "Gendering Violence: Masculinity and Power in Men's Accounts of Domestic Violence." *Gender and Society* 15: 358–380.

Andrus, Jennifer. 2015. *Entextualizing Domestic Violence: Language Ideology and Violence Against Women in the Anglo-American Hearsay Principle.* New York: Oxford University Press.

Anoka County Attorney's Office. n.d. "Domestic Violence Lethality Assessment Program." https://www.anokacounty.us/1543/Domestic-Violence-Lethality-Assessment-P, (accessed November 21, 2016).

Anoka County Community Corrections. n.d. "Adult Supervision and Programs: IDAPP." https://www.anokacounty.us/578/Adult-Supervision-and-Programs, (accessed November 21, 2016).

Anoka County Community Health and Environmental Services. 2015. *Community Health Improvement Plan 2015–2019.* https://www.anokacounty.us/DocumentCenter/Home/View/5588, (accessed November 21, 2016).

Aristotle. 1991. *The Rhetoric.* Transl. George Kennedy. New York: Oxford University Press.

Arnheim, Rudolf. 1969. *Visual Thinking.* Berkeley: University of California Press.

Arnold, Gretchen, and Jami Ake. 2013. "Reframing the Narrative of the Battered Women's Movement." *Violence Against Women* 19: 557–578.

Associated Press. 2014, December 16. "Le Center Residents Attend Public Hearing on Sex Offender Set to Be Transferred into Community." *StarTribune.* http://www.startribune.com/le-center-residents-voice-concerns-on-sex-offender/286049711/, (accessed November 21, 2016).

Association for the Treatment of Sexual Abusers. 2010, August 17. *Civil Commitment of Sexually Violent Predators*, Policy Paper. http://www.atsa.com/ppcivil commit.html, (accessed November 21, 2016).

Austin, John L. 1962. *How to Do Things with Words.* Cambridge, MA: Harvard University Press.

Baca, Maria Elena. 2011, February 28. "In Anoka County, a Sad Pattern of Abuse." *StarTribune.* http://www.startribune.com/local/north/117029298.html, (accessed November 21, 2016).

Baker, Katherine K. 2005. "Gender and Emotion in Criminal Law." *Harvard Journal of Law and Gender* 28: 447–466.

Barvir, Anna. 2007. "When Hysteria and Good Intentions Collide: Constitutional Considerations of California's Sexual Predator Punishment and Control Act." *Whittier Law Review* 29: 679–706.

Basile, Kathleen C., Jeffery H. Hall, and Mikel L. Walters. 2013. "Expanding Resource Theory and Feminist-Informed Theory to Explain Intimate Partner Violence Perpetration by Court-Ordered Men." *Violence Against Women* 19: 848–880.

Bawarshi, Anis. 2000. "The Genre Function." *College English* 62: 335–360.

Bawarshi, Anis, and Mary Jo Reiff. 2010. *Genre: An Introduction to History, Theory, Research, and Pedagogy*. West Lafayette, IN: Parlor Press.

Bazerman, Charles. 2003. "Textual Performance: Where the Action at a Distance Is." *Journal of Advanced Composition* 23: 379–396.

Beck, Ulrich. 1999. *World Risk Society*, Ciaran Cronin (transl.). Cambridge, UK: Polity Press.

Beck, Ulrich. 2000. "Risk Society Revisited: Theory, Politics and Research Programs." In *The Risk Society and Beyond: Critical Issues for Social Theory*, edited by Barbara Adam, Ulrich Beck, and Joost Van Loon, 211–229. London, UK: Sage Publications.

Beck, Ulrich. 2002. "The Terrorist Threat: World Risk Society Revisited." *Theory, Culture & Society* 19: 39–55.

Beck, Ulrich. 2007. *World at Risk*, Ciaran Cronin (transl.). Cambridge, UK: Polity Press.

Becker, Judith V., Jill Stinson, Shannon Tromp, and Gene Messer.2003. "Characteristics of Individuals Petitioned for Civil Commitment." *International Journal of Offender Treatment and Comparative Criminology* 47: 185–195.

Bell, Kathryn M., and Amy E. Naugle. 2008. "Intimate Partner Violence Theoretical Considerations: Moving Toward a Contextual Framework." *Clinical Psychology Review* 28: 1096–1107.

Benedikt, Amélia F. 2002. "On Doing the Right Thing at the Right Time: Toward an Ethics of *Kairos*." In *Rhetoric and Kairos: Essays in History, Theory, and Praxis*, edited by Phillip Sipiora and James S. Baumlin, 226–235. Albany: State University of New York Press.

Benson, Dennis. 2015, February 26. Videotaped Deposition Played as Direct Testimony by the Plaintiffs. *Karsjens et al. v. Jesson et al.* United States District Court, District of Minnesota. File No. 11-3659 (DWF/JJK).

Berkenkotter, Carol. 2008. *Patient Tales: Case Histories and the Uses of Narrative in Psychiatry*. Columbia: University of South Carolina Press.

Berkenkotter, Carol, and Cristina Hanganu-Bresch. 2011. "Occult Genres and the Certification of Madness in a 19th-Century Lunatic Asylum." *Written Communication* 28: 220–250.

Berkenkotter, Carol, and Thomas N. Huckin. 1995. *Genre Knowledge in Disciplinary Communication: Cognition/Culture/Power*. Hillsdale, NH: Lawrence Erlbaum.

Berman, Douglas A. 2015, September 12. "Federal Judge Finds Unconstitutional Missouri's Operation of Its Sex-Offender Civil Commitment Program." http://sentencing.typepad.com/sentencing_law_and_policy/2015/09/federal-judge-finds-unconstitutional-missouris-operation-of-its-sex-offender-civil-commitment-progra.html, (accessed November 21, 2016).

Berns, Nancy. 2001. "Degendering the Problem and Gendering the Blame." *Gender & Society* 15: 262–281.

Best, Joel. 1987. "Rhetoric in Claims-Making: Constructing the Missing Children Problem." *Journal of Social Problems* 34: 101–121.

Betzold, Don. June 30, 2015. "What the Minnesota Sex Offender Program Was Meant To Be." *StarTribune*. http://www.startribune.com/what-the-minnesota-sex-offender-program-was-meant-to-be/311061851/, (accessed November 21, 2016).

Bierschbach, Brianna. 2013, November 13. "Dayton Wants to Temporarily Suspend Provisional Release of Sex Offenders." *Capitol Report: Politics in Minnesota*. http://politicsinminnesota.com/2013/11/dayton-wants-to-suspend-provisional-release-of-sex-offenders/, (accessed November 21, 2016).

Biesecker, Barbara A. 1997. *Addressing Postmodernity: Kenneth Burke, Rhetoric, and a Theory of Social Change*. Tuscaloosa, AL: University of Alabama Press.

Bitzer. Lloyd. 1999. "The Rhetorical Situation." In *Contemporary Rhetorical Theory*, edited by John Louis Lucaites, Celeste Michelle Condit, and Sally Caudill, 217–225. New York, NY: Guilford Press.

Bizzell, Patricia, and Bruce Herzberg. 2000. "Introduction." In *The Rhetorical Tradition: Readings from Classical Times to the Present*, 2nd edition, edited by Patricia Bizzell and Bruce Herzberg, 1–16. Boston: Bedford/St. Martin's.

Bograd, Michele. 1999. "Strengthening Domestic Violence Theories: Intersections of Race, Class, Sexual Orientation, and Gender." *Journal of Marital and Family Therapy* 25: 275–289.

Boonzaier, Floretta. 2008. "'If the Man Says You Must Sit, Then You Must Sit': The Relational Construction of Woman Abuse: Gender, Subjectivity and Violence." *Feminist Psychology* 18: 183–206.

Brennaman, Nathan, Scott H. Ikeda, and Aaron Winter. 2015, September 21. "Defendants' Brief on Remedies." United States District Court District of Minnesota. Civil File No. 11-cv-3659 (DWK/JJK).

Britt, Elizabeth. 2001. *Conceiving Normalcy: Rhetoric, Law, and the Double Binds of Infertility*. Tuscaloosa: University of Alabama Press.

Brown, Carrie. 2008. "Gender-Role Implications on Same-Sex Intimate Partner Abuse." *Journal of Family Violence* 23: 457–462.

Brown, Jeffrey. 2015, July 2. "Minnesota Sex Offender Program: From Process to Politicization." *StarTribune*. http://www.startribune.com/readers-write-july-3-minnesota-sex-offender-program-iran-nuclear-negotiations-nicollet-mall-traffic-symbolism-and-atonement/311518321/, (accessed November 21, 2016).

Browning, Dan. 2013, October 1. "Cambridge Residents Speak Up to Keep Sex Offenders Out." *StarTribune*. http://www.startribune.com/local/north/226072301.html, (accessed November 21, 2016).

Buel, Sarah M. "Fifty Obstacles to Leaving, *a.k.a.*, Why Abuse Victims Stay." *The Colorado Lawyer* 28: 19–28.

Bureau of Justice Assistance. 2012. "Lethality Assessment Program (LAP)." Office of Justice Programs. https://www.bja.gov/SuccessStoryDetail.aspx?ssid=37, (accessed November 21, 2016).

Bureau of Justice Statistics. 2014, April 17. "Nonfatal Domestic Violence, 2003–2012." http://www.bjs.gov/index.cfm?ty=pbdetail&iid=4984, (accessed November 21, 2016).

Burke, Kenneth. 1969. *A Rhetoric of Motives*. Berkeley, CA: University of California Press.

Buss, David M., and Joshua D. Duntley. 2011. "The Evolution of Intimate Partner Violence." *Aggression and Violent Behavior* 16: 411–419.

Butler, Judith. 1990. *Gender Trouble: Feminism and the Subversion of Identity*. New York: Routledge.

Caldwell, Dean. 2015, February 23. Testimony for the Plaintiffs. *Karsjens et al. v. Jesson et al.* United States District Court, District of Minnesota. File No. 11-3659 (DWF/JJK).

Call, Gordon B. v. Maria Gomez, Commissioner of Human Services et al. 1995, August 4. 535 N.W.2d 312. Supreme Court of Minnesota.

Campbell, Jacquelyn. 2002. "Health Consequences of Intimate Partner Violence." *Lancet* 359: 1331–1336.

Campbell, Jacquelyn C. 2003. "Danger Assessment." http://www.dangerassessment.org/uploads/pdf/DAEnglish2010.pdf, (accessed November 21, 2016).

Campbell, Jacquelyn C. 2004. "Helping Women Understand Their Risk in Situations of Intimate Partner Violence." *Journal of Interpersonal Violence* 19: 1462–1477.

Campbell, Jacquelyn C. 2005. "Lethality Assessment Approaches: Reflections on Their Use and Ways Forward." *Violence Against Women* 11: 1206–1213.

Campbell, Jacquelyn C., et al. 2003. "Risk Factors for Femicide in Abusive Relationships: Results From a Multisite Case Control Study. "*American Journal of Public Health* 93: 1089–1097.

Campbell, Jacquelyn, Daniel W. Webster, and Nancy Glass. 2006. "The Danger Assessment: Validation of a Lethality Risk Assessment Instrument for Intimate Partner Femicide." *Journal of Interpersonal Violence* 42: 653–674.

Cann, K. S., et al. 2001. "Domestic Violence: A Comparative Survey of Levels of Detection, Knowledge, and Attitudes in Healthcare Workers." *Public Health* 115: 89–95.

Carlsmith, Keven M., John Monahan, and Alison Evans. 2007. "The Function of Punishment in the 'Civil' Commitment of Sexually Violent Predators." *Behavioral Sciences and the Law* 25: 437–448.

Cattaneo, Lauren Bennett, and Aliya R. Chapman. 2011. "Risk Assessment with Victims of Intimate Partner Violence: Investigating the Gap Between Research and Practice." *Violence Against Women* 10: 1286–1298.

CBS News: Local. 2012, March 12. "High-Risk Sex Offender Heads to Halfway House." http://minnesota.cbslocal.com/2012/03/12/high-risk-sex-offender-heads-to-halfway-house-this-week/, (accessed November 21, 2016).

CBS News: The Early Show. 2004, March 11. "Governor Pawlenty and Chris Lang Comment on Dru Sjodin's Disappearance." https://votesmart.org/public-statement/31876/cbs-news-the-early-show-transcript, (accessed November 21, 2016).

Ceccarelli, Leah. 2001. "Manufactured Scientific Controversy: Science, Rhetoric, and Public Debate." *Rhetoric & Public Affairs* 14: 195–228.

Center for Sex Offender Management. 2000, August. "Myths and Facts About Sex Offenders." http://www.csom.org/pubs/mythsfacts.html, (accessed November 21, 2016).

Centers for Disease Control. 2010. "Violence, Sexual Violence, and Stalking." National Intimate Partner and Sexual Violence Survey. http://www.cdc.gov/violenceprevention/pdf/nisvs-fact-sheet-2014.pdf, (accessed November 21, 2016).

Chanen, David. 2010, April 19. "After 30 Years, Will Killer Be Freed? Ming Sen Shiue's Sentence for Kidnapping, Murder and Rape Is Almost Up. A Trial Will Decide If He Still Is a Threat." *StarTribune*. http://www.highbeam.com/doc/1G1-224281903.html, (accessed November 21, 2016).

Chanen, David. 2010, September 29. "Judge: No Freedom for Shiue." *Star-Tribune*. https://www.highbeam.com/doc/1G1-224281903.html, (accessed November 21, 2016).

Chanen, David. 2012, March 29. "Fast Track for Domestic Violence Cases Is Paying Off in Anoka County." *StarTribune*. http://www.startribune.com/local/north/144745605.html, (accessed March 30, 2012).

Chekuru, Kavitha. 2013, March 10. "Violence Against Woman Act Includes New Protections for Native American Women." *Huffington Post Politics*. http://www.huffingtonpost.com/2013/03/10/violence-against-women-act-native-americans_n_2849931.html, (accessed November 21, 2016).

Cheng, Maria. 2013, June 20. "WHO: A Third of Women Suffer Domestic Violence." Associated Press. *StarTribune*. http://news.yahoo.com/study-third-women-suffer-domestic-violence-205228597.html, (accessed November 21, 2016).

Cherney, James L. 2011."The Rhetoric of Ableism." *Disability Studies Quarterly* 31: n.p. Online journal. http://dsq-sds.org/article/view/1665/1606, (accessed November 21, 2016).

Clair, Sharon. 2011, March. "Collaborative Results in IDAPP." *The Informant*. Anoka County Community Corrections, 2100 Third Ave, Anoka, MN 55303.

Clairmont, Susan. 2015, January 6. "'Pure Evil' Pedophile Released from Prison After 21 Years." *Hamilton Spectator*. http://www.thespec.com/news-story/5243545--pure-evil-pedophile-released-from-prison-after-21-years/, (accessed November 21, 2016).

Cohen, Stanley. 1980. *Folk Devils and Moral Panics: The Creation of the Mods and Rockers*. New York, NY: St. Martin's Press.

Collins, Patricia Hill. 1998. "The Tie That Binds: Race, Gender and US Violence." *Ethnic and Racial Studies* 21: 917–938.

Colorado Revised Statutes. 2002. "Crime of Violation of a Protection Order. Penalty. Peace Officers' Duties. Definitions" Section 18-6-803.5 (3)(a). http://www.womenslaw.org/statutes_detail.php?statute_id=512#statute-top, (accessed November 21, 2016).

Combe, Rosemary J. 2000. "Contingent Articulations: A Critical Cultural Studies of Law." In *Law in the Domains of Culture,* edited by Austin Sarat and Thomas R. Kearns, 21–64. Ann Arbor: University of Michigan Press.

Corsilles, Angela. 1994. "No Drop Policies in the Prosecution of Domestic Violence Cases: Guarantee To Action or Dangerous Solution?" *Fordham Law Review* 63: 853–881.

Cosgrove-Mather, Bootie. 2007, December 5. "Anger, Fear, Pain after Dru Found." *CBS News/AP*. http://www.cbsnews.com/2100-201_162-612796.html, (accessed November 21, 2016).

Criminal Justice Professionals of Anoka County, MN. 2010, February 17. "Application to The Community-Defined Solutions to Violence Against Women Grant Program." Anoka County Attorney's Office, 2100 Third Ave. South, Suite 720, Anoka, MN 55303-2235.

Criminal Justice Professionals of Anoka County, MN. 2012, March 23. "Application to The OVW Fiscal Year 2012 Grants to Encourage Arrest Policies Programs." Anoka County Attorney's Office, 2100 Third Ave. South, Suite 720, Anoka, MN 55303-2235.

Critcher, Chas. 2002. "Media, Government and Moral Panic: The Politics of Paedophilia in Britain. 2000–2001." *Journalism Studies* 3: 521–535. http://dx.doi.org/10.1080/1461670022000019182.

Crowley, Sharon, and Debra Hawhee. 2008. *Ancient Rhetorics for Contemporary Students,* 4th edition. White Plains, NY: Longman.

Daigle, Leah E., and Sadie J. Mummert. 2014. "Sex-Role Identification and Violent Victimization: Gender Differences in the Role of Masculinity." *Journal of Interpersonal Violence* 29: 255–278.

Davey, Monica. 2015, June 17. "Minnesota's Holding of Sex Offenders After Prison Is Ruled Unconstitutional." *The New York Times.* http://www.nytimes.com/2015/06/18/us/minnesotas-holding-of-sex-offenders-after-prison-is-ruled-unconstitutional.html?_r=0, (accessed November 21, 2016).

Davis, Robert C., Barbara E. Smith, and Heather J. Davies. 2001. "Effects of No-Drop Prosecution of Domestic Violence Upon Conviction Rates." *Justice Research and Policy* 3 (2): 1–13.

Dayton, Mark. 2013, November 13. Letter to Commissioner Lucinda Jesson, Minnesota Department of Human Services. http://stmedia.startribune.com/documents/GovernorDayton_Letter_SexOffenders.pdf, (accessed November 21, 2016).

DePrince, Anne P., Joanne Belknap, Jennifer S. Labus, Susan E. Buckingham, and Angela R. Gover. 2012. "The Impact of Victim-Focused Outreach on Criminal Legal Systems Outcome Following Police-Reported Intimate Partner Abuse." *Violence Against Women* 18: 861–881.

DeShaney v. Winnebago City Social Services Department. 1989, February 22. U.S. Court of Appeals, Seventh Circuit. No. 87–154. 489 U.S. 189.

Devitt, Amy J. 2004. *Writing Genres.* Carbondale: Southern Illinois University Press.

Dichter, Melissa E, and Richard J. Gelles. 2012. "Women's Perceptions of Safety and Risk Following Police Intervention for Intimate Partner Violence." *Violence Against Women* 18: 44–63.

Dienemann, Jaqueline, Jacquelyn Campbell, Karen Landerburger, and Mary Ann Curry. 2002. "The Domestic Violence Survivor Assessment: A Tool For Counseling Women in Intimate Partner Violence Relationships." *Patient Education and Counseling* 46: 221–228.

Ding, Huiling. 2013. "Transcultural Risk Communication and Viral Discourses: Grassroots Movements to Manage Global Risks to H1N1Flu Pandemic." *Technical Communication Quarterly* 22: 126–149.

Dixon, Louise, and Nicola Graham-Kevan. 2011. "Understanding the Nature of Etiology of Intimate Partner Violence and Implications for Practice and Policy." *Clinical Psychology Review* 31: 1145–1155.

Dobash, R. Emerson, and Russell P. Dobash. 2011. "What Were They Thinking?: Men Who Murder an Intimate Partner." *Violence Against Women* 17: 111–134.

Domestic Abuse Intervention Project. n.d. "Power and Control Wheel." http://www.theduluthmodel.org/pdf/powerandcontrol.pdf, (accessed November 21, 2016).

Domestic Abuse Project. 2013. *Annual Report Update.* http://www.domesticabuseproject.com/wp-content/uploads/2014/04/ann-report-update-2013.pdf, (accessed November 21, 2016).

Dunn, Jennifer L., and Melissa Powell-Williams. 2007. "'Everybody Makes Choices': Victim Advocates and the Social Construction of Battered Women's Victimization and Agency." *Violence Against Women* 13: 977–1001.

E.B. v. Verniero. 1997. 119 F.3d 1077 (3d Cir).

Editorial Board. 2015, June 17. "Cooperate, Don't Defy Federal Judge on Sex Offender Ruling: Policymakers Should Cooperate with Judge on Reforms, Not Defy Him." *StarTribune*. http://www.startribune.com/cooperate-don-t-defy-federal-judge-on-sex-offender-ruling/307997731/, (accessed November 21, 2016).

Egumenovska, Kristina K. 2012. "Black-Boxing Political Intersectionality: On 'Othering' That Deprives Individuals of Their Citizenship." *Social Identities* 18: 679–694.

Ellsberg, Mary. 2006. "Violence Against Women and the Millennium Development Goals: Facilitating Women's Access to Support." *International Journal of Gynecology and Obstetrics* 94: 325–332.

Ellsberg, Mary, Henrica Afm Jansen, Lori Heise, Charlotte H. Watts, and Claudia Garcia-Moreno. 2008. "Intimate Partner Violence and Women's Physical and Mental Health in the WHO Multi-Country Study on Women's Health and Domestic Violence: An Observational Study." *Lancet* 371: 1165–1172.

Elsen, Nicole. 2015, February 18. Direct Testimony. *Karsjens et al. v. Jesson et al.* United States District Court, District of Minnesota. File No. 11-3659 (DWF/JJK).

Enander, Viveka, and Carin Holmberg. 2008. "Why Does She Leave? The Leaving Process(es) of Battered Women." *Health Care for Women International* 29: 200–226.

Epstein, Deborah. 1999. "Effective Intervention in Domestic Violence Cases: Rethinking the Roles of Prosecutors, Judges, and the Court System." *Yale Journal of Law and Feminism* 11: 3050.

Evans, Ian. 2012, June 28. "Britain Denies Extradition of Minnesota Sex Suspect." *StarTribune*. http://www.startribune.com/local/160704485.html?refer=y, (accessed November 21, 2016).

Ferraro, Kathleen. 2006. *Neither Angels nor Demons: Women, Crime, and Victimization*. Lebanon, NH: University Press of New England.

Filler, Daniel M. 2003. "Terrorism, Panic and Pedophilia." *The University of Alabama School of Law* 10: 345–382.

Finley, Lucinda M. 1989. "Breaking Women's Silence in Law: The Dilemma of the Gendered Nature of Legal Reasoning." *Notre Dame Law Review* 64: 886–904.

Florida Misdemeanor Pretrial Diversion Program. 2015. http://www.sa18.state.fl.us/page/misdemeanor-diversion.html, (accessed November 21, 2016).

Florin, Karen. 2012, August 16. "Cops to Put It on the Line with Victims of Domestic Violence." *Safe Futures*. News and Press Section. http://www.safefuturesct.org/news-press/cops-to-put-it-on-the-line-with-victims-of-domestic-violence, (accessed November 21, 2016).

Follingstad, Dianne R., Ann P. Neckerman, and Julia Vormbrock. 1988. "Reactions to Victimization and Coping Strategies of Battered Women: The Ties that Bind." *Clinical Psychology Review* 8: 373–390.

Forliti, Amy. 2011, April 26. "Appeals Court Upholds Shiue's Civil Commitment." *Pioneer Press*. http://www.twincities.com/ci_17930854, (accessed November 21, 2016).

Forliti, Amy. 2012, February 15. "Commissioner Defends Provisioned Discharge of Minnesota Sex Offender." *Pioneer Press*. http://www.twincities.com/localnews/ci_19974550, (accessed November 21, 2016).

Forliti, Amy. 2012, March 5. "Golden Valley: 300 Attend Sex Offender Notification Meeting." *Pioneer Press*. http://www.twincities.com/localnews/ci_20108606/300-attend-sex-offender-notification-meeting-golden-valley, (accessed November 21, 2016).

Francis, Kelly. 2008, September. "Minnesota's New Domestic Abuse Strangulation Statute." *Bench & Bar of Minnesota*. http://www.mnbar.org/benchandbar/2008/sept08/strangulation.html, (accessed November 21, 2016).

Franks, Mary Anne. 2013–2014. "Real Men Advance, Real Women Retreat: Stand Your Ground, Battered Women's Syndrome, and Violence as Male Privilege." *University of Miami Law Review* 68: 1099–1128.

Freadman, Anne. 1994. "Anyone for Tennis?" In *Genre and the New Rhetoric*, edited by Aviva Freedman and Peter Medway, 43–66. London: Taylor & Francis.

Freadman, Anne. 2002. "Uptake." In *The Rhetoric and Ideology of Genre: Strategies for Stability and Change*, edited by Richard M. Coe, Lorelei Lingard, and Tatiana Teslenko, 39–53. Creskill, NJ: Hampton Press.

Freedman, Aviva, and Peter Medway. 1994. "Introduction: Locating Genre Studies: Antecedents and Prospects." In *Genre and the New Rhetoric*, edited by Aviva Freedman and Peter Medway, 1–20. London: Taylor & Francis.

Freeman, Michael O., John L. Kirwin, and Theresa Couri. 2015, September 14. "Amicus Curae Memorandum of Hennepin County Attorney Addressing Remedies." United States District Court District of Minnesota. Civil File No. 11-cv-3659 (DWK/JJK).

Freeman, Naomi H., Michael H. Miner, Deborah J. McCulloch, and Robin J. Wilson. 2014, November 17. Rule 706 Expert Report and Recommendations, Civil No. 11-3659 (DWF/JJK). http://stmedia.startribune.com/documents/Expert+panel+report+on+sex+offender+program.pdf, (accessed November 21, 2016).

Galano, Maria, Erin C. Hunter, Kathryn H. Howell, Laura E Miller, and Sandra Graham-Bermann. 2013. "Predicting Shelter Residence in Women Experiencing Recent Intimate Partner Violence." *Violence Against Women* 19: 518–535.

Gallagher, Kathryn E., and Dominic J. Parrott. 2011. "What Accounts for Men's Hostile Attitudes Toward Women? The Influence of Hegemonic Male Role Norms and Masculine Gender Role Stress." *Violence Against Women* 17: 568–583.

Garcia-Moreno, Claudia, Henriette Jansen, Charlotte Watts, Mary Ellsberg, and Lon Heise. 2005. *WHO Multi-County Study of Women's Health and Domestic Violence Against Women: Initial Results on Prevalence, Health Outcomes, and Women's Responses*. Geneva, Switzerland: World Health Organization.

Garland, David. 2008. "On the Concept of Moral Panic." *Crime, Media, Culture* 4: 9–30.

Garland, Tammy. 2009. "An Overview of Sexual Assault and Sexual Assault Myths." In *Sexual Assault: The Victims, the Perpetrators, and the Criminal Justice System*, 2nd edition, edited by Frances P. Reddington and Betsy Wright Kreisel, 3–24. Durham, NC: Carolina Academic Press.

Gerston, Larry N. 1997. *Public Policy Making: Process and Principles*. Armonk, NY: Sharpe.

Giles, Kevin. 2012, June 2. "New Washington County Program Aids Domestic Abuse Victims." *StarTribune*, from "U.S. Senator Amy Klobuchar: Working for the People of Minnesota" at: http://www.klobuchar.senate.gov/public/amy-in-the-news?ID=905261b0-ffb3-448e-a876-e815bc3397ca, (accessed November 21, 2016).

Gilles, Ingrid, et al. 2013. "Collective Symbolic Coping with Disease Threat and Othering: A Case Study of Avian Influenza." *British Journal of Social Psychology* 52: 83–102.

Gillespie, Lane Kirkland, Tara N. Richards, Eugena M. Givens, and M. Dwayne Smith. 2013. "Framing Deadly Domestic Violence: Why the Media's Spin Matters on Newspaper Coverage of Femicide." *Violence Against Women* 19: 222–245.

Gillis, Joseph Roy, et al. 2006. "Systemic Obstacles to Battered Women's Participation in the Judicial System: When Will the Status Quo Change?" *Violence Against Women* 12: 1150–1168.

Glaser, Barney, and Amselm Strauss. 2011. *The Discovery of Grounded Theory: Strategies for Qualitative Research*. New Brunswick, NJ: Aldine Transactions.

Glass, Nancy, Stephen Dearwater, and Jacquelyn Campbell. 2001. "Intimate Partner Violence Screening and Intervention: Data from Eleven Pennsylvania and California Community Hospital Emergency Departments." *Journal of Emergency Medicine* 27: 140–149.

Goetz, Aaron T., Todd K. Shackelford, Gorge A. Romero, Farnaz Kaighobadi, and Emily J. Miner. 2008. "Punishment, Proprietariness, and Paternity: Men's Violence Against Women from an Evolutionary Perspective." *Aggression and Violent Behavior* 13: 481–489.

Gonzales v. City of Castle Rock. 2002, October 15. U.S. Court of Appeals, Tenth Circuit. No. 01-1053. 307.F3d 1258.

Gonzales v. City of Castle Rock. 2004, April 29. U.S. Court of Appeals, Tenth Circuit. No. 01-1053. 366 F3d 1093.

Goode, Erich, and Nachman Ben-Yehuda. 2006. "Enter Moral Panics." In *Constructing Crime: Perspectives on Making New and Social Problems*, 2nd edition, edited by G. W. Potter and V. E. Kappeler, 21–28. Long Grove, IL: Waveland Press.

Goodman, Lisa, and Deborah Epstein. 2005. "Refocusing on Women: A New Direction for Policy and Research on Intimate Partner Violence." *Journal of Interpersonal Violence* 20: 479–487.

Gordon, Robert M. 1980. "Fear." *Philosophical Review* 89: 560–578.

Gover, Angela R., Dagmar Pudrzynska Paul, and Mary Dodge. 2011. "Law Enforcement Officers' Attitudes about Domestic Violence." *Violence Against Women* 17: 619–636.

Grabill, Jeffery T. 2000. "Shaping Local AIDS/HIV Services Policy through Activist Research: The Problem of Client Involvement." *Technical Communication Quarterly* 9: 29–50.

Grabill, Jeffrey T., and Michele Simmons. 1998. "Toward a Critical Rhetoric of Risk Communication: Producing Citizens and the Role of Technical Communicators." *Technical Communication Quarterly* 7: 415–441.

Gustafson, Daniel E., Karla M. Gluek, David A. Goodwin, and Raina C. Borrelli. 2015, August 19. "Plaintiffs' Remedies Proposal and Brief in Support of the Remedies Proposal." United States District Court District of Minnesota. Civil File No. 11-cv-3659 (DWK/JJK).

Hall, Stuart. 1978. *Policing the Crisis: Mugging, the State, and Law and Order.* New York, NY: Holmes & Meier.

Halverson, Nancy. 2014, September. "An Interview." The National Center for Victims of Crime, Stalking Resource Center, Practitioner Perspectives. http://www.victimsofcrime.org/docs/default-source/src/nancy-halverson.pdf?sfvrsn=0, (accessed November 21, 2016).

Hanna, Cheryl. 1997–1998. "The Paradox of Hope: The Crime and Punishment of Domestic Violence." *William and Mary Law Review* 39: 1505–1584.

Hassan, Anita, and Mike Ward. 2014, December 30. "Judge in Controversial Sex Offender Program under Fire." *Houston Chronicle.* http://www.houstonchronicle.com/news/houston-texas/houston/article/Judge-in-controversial-sex-offender-program-under-5986273.php, (accessed November 21, 2016).

Hassouneh, Dena, and Nancy Glass. 2008. "The Influence of Gender Role Stereotyping on Women's Experience of Female Same-Sex Intimate Partner Violence." *Violence Against Women* 14: 310–325.

Heln, Amy Holmes. 2014, November 11. "'Heartsick' Elias—Case Judge Challenges Domestic Violence Myths: Guest Opinion." *The Oregonian.* http://www.oregonlive.com/opinion/index.ssf/2014/11/heartsick_elias-case_judge_tak.html, (accessed November 21, 2016).

Hier, Sean P. 2002. "Conceptualizing Moral Panic through a Moral Economy of Harm." *Critical Sociology* 28: 311–334.

Hirsh, Elizabeth, and Gary A. Olson. 1995. "Starting from Marginalized Lives: A Conversation with Sandra Harding." *Journal of Advanced Composition* 15: 193–225.

Hollander, Jocelyn. 2001. "Vulnerability and Dangerousness: The Construction of Gender through Conversation about Violence." *Gender and Society* 15: 83–109.

Hyden, Margareta. 2005. "'I Must Have Been an Idiot to Let It Go On': Battered Women's Narratives of Leaving Agency and Positioning in Battered Women's Narratives of Leaving." *Feminism and Psychology* 15: 169–188.

Idaho Domestic Violence Court Website. 2015. https://www.isc.idaho.gov/domestic-violence/dvc-home, (accessed November 21, 2016).

Ingebretsen, Edward J. 2001. *At Stake: Monsters and the Rhetoric of Fear in Public Culture.* Chicago: University of Chicago Press.

In re Blodgett. 1994, January 14. 510 N.W.2d 910 (Minnesota).

In re Linehan. 1997. 118 S. Ct 596; 557 N.W.2d 171 (Minnesota).

In re the Civil Commitment of Ming Sen Shiue. 2011, April 26. Court of Appeals of Minnesota. No. A10-2006. http://caselaw.findlaw.com/mn-court-of-appeals/1564982.html, (accessed November 21, 2016).

In re the Matter of Clarence Joseph Opheim. 2011, April 20. Findings of Fact and Recommendations, State of Minnesota, County of Ramsey, Department of Human Services, Special Review Board. https://s3.amazonaws.com/s3.documentcloud.org/documents/289513/opheim-05-20-11-jap-notice.pdf, (accessed November 21, 2016).

In re the Matter of Leon James Preston. 2001, June 12. Court of Appeals of Minnesota. No. C5-00-1715. http://caselaw.findlaw.com/mn-court-of-appeals/1372823.html, (accessed November 21, 2016).

Irvine, Janice M. 2008. "Transient Feelings: Sex Panics and the Politics of Emotion." *GLQ: A Journal of Lesbian and Gay Studies* 14: 1–40.

Jackson, Rebecca L., and Derek T. Hess. 2007. "Evaluation for Civil Commitment of Sex Offenders: A Survey of Experts." *Sexual Abuse: A Journal of Research and Treatment* 19: 425–448.

Janus, Eric. 2006. *Failure to Protect: America's Sexual Predator Laws and the Rise of the Preventive State*. Ithaca, NY: Cornell University Press.

Jenkins, Philip. 1998. *Moral Panic: Changing Concepts of the Child Molester in Modern America*. New Haven, CT: Yale University Press.

Jesson, Lucinda. 2015, February 13. Cross-Examination by Defense. *Karsjens et al. v. Jesson et al.* United States District Court, District of Minnesota. File No. 11-3659 (DWF/JJK).

Johnson, Carol A. "'You Can Never Be Sure' You Won't Reoffend? Crucial Words." *StarTribune*. http://www.startribune.com/readers-write-feb-28-federal-deficit-sex-offenders-farmland-values-and-taxes-politics-and-religion/370333501/, (accessed November 21, 2016).

Johnson, Joy L., Joan L. Bottorff, Annette Browne, Sukhdev Grewal, B. Ann Hilton, and Heather Clarke. 2004. "Othering and Being Othered in the Context of Health Care Services." *Health Communication* 16: 255–271.

Johnston, Nancy. 2015, February 26. Direct Examination by the Plaintiffs. *Karsjens et al. v. Jesson et al.* United States District Court, District of Minnesota. File No. 11-3659 (DWF/JJK).

Kahn, Paul. 2003. "Freedom, Autonomy, and the Cultural Study of Law." In *Cultural Analysis, Cultural Studies, and the Law: Moving Beyond Legal Realism*, edited by Austin Sarat and Jonathan Simon, 154–187. Durham, NC: Duke University Press.

Kansas v. Crane. 2002. 534 U.S. 407.

Kansas v. Hendricks. 1997. 521 U.S. 346.

Kappeler, Victor E., and Gary W. Potter. 2005. *The Mythology of Crime and Criminal Justice*, 4th edition. Long Grove, IL: Waveland Press.

Karsjens et al. v. Jesson et al. 2015. "Findings of Fact, Conclusions of Law, and Order." United States District Court, District of Minnesota. File No. 11-3659 (DWF/JJK). https://www.docketalarm.com/cases/Minnesota_District_Court/0--11-cv-03659/Karsjens_et_al_v._Minnesota_Department_of_Human_Services_et_al/, (accessed November 21, 2016).

Kathman, Ryan. 2007, July 9. "Van Keuren Gets Life Without Parole for 2 Murders." *LillieNews.com*. http://lillienews.com/content/van-keuren-gets-life-without-parole-2-murders, (accessed November 21, 2016).

Kelly, Liz. 1988. *Surviving Sexual Violence*. Minneapolis: University of Minnesota Press.

Knievel, Michael S. 2008. "Rupturing Context, Resituating Genre: A Study of Use-of-Force Policy in the Wake of a Controversial Shooting." *Journal of Business and Technical Communication* 22: 330–363.

Kohn, Laurie S. 2008. "The Justice System and Domestic Violence: Engaging the Case but Divorcing the Victim." *NYU Review of Law and Social Change* 32: 191–252.

Konradi, Amanda. 1996. "Understanding Rape Survivors' Preparations for Court." *Violence Against Women* March: 25–62.

Kotb, Hoda. 2007, August 13. "Nowhere to Hide: When Teri Lee's Life Was Threatened by an Ex-Boyfriend, She Did Everything She Could to Protect Herself and Her Children. Would Anyone Help?" Dateline NBC. http://www.nbcnews.com/id/20252303/ns/dateline_nbc-crime_reports/t/nowhere-hide/#.VDf_Qued6Hk, (accessed November 21, 2016).

Krantz, G. 2002. "Violence Against Women: A Global Public Health Issue!" Editorial. *Journal of Epidemiology & Community Health* 52: 242–243.

Kress, Gunther, and Theo Van Leeuwen. 2001. *Multimodal Discourse: The Modes and Media of Contemporary Communication*. London, UK: Arnold Press; New York, NY: Oxford University Press.

Kristeva, Julia. 1982. *Powers of Horror: An Essay on Abjection*. Leon S. Roudiez (transl.). New York, NY: Columbia University Press.

Kytonen, Rachel. 2013, November 20. "Gov. Dayton Suspends State's Plan to Transfer Sex Offender Clients to Cambridge." *The ECM Post Review*. http://ecmpostreview.com/2013/11/20/gov-dayton-suspends-states-plan-transfer-sex-offender-clients-cambridge/, (accessed November 21, 2016).

LaFond, John Q. 2000. "The Future of Involuntary Civil Commitment in the U.S.A. after *Kansas v. Hendricks*." *Behavioral Science and the Law* 18: 153–167.

Lancaster, Roger. 2011. *Sex Panic and the Punitive State*. Berkeley, CA: University of California Press.

Lane, Charles. 2005, March 21. "Court Tackles Town's Role in Child Safety: 3 Daughters Died When Colorado Police Refused to Arrest Banned Father." *The Washington Post:* A02. http://www.washingtonpost.com/wp-dyn/articles/A52168-2005Mar20.html?nav=rss_nation/courts/supremecourt, (accessed November 21, 2016).

Larcombe, Wendy. 2012. "Sex Offender Risk Assessment: The Need to Place Recidivism Research in the Context of Attrition in the Criminal Justice System." *Violence Against Women* 18: 482–501.

Legal Information Institute. 2015a. "Lesser Included Offense." https://www.law.cornell.edu/wex/lesser_included_offense, (accessed November 21, 2016).

Legal Information Institute. 2015b. "Rule 706. Court-Appointed Expert Witnesses." https://www.law.cornell.edu/rules/fre/rule_706, (accessed November 21, 2016).

Leon, Chrysanthi. 2001. *Sex Fiends, Perverts, and Pedophiles: Understanding Sex Crime Policy in America*. New York, NY: New York University Press.

Lininger, Tom. 2009. "The Sound of Silence: Holding Batterers Accountable for Silencing Their Victims." *Texas Law Review* 87: 857–912.

Longo, Bernadette. 2000. *Spurious Coin*. Albany, NY: SUNY Press.

Lonsway, Kimberly A., and Louise F. Fitzgerald. 1994. "Rape Myths, In Review." *Psychology of Women Quarterly* 18: 133–164.

Magnuson, Eric. 2013, December 2. "Task Force Final Report." *StarTribune*. http://stmedia.startribune.com/documents/Final+Report+--+Sex+Offender+Task+Force.pdf, (accessed November 21, 2016).

Mahoney, Martha. 1991. "Legal Images of Battered Women: Redefining the Issue of Separation." *Michigan Law Review* 90: 1, 5–6, 65–76, 78–79.

Marin County Threat Advisory Team. n.d. http://www.studentthreatassessment.com/adult-threat-assessment, (accessed November 21, 2016).

Martin, Emily. 1998. *The Woman in the Body: A Cultural Analysis of Reproduction*. Boston, Mass: Beacon Press.
Martinez, Edecio. 2010, April 20. "Ming Sen Shiue Terrified Minnesota, Served 30 Years for Murder, Kidnapping; Will He Go Free?" CBS News. http://www.cbsnews.com/news/ming-sen-shiue-terrified-minnesota-served-30-years-for-murder-kidnappings-will-he-go-free/, (accessed November 21, 2016).
Martinez-Rumundo, Denise. 2010, June 22. "Ming Shiue: Inside the Mind of a Psychopathic Killer." ABC News. http://abcnews.go.com/Primetime/primetime-mind-games-1980-kidnapping-mary-stauffer-math/story?id=10979437, (accessed November 21, 2016).
Maryland Network Against Domestic Violence. n.d.a. "Domestic Violence Lethality Assessment Program: 'Something's Going to Happen.'" The Lethality Assessment Committee, and the Division of Public Safety Leadership of Johns Hopkins University. Compact Disc. MNADV, 6911 Laurel Bowie Road, Suite 309, Bowie, MN, 20715.
Maryland Network Against Domestic Violence. n.d.b. "Lethality Assessment Program for First Responders: Learning to Read the Danger Signs." Training Slides. MNADV, 6911 Laurel Bowie Road, Suite 309, Bowie, MN, 20715. http://mnadv.org/_mnadvWeb/wp-content/uploads/2011/10/LAP_Info_Packet--as_of_12-8-10.pdf, (accessed November 21, 2016).
Maryland Network Against Domestic Violence. 2014, October. "Revised Statistics Information." http://mnadv.org/_mnadvWeb/wp-content/uploads/2014/10/LAP-Public-Stats-Memo.pdf, (accessed November 21, 2016).
McCool, Daniel C. 1995. *Public Policy Theories, Models, and Concepts: An Anthology*. Upper Saddle River, NJ: Prentice Hall.
McCulloch, Deborah. 2015, February 10. Direct Examination by the Plaintiffs. *Karsjens et al. v. Jesson et al.* United States District Court, District of Minnesota. File No. 11-3659 (DWF/JJK).
McEnroe, Paul. 2001, April 17. "Sex-Offender System Casts Wide Net." *StarTribune*. http://www.startribune.com/politics/statelocal/120031999.html, (accessed November 21, 2016).
McEnroe, Paul. 2011, February 8. "Seven Sex Offenders Might Be Released." *StarTribune*. www.startribune.com/politics/115577344.html, (accessed November 21, 2016).
McEnroe, Paul. 2012, March 5. "Golden Valley Prepares for Sex Felon Moving into Halfway House." *StarTribune*. http://www.startribune.com/golden-valley-prepares-for-sex-felon-moving-into-halfway-house/141525463/, (accessed November 21, 2016).
McKinnon, Sara L. 2012. "Essentialism, Intersectionality and Recognition: A Feminist Rhetorical Approach to the Audience." In *Standing in the Intersection: Feminist Voices, Feminist Practices in Communication Studies*, edited by Karma R. Chávez and Cindy L. Griffin, 189–210. Albany: SUNY Press.
Meloy, Michelle L. 2006. *Sex Offenses and the Men Who Commit Them: An Assessment of Sex Offenders on Probation*. Lebanon, NY: University of New England Press.
Merry, Sally Engle. 2009. *Gender Violence: A Cultural Perspective*. Chichester, West Sussex, England: John Wiley.
Messing, Jill Theresa, and Jonel Thaller. 2013. "The Average Predictive Validity of Intimate Partner Violence Risk Assessment Instruments." *Journal of Interpersonal Violence* 28: 1537–1558.

Messing, Jill Theresa, Jacquelyn C. Campbell, Sheryll Brown, Beverly Patchell, David K. Androff, and Janet Sullivan Wilson. 2014. "The Association Between Protective Actions and Homicide Risk: Findings From the Oklahoma Lethality Assessment Study." *Violence and Victims* 29: 543–563.

Miller, Carolyn R. 1984. "Genre as Social Action." *Quarterly Journal of Speech* 70: 151–167.

Miller, Carolyn R. 1992. "*Kairos* in the Rhetoric of Science." In *A Rhetoric of Doing: Essays on Written Discourse in Honor of James L. Kinneavy*, edited by S. P. White, N. Nakadate, and R. D. Cherry, 310–327. Carbondale: Southern Illinois University Press.

Miller, Carolyn R. 1994. "Opportunity, Opportunism, and Progress: *Kairos* in the Rhetoric of Technology." *Argumentation* 8: 81–96.

Miner, Michael. 2015, February 13. Direct Testimony. *Karsjens et al. v. Jesson et al.* United States District Court, District of Minnesota. File No. 11-3659 (DWF/JJK).

Minnesota Bureau of Criminal Apprehension. 2010. *Minnesota Predatory Offender Registration.* https://por.state.mn.us/predatorfaq.aspx, (accessed November 21, 2016).

Minnesota Coalition for Battered Women, 2005, March. "Facts About Intimate Partner Strangulation." http://media.wix.com/ugd/f4bdb8_3e221245c0b2069dd34ae333c2d65ab2.pdf, (accessed November 21, 2016).

Minnesota Coalition for Battered Women. 2015. "Femicide Report." http://media.wix.com/ugd/f4bdb8_b249771454f247d6bd2e9bb4037bc671.pdf, (accessed November 21, 2016).

Minnesota Court Rules. 2014, August 1. "Sentencing Guidelines." https://www.revisor.mn.gov/court_rules/rule.php?name=sg-toh, (accessed November 21, 2016).

Minnesota Department of Corrections. 2014. "Level 3 Predatory Offender Search." https://coms.doc.state.mn.us/Level3/SearchResults.asp?SearchType=City&City=St.+Paul, (accessed November 21, 2016).

Minnesota Department of Human Services. 2014. "Minnesota Sex Offender Program. Frequently Asked Questions." https://mn.gov/dhs/people-we-serve/adults/services/sex-offender-treatment/faqs.jsp, (accessed November 21, 2016).

Minnesota House File 6. 2011, May 5. Sex Offender Sentencing. http://www.house.leg.state.mn.us/hrd/bs/87/HF0006.pdf, (accessed November 21, 2016).

Minnesota House Health and Human Services Reform Committee. 2012, February 15. Meeting video. http://www.house.leg.state.mn.us/htv/programa.asp?ls_year=87&event_id=4028, (accessed November 21, 2016).

Minnesota Legislative Auditor. 2011, March 3. *Evaluation Report: Civil Commitment of Sex Offenders*, Program Evaluation Division, Department of Corrections, 1450 Energy Park Drive, Suite 200. http://www.auditor.leg.state.mn.us/ped/pedrep/ccso.pdf, (accessed November 21, 2016).

Minnesota Public Radio. 2004, January 8. "Pawlenty Outlines Proposal for Dealing with Sex Offenders." http://news.minnesota.publicradio.org/features/2004/01/08_scheckt_prison/, (accessed November 21, 2016).

Minnesota Sentencing Guidelines & Commentary. 2013, August 1. https://www.revisor.mn.gov/statutes/?id=244.09, (accessed November 21, 2016).

Minnesota Sentencing Guidelines Grid. 2014, August 1. https://mn.gov/sentencing-guidelines/guidelines/, (accessed November 21, 2016).

Minnesota Sex Offender Grid. 2016, August 1. http://mn.gov/msgc-stat/documents/2016%20Guidelines/2016%20Sex%20Offender%20Grid.pdf, (accessed November 21, 2016).

Minnesota Statutes 244.052. 2014. "Predatory Offenders; Notice." https://www.revisor.mn.gov/statutes/?id=244.052, (accessed November 21, 2016).

Minnesota Statutes 244.09. 2014 "Minnesota Sentencing Guidelines Commission." https://www.revisor.mn.gov/statutes/?id=244.09, (accessed November 21, 2016).

Minnesota Statutes 253B.18. Subd.15. 2014. "Persons Who Are Mentally Ill and Dangerous to the Public. Discharge." https://www.revisor.mn.gov/statutes/?id=253B.18, (accessed November 21, 2016).

Minnesota Statutes 253D.02. Subd. 15. 2014. "Sexual Psychopathic Personality." https://www.revisor.mn.gov/statutes/?id=253D.02, (accessed November 21, 2016).

Minnesota Statutes 253D.02. Subd. 16. 2014. "Sexually Dangerous Person." https://www.revisor.mn.gov/statutes/?id=253D.02, (accessed November 21, 2016).

Minnesota Statutes 253D.29. 2014. "Provisional Discharge." https://www.revisor.mn.gov/statutes/?id=253D.30, (accessed November 21, 2016).

Minnesota Statutes 518B.01. 2014. Subd. 4. "Domestic Abuse Act: Order for Protection." https://www.revisor.mn.gov/statutes/?id=518B.01, (accessed November 21, 2016).

Minnesota Statutes 518B.01. 2014. Subd. 14 "Domestic Abuse Act: Violation of an Order for Protection." https://www.revisor.leg.state.mn.us/statutes/?id=518B.01, (accessed November 21, 2016).

Minnesota Statutes 609.2247. 2014. "Domestic Assault by Strangulation." https://www.revisor.mn.gov/statutes/?id=609.2247, (accessed November 21, 2016).

Moniz, Josh. 2014, December 16. "Tense But Civil Le Center Sex Offender Hearing." *Mankato Free Press*. http://www.mankatofreepress.com/news/local_news/tense-but-civil-le-center-sex-offender-hearing/article_a9c3cddc-ce1a-5e70-a295-3d970947ee4e.html, (accessed November 21, 2016).

Moracco, Kathryn E., Kathryn Andersen, Rebecca M. Buchanan, Christina Espersen, J. Michael Bowling, and Courtney Duffy.2010. "Who Are the Defendants in Domestic Violence Protection Order Cases?" *Violence Against Women* 16: 1201–1223.

Morgan, Allison. 2006. "Civil Confinement of Sex Offenders: New York's Attempt to Push the Envelope in the Name of Public Safety." *Boston University Law Review* 86: 1001–1035.

Morris, A. Thomas. 1988. "The Empirical, Historical and Legal Case Against the Cautionary Instruction: A Call for Legislative Reform." *Duke Law Journal* 37: 154–173.

Morse, Stephen J. 1998. "Fear of Danger, Flight from Culpability." *Psychology, Public Policy, and Law* 4: 250–267.

Muehlenhard, Charlene L., and Leigh Ann Kimes. 1999. "The Social Construction of Violence: The Case of Sexual and Domestic Violence." *Personality and Social Psychology Review* 3: 234–245.

National Center for Victims of Crime. 2015. "Stalking Fact Sheet." https://www.victimsofcrime.org/docs/default-source/src/stalking-fact-sheet-2015_eng.pdf?sfvrsn=2, (accessed November 21, 2016).

NBC News, KARE 11. 2012, February 15. "House Committee Examines Sex Offender Discharge." http://minnesota.cbslocal.com/2012/02/15/house-committee-examines-sex-offender-discharge/, (accessed November 21, 2016).

New York Times, The. 2007, March 13. "Wrong Turn on Sex Offenders." http://www.nytimes.com/2007/03/13/opinion/13tue1.html?_r=0, (accessed November 21, 2016).

Nichols, Andrea J. 2013. "Survivor-Defined Practices to Mitigate Revictimization of Battered Women in the Protective Order Process." *Journal of Interpersonal Violence* 28: 1403–1423.

Oakes, Larry. 2008, June 9. "They're All Close Calls Now." *StarTribune.* http://www.startribune.com/local/19645554.html?page=1&c=y&refer=y, (accessed November 21, 2016).

Oakes, Larry. 2011, March 23. Updated from 2008, September 16. "Locked in Limbo." *StarTribune.* http://www.startribune.com/local/19615459.html, (accessed November 21, 2016).

Oakes, Larry. 2012, August 17. "Minnesota Must Change Sex Offender Program, Judge Orders." *StarTribune.* http://www.startribune.com/local/166497216.html, (accessed 2011).

Offen, Karen. 1988, Autumn. "Defining Feminism: A Comparative Historical Approach." *Signs: Journal of Women in Culture and Society* 14: 119–157.

Ombudsman, Office of, for Mental Health and Developmental Disabilities. 2010, July. "Sex Offender Civil Commitment Fact Sheet." Civil Commitment Training and Resource Center. https://mn.gov/omhdd/assets/sex-offender-cc-fact-sheet-2010_tcm23-27594.pdf, (accessed November 21, 2016).

Pajak, Carla Rose, Farah Ahmad, Angelique Jenney, Penny Fisher, and Linda M. Y. Chan. 2014. "Survivor's Cost of Saying No: Exploring the Experience of Accessing Services for Intimate Partner Violence." *Journal of Interpersonal Violence* 29: 2571–2591.

Paul P. v. Verniero. 1999. 170 F.3d 396 (3d Cir.).

Personal correspondence. 2014, June 4. Phone call with Mary L. Schuster.

Pfau, Michael William. 2007. "Who's Afraid of Fear Appeals? Contingency, Courage, and Deliberation in Rhetorical Theory." *Philosophy & Rhetoric* 40: 216–237.

Picart, Caroline Joan. 2003. "Rhetorically Reconfiguring Victimhood and Agency: The Violence Against Women Act's Civil Rights Clause." *Rhetoric & Public Affairs* 6: 97–125.

Pirius, Rebecca. 2012, November. "Domestic Abuse Laws in Minnesota: An Overview." Minnesota House of Representatives, Research Department. http://www.house.leg.state.mn.us/hrd/pubs/domabuse.pdf, (accessed November 21, 2016).

Pleck, Elizabeth. 2004. *Domestic Tyranny: The Making of American Social Policy Against Family Violence from Colonial Times to the Present.* Urbana: University of Illinois Press.

Poulakos, John. 1999. "Toward a Sophistic Definition of Rhetoric." In *Contemporary Rhetorical Theory*, edited by John Louis Lucaites, Celeste Michelle Condit, and Sally Caudill, 25–34. New York, NY: Guilford Press.

Prelli, Lawrence J. 1989. "The Rhetorical Construction of Scientific Ethos." *Evolution* 34 (5): 87–104.

Prince William County Government. 2015. "Pretrial Supervision." http://www.pwcgov.org/government/courts/cjs/Pages/Pretrial-Supervision.aspx, (accessed November 21, 2016).

Propen, Amy, and Mary Lay Schuster. 2008. "Making Academic Work Advocacy Work: Technologies of Power in the Public Arena." *Journal of Business and Technical Communication* 22 (July): 299–329.

Propen, Amy D., and Mary Lay Schuster. 2010. "Understanding Genre through the Lens of Advocacy: The Rhetorical Work of the Victim Impact Statement." *Written Communication* 27 (1): 3–35.

Ptacek, James. 1999. *Battered Women in the Courtroom: The Power of Judicial Responses.* Boston: Northeastern University Press.

Ratcliffe, Krista. 2005. *Rhetorical Listening: Identification, Gender, Whiteness.* Carbondale, IL: Southern Illinois University Press.

Reddington, Francis F. 2009. "A Brief History of Rape Law and Rape Law Reform in the United States." In *Sexual Assault: The Victims, the Perpetrators, and the Criminal Justice System*, 2nd edition, edited by Frances P. Reddington and Betsy Wright Kreisel, 319–333. Durham, NC: Carolina Academic Press.

"Relationship Assessment Tool." 2015. https://multco.us/file/8926/download, (accessed November 21, 2016).

Remsberg, Charles. 2007, December 11. "'Lethality Assessment' Helps Gauge Danger from Domestic Disputes." *PoliceOne.com.* http://www.policeone.com/patrol-issues/articles/1638964--Lethality-Assessment-helps-gauge-danger-from-domestic-disputes/, (accessed November 21, 2016).

Robson, Britt. 2004, January 28. "Capital Offenses: State Legislators Are Poised for a Spending Spree—On Stadiums and Prisons." *City Pages News.* http://www.citypages.com/2004-01-28/news/capitol-offenses/, (accessed 2011).

Rosenberg, Rosalind. 1982. *Beyond Separate Spheres: Intellectual Roots of Modern Feminism.* New Haven: Yale University Press.

Rosenblum, Gail. 2012, March 13. "Education, Empathy Useful for Legislators Weighing Sex Offender Program." *StarTribune.* http://www.startribune.com/rosenblum-education-empathy-useful-for-legislators-weighing-sex-offender-program/197902301/?refer=y, (accessed November 21, 2016).

Sadusky, Jane M. 2006. "Pretrial Release Conditions in Domestic Violence Cases: Issues and Context." Battered Women's Justice Project. http://www.bwjp.org/assets/documents/pdfs/pretrial_release_conditions_domestic_violence_cases.pdf, (accessed November 21, 2016).

Sakry, Tammy. 2012, April 19. "The 13 Questions That Could Save a Life." ABC Newspapers. http://abcnewspapers.com/2012/04/19/the-13-questions-that-could-save-a-life/, (accessed November 21, 2016).

Sakry, Tammy. 2012, June 29. "Program Helps Offenders Break the Cycle." ABC Newspapers. http://abcnewspapers.com/2012/06/29/program-helps-offenders-break-the-cycle/, (accessed November 21, 2016).

Salzhauer, Eliana, and Claire Gordon. 2014, April 5. "Florida Becomes the Harshest State for Sex Offenders." Aljazeera America. http://america.aljazeera.com/watch/shows/america-tonight/articles/2014/4/5/florida-becomes-theharsheststateforsexoffenders.html, (accessed November 21, 2016).

Sample, Lisa L., and Colleen Kadleck. 2008. "Sex Offender Laws: Legislators' Accounts of the Need for Policy." *Criminal Justice Policy Review* 19: 40–62.

Sarat, Austin, and Thomas R. Kearns. 2000. "The Cultural Lives of Law." In *Law in the Domains of Culture*, edited by Austin Sarat and Thomas R. Kearns, 1–20. Ann Arbor: University of Michigan Press.

Sarat, Austin, Marianne Constable, David Engel, Valerie Hans, and Susan Lawrence. 1998. "The Concepts of Boundaries in the Practices and Products of Sociolegal Scholarship: An Introduction." In *Crossing Boundaries: Traditions and Transformation in Law and Society Research*, edited by Austin Sarat et al. 1–17. Evanston, IL: Northwestern University Press.

Sargent, David. 2011, May. "Interview," Center for Court Innovation. http://www.courtinnovation.org/research/11-questions-officers-assess-homicide-risk, (accessed November 21, 2016).

Sartre, Jean-Paul. 1956. *Being and Nothingness: A Phenomenological Essay on Ontology*. Hazel Barnes (transl.). New York: Simon and Schuster.

Savage, Jessica. 2006. "Battered Woman Syndrome." *Georgetown Journal of Law and Gender* 7: 761–769.

Schade, Brad. 2013, March 4. "Minnesota Sex Offenders Program at Risk of Court Takeover." *StarTribune*. http://www.startribune.com/minnesota-sex-offender-program-at-risk-of-court-takeover/195182761/, (accessed November 21, 2016).

Schafron, Lynn Hecht. 1992. "Maiming the Soul: Judges, Sentencing and the Myth of the Nonviolent Rapist." *Fordham Urban Law Review* 20: 439–453.

Scheppele, Kim. 1992. "Just the Facts, Ma'am: Sexualized Violence, Evidentiary Habits, and the Revision of Truth." *New York Law Review* 37: 123–172.

Schneider, Elizabeth. 2000. *Battered Women and Feminist Lawmaking*. New Haven, CT: Yale University Press.

Schneider, Elizabeth. 1993. "Feminism and the False Dichotomy of Victimization and Agency." *New York Law School Law Review* 38: 387–399.

Schuster, Mary Lay, and Amy D. Propen. 2011. *Victim Advocacy in the Courtroom: Persuasive Practices in Domestic Violence and Child Protection Cases*. Boston, MA: Northeastern University Press.

Scott, J. Blake. 2006. "Kairos as Indeterminate Risk Management: The Pharmaceutical Industry's Response to Bioterrorism." *Quarterly Journal of Speech* 92: 115–143.

Searle, John R. 1995. *The Construction of Social Reality*. New York: The Free Press.

Segal, Judy Z. 2005. *Health and the Rhetoric of Medicine*. Carbondale: University of Southern Illinois Press.

Serran, Geris, and Philip Firestone. 2004. "Intimate Partner Homicide: A Review of the Male Proprietariness and the Self-Defense Theories." *Aggression and Violent Behavior* 9: 1–15.

Serres, Chris. 2014, January 15. "Lawmakers Weigh Changes to Minnesota's Sex-Offender Program." *StarTribune*. http://www.startribune.com/lawmakers-weigh-changes-to-minnesota-s-sex-offender-program/240347761/, (accessed November 21, 2016).

Serres, Chris. 2014, February 20. "Federal Judge Questions Legality of Minnesota's Sex Offender Program." *StarTribune*. http://www.startribune.com/politics/statelocal/246389931.html, (accessed November 21, 2016).

Serres, Chris. 2015, March 12. "Rape Survivor Recounts Night of Horror, Warns Against Release of Offenders." *StarTribune*. http://www.startribune.com/

rape-survivor-warns-against-releasing-sex-offenders/296135791/, (accessed November 21, 2016).

Serres, Chris. 2015, June 17. "Minnesota Sex Offender Program Is Ruled Unconstitutional." *StarTribune.* http://www.startribune.com/judge-expected-to-rule-today-in-lawsuit-challenging-minnesota-s-sex-offender-program/307884871/, (accessed November 21, 2016).

Serres, Chris. 2015, July 24. "Eric Magnuson, Former Chief Justice of Minnesota, Selected for Key Role in Sex Offender Lawsuit." *StarTribune.* http://www.startribune.com/former-minnesota-supreme-court-chief-magnuson-picked-for-key-role-in-sex-offender-lawsuit/318368841/, (accessed November 21, 2016).

Serres, Chris. 2015, August 11. "Thrice-Convicted Rapist Granted Provisional Discharge from Minnesota Sex Offender Program." Star Tribune. 11 August 2015. http://www.startribune.com/68-year-old-rapist-granted-provisional-discharge-from-minnesota-sex-offender-program/321450821/, (accessed November 21, 2016).

Serres, Chris. 2015. August 26. "Man Convicted of Raping Girls is given Conditional Release, but State Vows Appeal." Star Tribune. 26 August 2015. http://www.startribune.com/man-convicted-of-raping-girls-granted-release-but-state-vows-appeal/323024251/, (accessed November 21, 2016).

Serres, Chris. 2016, February 10. "Rapist Heading to St. Paul, Joins Ranks of Sex Offenders Being Released." *StarTribune.* http://www.startribune.com/rapist-heading-to-st-paul-joins-ranks-of-sex-offenders-being-released/368264781/, (accessed November 21, 2016).

Serres, Chris. 2016, February 11. "Release of Convicted Rapist Draws a Crowd to St. Paul Meeting." http://www.startribune.com/release-of-convicted-rapist-expected-to-draw-big-crowd-tonight-at-public-meeting-in-st-paul/368353651/, (accessed November 21, 2016).

Serres, Chris. 2016, February 20. "As Door Inches Open from SMOP, a Sex Offender Ponders Being Free." *StarTribune.* http://www.startribune.com/as-door-inches-open-from-msop-a-sex-offender-ponders-being-free/369509232/, (accessed November 21, 2016).

"Sex Offender Civil Commitment in Minnesota: Challenges and Opportunities." 2012, January 19. Public Symposium at Mitchell Hamline School of Law. http://calendar.wmitchell.edu/calendar/EventList.aspx?fromdate=1/19/2012&todate=1/19/2012&display=Day&type=public&eventidn=23371&view=EventDetails&information_id=69101, (accessed January 2012).

"Sex Offender Notification." 2014. http://www.stpaul.gov/index.aspx?NID=1811, (accessed November 21, 2016).

Sharps, Phyllis W., Jane Koziol-McLain, Jacquelyn C. Campbell, and Xiao Xu. 2001. "Health Care Providers' Missed Opportunities for Preventing Femicide." *Preventative Medicine* 33: 373–380.

Shenoy, Rupa. 2011, March 11. "Audit: Inconsistencies, High Cost in Minn. Sex Offender Treatment." Minnesota Public Radio. http://minnesota.publicradio.org/display/web/2011/03/11/sex-offender-report/, (accessed November 21, 2016).

Shepard, Melanie F., Barbara A. Elliott, Dennis R. Falk, and Ronald R. Regal. 1999. "Public Health Nurses' Responses to Domestic Violence: A Report from the Enhanced Domestic Abuse Intervention Project." *Public Health Nursing* 16: 359–366.

Sheridan, Lorraine, and Karl Rogers. 2011. "Key Questions to Consider in Stalking Cases." *Behavior Sciences and the Law* 29: 255–270.

Smith, Barbara E., and Robert C. Davis. 2004. "An Evaluation of Efforts to Implement No-Drop Policies: Two Central Values in Conflict." National Criminal Justice Reference Center. https://www.ncjrs.gov/pdffiles1/nij/199719.pdf, (accessed November 21, 2016).

Smith, John. 2002. "Time and Qualitative Time." In *Rhetoric and Kairos: Essays in History, Theory, and Praxis*, edited by Phillip Sipiora and James S. Baumlin, 46–57. Albany: State University of New York Press.

Smith, Mary Lynn, and Dave Hage. 2012, July 25. "Minnesota Sex-Offender Lawsuit Takes Step Forward; Class-Action Case Questions Legality of the State Program." *StarTribune*. http://www.highbeam.com/doc/1G1-297569463.html, (accessed November 21, 2016).

Sokoloff, Natalie J. 2004. "Domestic Violence at the Crossroads: Violence Against Poor Women and Women of Color." *Women's Studies Quarterly* 32: 139–147.

Spears, Jeffrey W. 2005. "Prosecution of Sex Crimes." In *Sexual Assault: The Victims, the Perpetrators, and the Criminal Justice System*, edited by Frances P. Reddington and Betsy Wright Kreisel, 281–297. Durham, NC: Carolina Academic Press.

Spinuzzi, Clay. 1996. "Pseudotransactionality, Activity Theory, and Professional Writing." *Technical Communication Quarterly* 5: 295–308.

Spinuzzi, Clay. 2003. *Tracing Genres through Organizations: A Sociocultural Approach to Information Design*. Cambridge, MN: MIT Press.

Sreenivasan, Shoba, Linda E. Weinberger, and Thomas Garrick. 2003. "Expert Testimony in Sexually Violent Predator Commitments: Conceptualizing Legal Standards of 'Mental Disorder' and 'Likely to Reoffend.'" *Journal of the American Academy of Psychiatry and the Law* 31: 471–485.

Stahl, Brandon, and Maya Rao. 2013, April 15. "A Backlash Against Minnesota's Growing Ranks of Level Three Sex Offenders." *StarTribune*. http://www.startribune.com/backlash-grows-against-minnesota-level-three-sex-offenders/202872731/, (accessed November 21, 2016).

StarTribune. 1999, December 9. "Dangerous Folks: Linehan Stays Where He Belongs." http://www.highbeam.com/doc/1G1-86870439.html, (accessed November 21, 2016).

StarTribune. 2012, February 8. "Keep Politics Out of Sex Offender Release." http://www.startribune.com/editorial-keep-politics-out-of-sex-offender-release/138896229/, (accessed November 21, 2016).

StarTribune. 2012, November 30. "High-Risk Sex Offender to Move from Golden Valley to Minneapolis." http://minnesota.cbslocal.com/2012/11/30/high-risk-sex-offender-to-move-from-golden-valley-to-mpls/, (accessed November 21, 2016).

StarTribune. 2013, March 30. "Minnesota Sex Offender Program Needs Calm Reform." Editorial Board. http://www.startribune.com/minnesota-sex-offender-program-needs-calm-reform/200654681/, (accessed November 21, 2016).

StarTribune. 2013, October 5. "Minnesota Sees an Outbreak of Domestic Violence: Reported Deaths Have Already Doubled over 2012." Editorial Board http://www.startribune.com/opinion/editorials/226530621.html, (accessed November 21, 2016).

Starzonski, Andrew, and David Nussbaum. 2000. "The Self and the Psychology of Domestic Homicide-Suicide." *International Journal of Offender Therapy and Comparative Criminology* 4: 468–479.

State of Minnesota, Respondent, v. Steven Van Keuren, Appellant. 2008, December 18. No. A07-1842. http://caselaw.findlaw.com/mn-supreme-court/1029745.html, (accessed November 21, 2016).

State v. Norman. 1989. 324 N.C. 253, 378 S. E. 2d 8.

Stern, Paul. 2000. "The Civil Commitment of Sexually Violent Predators: When We Know the Danger We Face, What Should Our Response Be?" *Trauma, Violence, Abuse* 1: 99–102.

Swales, John M. 1990. *Genre Analysis: English in Academic and Research Settings.* Cambridge: Cambridge University Press.

Tallian, Karen. 2013, February 20. "Sex Offender Laws Are Not the Best Way to Protect Children." *The New York Times.* http://www.nytimes.com/roomfordebate/2013/02/20/too-many-restrictions-on-sex-offenders-or-too-few/sex-offender-laws-are-not-the-best-way-to-protect-children, (accessed November 21, 2016).

Texas Council on Family Violence. n.d. "Domestic Violence Personal Safety Plan." http://tcfv.org/pdf/PSP%20ENGLISH.pdf, (accessed November 21, 2016).

Thapar-Björkert, Suruchi, and Karen J. Morgan. (2010). "'But Sometimes I Think ... They Put Themselves in the Situation': Exploring Blame and Responsibility in Interpersonal Violence." *Violence Against Women* 16: 32–59.

Threat Assessment Twin Cities. n.d. "Violence Prevention Through Threat Management." https://threatassessmenttc.wordpress.com/, (accessed November 21, 2016).

Tice, D. J. 2013, January 23. "Minnesota's Sex Offenders—Dealing with the Worst in a Better Way." *StarTribune.* http://www.startribune.com/minnesota-s-sex-offenders-dealing-with-the-worst-in-a-better-way/137927713/, (accessed November 21, 2016).

Tice, D. J. 2014, February 1. "Tough Thing, Isn't It, This 'Due Process?'" *StarTribune.* http://www.startribune.com/opinion/commentaries/243012671.html, (accessed November 21, 2016).

Tomljanovich, Esther M. 2005, January. *Governor's Commission on Sex Offender Policy: Final Report.* https://www.leg.state.mn.us/docs/2005/other/050099.pdf, (accessed November 21, 2016).

Totenberg, Nina. 2010, January 12. "Federal Prisoners Kept Beyond Their Sentences." National Public Radio. http://www.npr.org/templates/story/story.php?storyId=122452485, (accessed November 21, 2016).

Town of Castle Rock, Colorado v. Gonzales. 2005, June 27. 545 U.S. 748.

Training Institute on Strangulation Prevention. 2013, July 22. "Life and Death in Your Hands: Strangulation More Common in Domestic Abuse Cases." https://www.strangulationtraininginstitute.com/life-and-death-in-your-hands-strangulation-more-common-in-domestic-abuse-cases/, (accessed November 21, 2016).

Trinch, Shonna. 2010. "Forging Violence Against Women: Documents, Regimes of Family and Intimate-Partner Violence." *Law, Culture and the Humanities* 7: 394–412.

Tubman Family Crisis and Support Services, n.d. "Supportive Information for Victims of Domestic Violence." http://www.tubman.org/documents/supportive_info_booklet.pdf, (accessed November 21, 2016).

Tullock, J. 1999. "Fear of Crime and the Media: Sociocultural Theories of Risk." In *Risk and Sociological Theory: New Directions and Perspectives*, edited by Deborah Lupton, 34–58. Cambridge, UK: Cambridge University Press.

US v. Comstock. 2009. 551 F.3d 274, 275–276 (4th Circuit).

U.S. Department of Justice, 2005. *Family Violence Statistics: Including Statistics on Strangers and Acquaintances*. Office of Justice Programs, Bureau of Justice Statistics. bjs.ojp.usdoj.gov/content/pub/pdf/fvs.pdf, (accessed November 21, 2016).

Vainik, Jennifer. 2006–2007. "Kiss, Kiss, Bang, Bang: How Current Approaches to Guns and Domestic Violence Fail to Save Women's Lives." *Minnesota Law Review* 91: 1111–1154.

Vandello, Joseph A., and Dov Cohen. 2003. "Male Honor and Female Fidelity: Implicit Cultural Scripts That Perpetrate Domestic Violence." *Journal of Personality and Social Psychology* 84: 997–1010.

Van Houtum, Henk, and Ton Van Naerssen. 2001. "Bordering, Ordering and Othering." *Royal Dutch Geographical Society* 93: 125–136.

Van Orden et al. v. Schafer et al. 2015, September 11. United States District Court Eastern District of Missouri, Eastern Division. http://law.justia.com/cases/federal/district-courts/missouri/moedce/4:2009cv00971/100544/467/, (accessed November 21, 2016).

Vess, James. 2009. "Fear and Loathing in Public Policy: Ethical Issues in Laws for Sex Offenders." *Aggression and Violent Behavior* 14: 264–272.

Vinton, Linda, and Dina J. Wilke. 2014. "Are Collaborations Enough? Professionals' Knowledge of Victim Services." *Violence Against Women* 20: 716–729.

Violence Policy Center. 2012, May. *American Roulette: Murder-Suicide in the United States*, 4th edition. Violence Policy Center, 1730 Rhode Island Ave., NW, Suite 1014, Washington, D.C., 20036. http://www.vpc.org/studies/amroul2012.pdf, (accessed November 21, 2016).

Virginia Department of Criminal Justice Services. 2013, October. *Review of Lethality Assessment Programs (LAP)*. http://www.postandcourier.com/tilldeath/assets/d1-25.pdf, (accessed November 21, 2016).

Vokey, Megan, Bruce Tefft, and Chris Tysiaczny. 2013. "An Analysis of Hyper-Masculinity in Magazine Advertisements." *Sex Roles* 68: 562–576.

Walker, Leonore A. 1991. "Post-traumatic Stress Disorder in Women: Diagnosis and Treatment of Battered Woman Syndrome." *Psychotherapy: Theory, Research, Practice, Training* 28: 21–29.

Walton, Douglas. 2000. *Scare Tactics: Arguments that Appeal to Fear and Threats*. Boston: Kluwer Academic Publishers.

Washington County. n.d. "Conducting a Lethality Screen for First Responders." Laminated card.

Websdale, Neil. 2000, February. "Lethality Assessment Tools: A Critical Analysis." National Online Resource Center on Violence Against Women. http://vawnet.org/material/lethality-assessment-tools-critical-analysis, (accessed November 21, 2016).

Welch, Michael, Eric A. Price, and Nana Yankey. 2002. "Moral Panic over Youth Violence: Wilding and the Manufacture of Menace in the Media." *Youth Society* 341: 3–30.

Weldon, Laurel S. 2006. "Inclusion, Solidarity, and Social Movements: The Global Movement against Gender Violence." *Perspectives on Politics* 4: 55–74.

West-Newman, Catherine Lane. 2005. "Feeling for Justice? Rights, Laws, and Cultural Contexts." *Law and Social Inquiry* 30: 305–335.

White, James Boyd. 1990. *Justice as Translation: An Essay in Cultural and Legal Criticism*. Chicago: University of Chicago Press.

Wilcox, Pamela, C. E. Jordan, and Adam J. Pritchard. 2006. "Fear of Acquaintance Versus Stranger Rape as a 'Master Status': Towards a Refinement of the 'Shadow of Sexual Assault.'" *Violence and Victims* 21: 357–373.

Wilkinson, Deanna L., and Susan J. Hamerschlag. 2005. "Situational Determinants in Intimate Partner Violence." *Aggression and Violent Behavior* 10: 333–361.

Williams, Clare, Jenny Kitzinger, and Lesley Henderson. 2003. "Envisaging the Embryo in Stem Cell Research: Rhetorical Strategies and Media Reporting of the Ethical Debates." *Sociology of Health & Illness* 25: 793–814.

Wilson, Franklin T. 2004. "Out of Sight, Out of Mind: An Analysis of *Kansas v. Crane*, and the Fine Line between Civil and Criminal Sanctions." *The Prison Journal* 84: 379–394.

Wisconsin State Legislature. 2015. "Stalking." Statute 940.32. https://docs.legis.wisconsin.gov/statutes/statutes/940/II/32, (accessed November 21, 2016).

Wolfe, Warren. 2012, February 15. "Intense Scrutiny 'Will Never End' for Sex Offender." *StarTribune*. http://www.startribune.com/printarticle/?id=139410548, (accessed November 21, 2016).

Wolfe, Warren. 2012, February 19. "A Turning Point for State's Sex Offender Program." *StarTribune*. http://www.startribune.com/local/stpaul/139595093.html, (accessed November 21, 2016).

Women's Advocates, Inc. 2014. "The History of Women's Advocates, Inc." http://www.wadvocates.org/about-us/history/, (accessed November 21, 2016).

Wood, Jennifer K. 2005. "'In Whose Name'? Crime Victim Policy and the Punishing Power of Protection." *National Women's Studies Association Journal* 17: 1–17.

World Health Organization (WHO). 2004. "Preventing Violence: A Guide to Implementing the Recommendations of the *World Report on Violence and Health*." Avenue Appia 20, 1211 Geneva 27, Switzerland. http://apps.who.int/iris/bitstream/10665/43014/1/9241592079.pdf, (accessed November 21, 2016).

Zander, Thomas K. 2008. "Commentary: Inventing Diagnosis for Civil Commitment of Rapists." *Journal of the American Academy of Psychiatry and the Law* 36: 459–469.

Zatz, Marjorie S. 1987. "Chicano Youth Gangs and Crime: The Creation of a Moral Panic." *Contemporary Crises* 11: 129–158.

Zellers, Kurt, and Matt Dean. 2012, February 6. Letter to Governor Mark Dayton. https://docs.google.com/file/d/0B1H7-K2-axccZmQzMGU2NDYtZGJhYS00YWMzLWI3ZTEtYmNiZTAzMWRjN2Q1/edit?hl=en_US&pli=1, (accessed November 21, 2016).

Zennie, Michael. 2015, April 15. "Serial Pedophile 'Molested SEVEN Children' Just 18 Months After Psychologists Gave Him a Second Change and Helped Him to Get Released from Prison." *Daily Mail*. http://www.dailymail.co.uk/news/article-3047047/Serial-pedophile-molested-SEVEN-children-just-18-months-psychologists-gave-second-chance-recommended-release-prison.html, (accessed November 21, 2016).

Zilney, Lisa Anne, and Laura J. Zilney. 2009. *Reconsidering Sex Crimes and Offenders: Prosecution or Persecution?* Lanham, UK: Scarecrow Press.

Zonana, Howard, et al. 1999. *Dangerous Sex Offenders: A Task Force Report of the American Psychiatric Association*. Washington, DC: American Psychiatric Press.

Index

www.ingramcontent.com/pod-product-compliance
Ingram Content Group UK Ltd.
Pitfield, Milton Keynes, MK11 3LW, UK
UKHW022000180926
475701UK00003B/109
9780367887049